MW01175013

A Look at Modern Social Issues

Buddhism and Our Changing Society (1)

By
Venerable Master Hsing Yun

Translated by Tom Graham

By Venerable Master Hsing Yun
Translated by Tom Graham
Edited by Edmond Chang and Robin Stevens
Book and cover designed by Dung Tuyet Trieu
Calligraphy Seal Engraving by Yiu Yanchen

Published by Buddha's Light Publishing
3456 S. Glenmark Drive,
Hacienda Heights, CA 91745, U.S.A.
Tel: (626) 923-5144
Fax: (626) 923-5145
E-mail: itc@blia.org
Website: www.blpusa.com

ISBN-10: 1-932293-22-1
ISBN-13: 978-1-932293-22-7

Contents

$\mathcal{P}$reface

This volume gives a partial record of an extraordinary series of lectures given by Venerable Master Hsing Yun parallel to those delivered on the campus of the University of the West in 2004 and 2005. His classes have been a way for him to give a full explanation of his insights regarding many of the social issues of our time. The classes attracted hundreds of students on both the Rosemead campus as well as in more than 20 centers around the world participating through live internet. The lecture series, part of the regular course work of the university, took place each semester for five days. Not only did the audiences get to hear the Master's class remarks, time was provided for questions from all of the sites. An indication of the intense interest on the part of the listeners was the numbers of questions that people wanted to ask. From the internet groups, there were dozens of questioners standing in a "virtual" line waiting for an opportunity to have contact with the Master. These have been inspiring events as we see how many people are willing to take the time to think deeply about the problems and issues of our world.

Master Hsing Yun took on this task with his usual dedication. He addressed difficult and controversial subjects and opened up to the worldwide audience for questions on any of the topics. It was a brave step on his part to share thoughts on matters that often stir intense emotions. The fact that questions could be directed to the Master was an innovation. Speaking to large audiences, he is seldom able to make himself available for face to face dialogue. Now, we have this volume taken from the recordings of his lectures for those who could not take part in the live event and for those who wish to review and relive the experience.

The topics that are covered in these teachings range from the ethical concerns in biological sciences such as euthanasia to personal challenges associated with suicide and depression. Family management in contemporary life has been addressed, especially in regard to dealing with problems of aging and hospice care. We have entered into a new era of cloning, virtual reality, internet commerce, and global life. As you will see in the following pages, Master calmly addresses these potentially troubling issues. He continually urged the audiences not to turn their back on the new age of technology but to deal with it in a reasoned and insightful manner. As I listened to his lectures and answers, I was reminded of passages in the Prajnaparamita sutras that state: the "perfections" give the Bodhisattva the ability to keep concentration and focus even in the face of extreme distractions. It seemed that the Master was reminding the group to be fully present in body and mind at every moment and not allow problems and confusions to overwhelm judgment and tranquility.

One of the important messages coming from the Master was the need for individual decision making. His stories reminded people that we cannot always follow the dictates of others when charting the course we take in relationship to life's activities. Similarly, he urged the group to be careful of intruding into the space of another person when such an action is inappropriate.

A number of people raised their own personal situations during the question periods asking for support and help in confronting problems in their lives. The answers from Master, were sometimes confronting. He asked individuals to give up reliance on solutions that do not involve them in moving toward a more enlightened state. One evening, he presented a masterful account of the meaning of "emptiness." The gist of his remarks were a warning about clinging to beliefs and practices that are external rather than inner growth.

As with all his teaching, Master Hsing Yun holds to his principle that Buddhism speaks to the human condition. This means for him that Buddhist values inform believers about all aspects of their lives. Even the mundane tasks or the decisions that have to be made in day to day relationships are dealt with through interpretation and understanding of the Buddhist tradition. Personal development and ability to handle emotional states are equally involved in Humanistic Buddhism.

The students who were fortunate enough to join in this class know that they have been challenged to rethink the ways in which they react to the stresses of living. This volume now makes this information available for the reading audience.

Lewis Lancaster
President
University of the West

$\mathcal{A}$cknowledgments

We received a lot of help from many people and we want to thank them for their efforts in making the publication of this book possible. We especially appreciate Venerable Tzu Jung, the Chief Executive of the Fo Guang Shan International Translation Center (F.G.S.I.T.C.), Venerable Hui Chi, Abbot of Hsi Lai Temple; Venerable Yi Chao and Venerable Miao Hsi for their support and leadership; Tom Graham, for his translation; Edmond Chang and Robin Stevens and for their editing; Venerable Man Jen, Mu-Tzen Hsu, Pey-Rong Lee, and Kevin Hsyeh for proofreading and preparing the manuscript for publication; Dung Trieu for her cover and book design. Our appreciation also goes to everyone who has supported this project from its conception to its completion.

A Look at Modern Social Issues

Buddhism and Our Changing Society (1)

Life Education

From the moment we are born, people must contend with questions pertaining to their existence and to the very significance of life itself. The meaning of human life can be found neither in the security of an easy job, nor in the pursuit of basic necessities, for life's most profound value appears only when we live in such a way that benefits ourselves and others. In other words, it is to live a life of meaning, value, and dignity.

What is the significance and value of life? How can we live in such a way that our lives are marked by significance, value, and dignity? What is the essential nature of life? What is the true characteristic of life? Each of these topics is fundamental to the question of "life education." Even when we realize our own life's significance, we should consider how to coexist in mutual respect and harmony with all sentient beings, the natural environment, and other manifested conditions. These are all within the parameters of life education.

Life education has become an important topic of concern in society today. Yet in the Buddhist tradition, when the Buddha spoke of "dependent origination" as early as 2,000 years ago, he was already explaining how all life exists on the basis of mutual interdependence.

In his "twelve links of dependent origination" explanation of the cycle of birth and death, the Buddha explained where life comes from and how it cycles through the three periods of time. This explanation helps us understand the mystery of where life comes from and where it goes. The Buddha's explanations of the Three Dharma Seals, the Four Noble Truths, the Noble Eightfold Path, the Law of Dependent Origination, the Middle Way, and the truth of Emptiness help us understand the essential nature and significance of life, so as to establish its value and realize its potential.

Since the Buddhist tradition has many answers to the question of life education, the Taiwan Ministry of Education, together with Buddha's Light International Association (BLIA), has for many years held "Study of Life Education" seminars for all teachers of the Republic of China during winter and summer school vacations. These seminars have consistently been held at Fo Guang Shan. On August 23, 2003, over 2,000 teachers participated in a seminar held at Fo Guang Shan's Tathagata Auditorium, where they were given the chance to participate with many of Fo Guang Shan's lay and monastic leaders in a discussion presided over by Master Hsing Yun on the subject of life education.

Master Hsing Yun opened with the statement, "People come into this world because they have a life to live. If they had no life to live, they would not have a body and they would not be active. Since people do have lives to live, the world exists, people exist, happiness exists, and joy exists. And in this we can see the importance of life itself."

According to Master Hsing Yun, life is not confined to human beings, but is in fact the mind of all sentient beings. Indeed, all things in the universe–including mountains, streams, flowers, grass, sand, and rocks, and even clothing and tables–have a life of their own. An article of clothing, for example, if worn by someone who does not know how to care for it, may last only a few months. But if it is worn by someone who knows how to care for it, it may last as long as ten or twenty years, naturally enjoying a longer lifespan. From this we can see how the life of that article of clothing might be either long or short, depending on conditions.

If a table is cared for properly and moved around carefully, it might last for decades without showing any signs of damage. In contrast, a new sofa might last just a few days if children are allowed to jump up and down on it, and its life will come to an early demise. But these are shallow examples of life–for real life is the mind, and the mind never dies. Thus, Master Hsing Yun believes that life can be found everywhere in nature, for life flows through all time and space. Indeed, life flows through sentiments as well–it is just a matter of how we look at it.

During the seminar, Master Hsing Yun emphasized that

Buddhism advocates not killing, as this is a form of compassion. Yet while it is important not to kill, it is also important to protect life and to progress toward espousing the equality of all forms of life–these all encapsulate today's global concerns about environmental protection, which is itself a very positive kind of life education.

During two hours of discussion, Master Hsing Yun directed people to a new understanding of life from a Buddhist perspective. He showed the audience how to better respect and care for life and to further enhance the value and significance of a full life. Below is a record of the discussion that took place that day.

Understanding life

Recently, Taiwan's Ministry of Education has been actively promoting life education. When the subject of life arises, however, most people wonder: where does life come from and where is it going to? And can the teachings of the Buddha help us understand the question of life and death?

The questions of life have puzzled philosophers and thinkers from the very birth of human civilization. Though there have been many who have spent their entire lives trying to solve this riddle from ancient times to the present, only Sakyamuni Buddha and the enlightened Chan masters of history have ever succeeded in fully untangling it, showing how difficult it is to fully comprehend.

Most people answer the question of where life comes from as the ancients did, by saying: "Whatever lives must die. It does not matter if one is wise or foolish, wealthy or poor. Some will die in ten years, others in one hundred. It does not matter, for the benevolent sages must die as surely as the evil and violent. The sagely Chinese emperors Yao and Shun were born and, once dead, their corpses rotted. Likewise, the despotic emperors Jie and Zhou were born and, once dead, their corpses rotted. Since all that rots is the same, is there anyone who can tell between them now?"

Since people throughout history were largely ignorant of

the origins of life, they often thought of the course of life in this way: "We come by chance alone, but our leaving is certain. While here, we do what we must and follow what is natural." Some also said: "People are born amidst conditions over which they have no choice; they pass their lives amidst many unavoidable conditions; and at last they die after a struggle they cannot refuse." Even Confucius taught his disciples: "As we do not yet understand life, how can we expect to understand death?" And if even he could not understand, how are ordinary people supposed to?

Actually, a truly wise person should recognize the need to seek the source of life, raising the question of where life comes from and where it is going. Life surely does not arise as it did for Sun Wukong, the legendary monkey king who suddenly emerged from some rocks. People normally do not pop out of rocks and they do not fall from the sky. Well then, where do they come from? Most people in this world would answer: from their parents! Well then, where do the parents come from? From their grandparents! And where do they come from? From their great-grandparents! And where do they come from? No matter how many generations we trace back, we will never obtain a satisfying answer to the question in this way.

Then where do people come from? Anthropologists say that people evolved from apes and monkeys. Then, where do apes and monkeys come from? They evolved from reptiles! Where do reptiles come from? They are made of cells. Where do cells come from? No matter how far back we keep going, we will never find a conclusive answer to our questions.

Where do people come from? Christians say that God made them! But then, where does God come from? Where do people come from? Some Hindu teachings say that they issued from the mouth of Brahma! But then the same question arises—where does Brahma come from? Where do people come from? Buddhism says that life originates from arising conditions. But what does this mean? It means that things arise due to many complex causes and conditions, and that they do not arise for just one reason or suddenly come out of nothing.

According to the Buddha's explanation of the "twelve links of dependent origination," sentient beings arise out of the accumulated afflictions of ignorance, and this ignorance gives rise to actions, which produce consciousness. Following that, the "storehouse consciousness" directs the growth of the embryo in the mother's womb leading to development of the physical mind and the body of life, which are known as the link of "name and form." The word "name" here means the mental part of "body of life," while "form" refers to the physical part.

After some months, the eyes, ears, nose, tongue, and body of the "body of life" mature enough to be called the "six organs." After birth, the being leaves its mother and gradually develops contact with the environment. This contact leads it to have sensations of liking or disliking the things in which it comes into contact; and these sensations lead to the development of feelings of desire or repulsion toward those things. Desire leads to grasping, leading to the generation of karma, which now exists as "being" of the "body of life." This leads to the "birth" of new conditions or of a new life, and birth leads to old age and death. And death marks the start of a new body of life.

Thus, because there is ignorance, there are actions. And because there are actions, there is consciousness. And because there is consciousness, there is the mental and physical "name and form." And because there is "name and form," there are the six organs–eye, ear, nose, tongue, body, and thought. And due to the activities of the six organs, there is contact. And because there is contact, there is sensation. And because there is sensation, there is desire. And because there is desire, there is grasping. And because there is grasping, there is the "being" of the future state of the "body of life." And because there is the "being" of further causes and conditions, there arises a new "birth," which eventually attains old age and death.

Due to the cyclical nature of the twelve links of dependent origination, sentient beings are born again and again into this world in a cycle of birth and death that continues without end. Thus, Buddhism's twelve links of dependent origination theory explains that life cycles endlessly through time, always moving from the past to the present to the future. The question of the origin of life is one area wherein the perspective of Buddhism is quite different from those of other religions.

Most religions approach this question using a linear paradigm, while Buddhism employs a circular rationale. For example, Christians say something like this: "Where do people come from? They come from God. And where does God come from? God has always been and He has no need to come from anywhere." This kind of thinking cannot be applied universally nor equally, and thus is not very convincing.

The Buddhist position is as follows: "Where do people come from? People come from death. And where does death come from? Death comes from birth!" People are born, they live, they become old and sick, and they die. The world itself also comes together, abides for a time, declines, and is extinguished. Our minds are born, they abide for a time, they change, and then they cease. The cycle of birth and death never ceases; it is like a clock hand that turns from one to twelve, and then from twelve to one–there is no end to its cycling. So, where is the beginning? Where is the end? The truth is–there is no beginning and no end. This is like the old question of which came first, the chicken or the egg. If the chicken came first, then there must not have been an egg, and if so, how did the chicken appear? If the egg came first, then there must not have been a chicken. Well then, how did the egg appear?

Buddhists believe that "dharmas do not arise alone, but depend on many conditions before they can arise." Buddhists believe that life is beginningless and endless, and situate human beings at the pivot of the cycle of birth and death that operates within the six realms. The six realms are the realms of hell, ghosts, animals, humans, asuras, and devas. Human beings cycle through these six realms due to their karma. The string of lives generated by karma within the six realms can be compared to a string of prayer beads–one bead equals one life. The lives are strung together by karma just as the beads are strung together by the string, and once they have been strung, they can never be disbanded. This is why Buddhists say that human beings move within the cycle of birth and death through time that is both beginningless and endless.

There is a song, "*A River of Spring Water Flows Toward the East*"–but, no matter in which direction it flows, it will always flow back again. Not only is the cycle of birth and death unceasing in the six realms, but Buddhist sutras also describe it as dependent on the Law of Cause and Effect, which is expressed in the statement: "Because there is this, there is that; if there were not this, there would not be that." Our lives do not come about randomly and cannot exist independently. For example, we are all dependent on farmers for the food we consume and on textile workers for the clothes we wear.

Consider also that aside from being dependent on our parents to raise us, on our teachers to teach us, and on the collective accomplishments of people in society, our existence is also dependent on sunlight, water, and air in addition to the many other conditions that support us. If any one of the myriad conditions in the universe were missing, none of us might exist.

Thus, a person's life is not built upon his body alone, for it depends upon many other factors as well–upon farmers, workers, and the realization of our conditions with people in society. If any of our conditions with others is removed, we will find it very difficult to sustain our lives. This is especially true of the conditions that brought our parents together, making them fall in love, and combining with our own karmic causes that allowed them to give us life and raise us. Thus, if we want to answer the question of where life comes from, we can answer most simply by saying that it comes from causes and conditions, from the karma that generates these, from the actions that generated that karma, and then, ultimately, from the fruits of that karma. In this sense, life is essentially the karmic fruit of causes and conditions. Once present, life proceeds through the cycle of birth and death according to its karma, which answers the question of where life goes.

When people are born, where do they come from? When they die, where do they go? How is human life within the universe formed? The Tiantai School answers this question best with the saying: "One hundred realms, one thousand essential qualities." This statement means that each one of us holds ten dharma realms within our minds and that each of these realms contains ten essential factors–therefore "one hundred realms" and "one thousand essential qualities" are contained within each of our minds. In terms of time, our minds "encompass all three periods of time." In terms of space, our minds "pervade all ten directions." For this reason, when "the mind can embrace all space and recognize all worlds, as numerous as grains of sand," the origin of all things within the universe lies within our own minds.

There is a Buddhist text, the *Awakening of Faith*, that asks us to believe in our true mind. The true mind is like a piece of gold–no matter into what shape it is formed, its basic nature and value is never changed. It does not matter if we shape the gold into a ring, some earrings, an ornament, or utensils for dining; it does not matter if we throw it into a gutter or onto a pile of garbage, for though its shape may change endlessly, the nature of the gold itself will not change. This is just the way our true mind is, for no matter where we are within the cycle of birth and death, our true mind pervades all things and never changes. It does not matter if we are in the nether world between lives, or that once we have been born we will age, or that once we age we will become sick, or that once we become sick we will die, for the true mind–though it may cycle endlessly–never changes and it pervades all things.

The world can be destroyed, but our true mind will not be. Though the forms our lives take may hold countless differences among them, the essential nature of life will always be the same.

However, when ordinary people distinguish life and death, they are almost always deluded due to the "confusion of birth," which separates one lifetime from the next. Thus, by changing "bodies," we completely forget our past. Throughout history people have come to all sorts of conclusions about what life is and where it must come from. No matter, for the truth is that life simply has no beginning or end. Life follows conditions and is transformed by them; our lives follow our karma endlessly without interruption. As long as we understand the Buddha's teachings on dependent origination, emptiness, the Three Dharma Seals, karma, consciousness, and the Law of Cause and Effect, the question of where life comes from and where it is going will be self-evident.

What is life education?

Given the Buddhist perspective on where life comes from and where it goes, what is the real meaning of life education? What light can Buddhism shed on this subject that is stimulating and conducive to positive reflection?

These questions remind me of a story. The former Minister of Education in Taiwan, Cheng Ziliang, said that when he once asked some elementary school second-graders to tell him their ideas on death, one of them said: "Death is like going to sleep at night; the next day we just wake up again." The children had been watching so much TV, where people constantly die and come back to life, that they thought life was like a movie. Cheng was very concerned about their attitudes, for he thought that if their understanding of life was that shallow, how could they be expected to show proper respect for their own lives or those of others?

This is a valid concern, for if someone has a poor understanding of life, he will be unlikely to respect the lives of others and find it difficult to discover a sense of dignity within his own. This problem is exacerbated by what some parents do these days—they allow their children to play with small living creatures—dragonflies, spiders, little fish, and shrimp—with the full understanding that these sentient beings will die in the game. When children are taught from a young age to be unconcerned about the lives of small animals, why are we surprised when they grow up and kill human beings?

Life is the most precious thing in the world, and killing is the cruelest. Though some people are rich, some poor, some high, and some low—life is equally precious to all of them. We should be concerned about the well-being of all living things on the planet.

That which we call life is the body that experiences the results of the good and bad karmic causes that were generated in the past. Some beings fly in the sky, some swim in the water, some crawl on the earth, some run in the hills, some live in the water and on land, some have no legs, some two legs, and some many legs. Some lives are lived independently, some are lived cooperatively among others, and some are parasitic. Some lives have form, some have no form, some can move, and some cannot.

It can be said that life appears everywhere in nature. A drop of water has its life, as a leaf has its own; both need to be cared for. The rivers and mountains, pines and cypresses, sun and moon, and the passage of time itself all are forms of life. Buddhists say: "The three realms are in the mind, and all things are nothing more than mind." If I take great care to make a clock, and if I put all of my mind and wisdom into it, then the clock will contain something of my life. If I plan and build a house, its rooms will hold something of my life. The people who work against environmental pollution and help to clean the environment become part of that environment, and their caring takes on a life of its own.

All life between heaven and earth arise ceaselessly. Students of life cannot confine themselves to the study of human life alone, for all subjects are valuable to our understanding of life. Geologists study the earth's crust, astronomers investigate the stars, meteorologists study the weather, botanists plants, microbiologists study cells and their components, and historians study the development of human civilizations—and each of these areas of study has value and significance for all life.

The value of life is love, and its significance is gratitude. If there is love, there is life, for if there is love, there is the chance to be born; and if there is love, there is existence; and if there is love, there is the continuance of existence. Life does not appear only after birth, and it is not over at the time of death. Life is beginningless and endless, and it has no inside or outside.

Life is vital, flexible, and versatile. Life requires versatility, vitality, and flexibility for us to establish good relations with others. For example, rain nourishes the trees in the woods, and those trees, in turn, help retain water. After human beings have consumed food, they in turn produce nutriments that support the growth of more food sources. Life is a mutual, give-and-take enterprise that depends on many causes and conditions. If you try to live completely alone and for yourself, you will find that you soon will have no life at all!

Life is very hard to understand, but no matter how we look at it, our analysis will reveal that its most important aspects are birth and death. Buddhism pays close attention to the questions of birth and death. Indeed, Buddhism is essentially little more than the study of birth and death. The vow of Avalokitesvera Bodhisattva to "aid all sentient beings who are suffering" is a vow to alleviate problems associated with birth, while the vow of Amitabha Buddha to "receive those who are dying" is a vow that alleviates the problems associated with death.

Not only does Buddhism answer questions on birth and death, but it also honors and cares for life deeply. The Buddhist tradition emphasizes cherishing conditions, good fortune, birth, and life itself. The Buddha's compassion and care for all sentient beings has been recorded in many sutras–all one needs to do is look and one will find many such references. For example, he is said to have once cut his own flesh to feed an eagle, sacrificed himself to feed a tiger, given up food to feed some fish, and taught the Dharma to foxes. He melded his life with the truth, and with this truth he nourishes all sentient beings.

The Buddha stressed the life of the greater self–he said: "I am also a sentient being," and he regarded all sentient beings as self. Since he knew that all things that have form must eventually decay, he used his own form and his own limited lifespan to enter into the great transformation of all things, and in this capacity–in his wise and formless Dharma body–he cares for all sentient beings. This is how it is that the life of his teachings is able to pervade all things. Indeed, it pervades not only all human beings but all animals, and so there is the saying: "Both sentient and non-sentient beings attain perfect wisdom of all things." Indeed, even "icchantika will one day become Buddhas." This truth is also revealed in the later Chinese saying: "When Daosheng spoke the Dharma, even the stones nodded in assent."

More than once–to protect his ancestral state of Kapilavastu from annihilation–the Buddha sat in meditation in the middle of the road to stop the armies of King Virudhaka. At another time, he spoke the Dharma to Varsakara, thereby preventing a war between Magadha and Vrji. These examples clearly show that he deeply respected and cherished life. His hope was to inspire everyone to love peace, so as to protect them from the casualties and plight of war.

His method of caring for life was not to use weapons to oppose the enemy, but rather to use compassion as protection. An example of this is the time that Devadatta attacked the Buddha; Ananda immediately exhorted those around to grab weapons to protect the Buddha, but the Buddha stopped them and replied that if he needed weapons to protect himself, how could he be considered an authentic Buddha?

The Buddha's life is limitless and eternal; it is not something transitory or spanning just one lifetime. His life was so infused with compassion that a drunken elephant once relinquished its animal nature and began to weep when it saw the Buddha; another time, some exhausted pigeons landed near him and remained motionless as if having found their protector. Even a criminal, filled with the intention to kill and planning to assassinate the Buddha, instinctively dropped his knife when he encountered the Buddha and asked if he could take refuge with him as his disciple. These examples clearly reveal the effects the Buddha's immense compassion had on others.

"*The Method for Purifying the Mind and Contemplating the Truth*" says: "There are many ways to become enlightened, but the quickest is through compassion." The subject of the Buddha's compassion reminds me of an article I once read in an issue of *National Geographic* that claimed "killing is the only way to survive." It reasoned that since all beings compete and the process of natural selection occurs constantly, those that adapt well survive, while those that do not are eliminated. Therefore, the law of evolution that applies to all animals is that the weak become food for the strong, which relies on killing as the inevitable means for survival. This is quite the opposite of the Buddhist tradition's emphasis on using compassionate means to protect sentient beings. The contrast between these two ways of thinking constitutes the profound difference between Buddhas and demons.

The Buddhist tradition of respecting all life is not confined to protecting only one's own life. The Ksitigarbha Bodhisattva descended into hell to save all sentient beings who are forced to suffer there, while the Avalokitesvera Bodhisattva roams many worlds seeking to answer pleas for help. Even at the most minute level, "when the Buddha contemplates a bowl of water, he sees 84,000 kinds of micro-organisms." Compassion in Buddhism can thus be said to be all-inclusive and all-pervasive.

When Buddhism discusses the four elements—earth, water, fire, and wind—the life of the earth is solid, but the life of water flows. Water that does not flow is dead water. Air, too, must flow to exist, while the life of light is found in radiating warmth.

When the Buddhist tradition talks about the cycle of birth and death and dependent origination, it is talking about life. The cycle of birth and death describes a life that has no death, while dependent origination describes the "conglomerate body" of all life taken as a whole. The Buddhist tradition also calls on us to build a universal life that has no limits. For example, when we chant the name of Amitabha Buddha, we are chanting a name that means boundless light and boundless life, and the meaning of this transcends both time and space.

What can transcend time and space? Truth can, and for this reason it can be said that truth is a universal and boundless kind of life. The Buddha has three bodies, and among these three, his transformation body was conditioned and it came and went, but his Dharma body is not conditioned by anything and thus it is able to enter the boundlessness of time and space of the universe. From this we can see that only truth has a life that is without limit, for all other forms of life are always marked by stages and cycles.

The purpose of religion is to promulgate the truth and for this reason the life of religions can be maintained for a long time. For example, many Buddhist temples date back thousands of years, and will survive for even more. Buddhist sutras must be periodically dried out and maintained, and special libraries must be made to preserve them, though the notion of protecting these things is something that belongs mainly to people of the modern era.

Buddhism pursues a mission of performing benevolent deeds, and Buddhist monastics give their all to sentient beings for the purpose of fulfilling life. Buddhists are concerned about the environment and want to protect it; they build bridges, and put out food and water for travelers–all of this is for the purpose of caring for life. Among the Buddha's disciples, we have the example of the "novice monk who saved the ants" that demonstrates the virtue of protecting life. "Nanchuan who killed a cat" is a paradoxical Chan koan that conveys this truth.

Buddhist monastics carry the sutras respectfully in both hands and take great care not to desecrate them in any way. This sort of caring reveals how they cherish the truths the sutras contain; this, in turn, shows how they cherish all of life. The custom of traveling monks clutching their staffs and wandering in search of corpses of dead animals to bury also shows the deep concern and reverence that Buddhist monastics have for all life. Some Buddhist monastics vow to give their whole lives to great monks, and by this vow lengthen and expand their own lives. This is what is meant by the sayings: "giving the small to the great, giving the self to the other" and "giving the phenomenon to the law that underlies it."

Since the life of a religion is passed on—as one lamp lighting another—from generation to generation, its light burns brightly and continuously. In this sense, the life of the Buddha will last as long as his teachings are passed from one generation to the next. The life of the Dharma will span great distances and be without end as it flows everywhere with the truth. As long as it emulates the virtue and demeanor of the great monks—such as Subhuti and Maudgalyayana—the life of the Sangha also exhibits such spirit.

Even today, we can still feel the rigor of life in Master Sheng Hui's incomparable spirit when he roared like a lion at the Great Assembly at Hua Tai to inaugurate the Sixth Patriarch. Do we not, some one thousand years later, still feel the lingering shadow of the Tang Dynasty translator-monk Xuanzang, who walked eight hundred arduous miles across sandy desert to obtain sutras in India?

The texts on freeing animals by great Buddhist masters teach a kind of life education. Likewise, the Confucian admonition "not to light a candle out of pity for the moths and always to leave food out of love for the mouse" also shows the way that they care for life. During the 2004 New Year's Arts and Crafts Show, Fo Guang Shan designed a special "Herbivore Zone" not only to teach people to care for life, but also to provide the best teaching material on "Nature and Life." In addition, Fo Guang Shan Cultural Foundation's publication of renowned Chinese artist Feng Zikai's "*Collection of Paintings on Protecting Life*" further serves as an educational resource to promote life education.

In 2002, when Fo Guang Shan hosted a visit from Mainland China of the relic of the Buddha's finger, many people fell to their knees and touched their heads to the ground; others wept openly; others were overwhelmed by feelings of joy, while still others felt as if they were meeting the Buddha himself after 2,500 years. These sorts of emotional responses explain what we mean when we say that the Buddha is still alive, for his relics are clearly living. And not only do relics of the Buddha have life, for all things that remind us of him—a canvas portraying a sage or a block of wood carved into a Buddha—all capture his awakened and fulfilled life.

There have also been many noble Buddhist monks who have sacrificed their lives as martyrs to protect the religion. During the Great Proletariat Cultural Revolution in Mainland China, many temples and Buddhist religious objects were saved from destruction by the spirit of martyrdom, exhibited by monastics willing to sacrifice their lives so that the Buddhist tradition could be preserved. In Vietnam in 1963, President Ngo Dinh Diem tried to destroy Buddhism to help the Catholics. By his orders the Buddhist flag was not allowed to be hung at celebrations of the Buddha's birthday—and due to this, Master Guangde and six other monastics burned themselves alive. While it is true that in ordinary times we must do all that we can to preserve our lives, the willingness to sacrifice our lives when it is necessary to fulfill one's duty can render life even more precious.

There is the saying: "Do not save your life if it means compromising one's humanity; sacrifice your life if it means fulfilling one's humanity." Those who seek to preserve life at the expense of one's humanity are as good as dead; those who die for the sake of one's humanity are truly alive. The Confucians say: "Death can be as heavy as Mt. Tai or as light as a goose feather." And there is the ancient proverb: "When a person dies, he leaves behind his reputation; when a tree dies it leaves behind its bark." The Confucians say: "Establish virtue, establish your words, establish your deeds." Clearly, the point of all of this is to leave behind a life that endures.

Life can be forged and conditioned by its environment; people in cold and snowy places naturally develop a strong and resilient life force. A tuft of grass on the top of a wall or a clump of wildflowers by the side of the road reveal the strength of their life force by bravely withstanding gusty winds.

The strength of life comes from the ability to leave one's own legacy, to endow society with compassion, to instill faith in oneself, and to offer contributions to humanity. For this reason, the most important aspects of life education should be to teach students to respect life, to teach them how to live in such a way that they manifest the dignity of life itself, and to teach them how to create value and significance within their own lives. Dignity is the best form of capital we can have in this life. The worst thing that can happen to a people is to sweep away their dignity. Today, people not only wish to live with dignity, but they also want to die with dignity, as can be found among those who advocate euthanasia.

Dignity is not arrogance, nor is it based on self-importance or conceit. It is not an act, nor is it a delusion. Dignity must stand before a powerful force, and not bow to it or bend under pressure. It allows us to abide by our beliefs and principles, preserving our character and integrity.

Beyond having dignity, people also need to lead lives that have value and significance. The late Chiang Kai-shek once said: "The significance of human life is to create the continuance of the life of the universe; and the purpose of human life is to increase the sum total of human happiness." Mao Zedong stated: "Of all of the things in this world, human beings are the most precious." In his opinion, the value of life lies in its contribution to society and the masses, and not in what it can ask from society. This is the reason he so often exhorted others to lead lives of purpose and signifi-cance, and why he often used the slogan: "With all of our minds and all of our hearts, we serve the masses." In the Buddhist tradi-tion, the significance of life is found in bringing more truth, whole-someness, and beauty into this world. And to do this we must understand the eternal nature of life. Though our physical bodies become old and die, our true lives never die, just as a flame that passes from one log to another.

The meaning of life is thus found in what we contribute to and how we benefit humanity, and not in how long we live. The sun shines its light throughout the world, so people everywhere love the sun. Running water nourishes a myriad of things, and so all things love running water. If a person can live meaningfully and usefully, his life will have value.

Even though "The mayfly is born in the morning and dies in the evening, and a human life does not exceed one hundred years," the death and decay of the body is not the end of life! There is the saying: "Contemplate the vastness of heaven and earth, and you will realize the boundlessness of life." The length of a life is insignificant compared to what that life has brought into the world, and what it encompasses. It is especially important to expand our perspective in life, to nurture quality in the substance of life, and to establish a wholesome view on life, morality, and value. These should be the concerns of those who advocate life education.

Is there eternal life?

The Christians say: "If we believe in God, we will attain eternal life." The Daoists say that if a person has the proper training, he will be able to live forever. So, is it possible for people to live forever and never die?

Eternal life is a wonderful term for it means roughly the same thing as eternity. The problem is that there is nothing in this realm that is eternal and does not change. Buddhist teachings hold that both this world and human life are impermanent. Impermanence means that life is constantly flowing and changing. Our thoughts are an example of this, for they change from moment to moment, constantly, with the speed of a rushing waterfall. And according to scientific research, the cells that make up our bodies are constantly being replaced in intervals of either seven days or seven years. Every seven years, the cells in our bodies regenerate at least once—almost as if taking on a new body, like turning into someone new.

Impermanence is one of the profound truths of Buddhism, but since many people do not understand the true meaning of this term, they fear and shy away from it. Truthfully, there is nothing frightening about this concept as long as we understand what it means. Because there is impermanence, there can be hope; because there is impermanence, there can be a future. For example, in the past people were ruled by emperors and they lacked freedom—if impcrmanence did not exist, that situation might still prevail, and we may never have developed the democracies we have today. During the Stone Age, when people had yet to develop wisdom, they ate raw meat and lived primitively–if there were no impermanence, things may never have changed and we might still be living in the same savage conditions.

Impermanence is not something that is confined to one event or person, for it is universal and touches everything. Impermanence is equally present in all things and is impervious to external forces great and small. Impermanence is not a completely passive concept. If I am poor, I know that one day my conditions will change; if I am stupid, I know that if I work and study hard, I will become more intelligent.

Taiwan had a terrible earthquake on September 21, 1999, in which countless buildings collapsed and many people were killed and injured–it was truly a disaster. But it is also true that due to the destruction of so many buildings, most businesses and schools had to rebuild and improve their facilities. If nothing is ever destroyed, how can anything new be made? If there were no impermanence, how could there be improvement? Because there is impermanence, everything can be changed for the better. And because there is impermanence, our futures hold boundless promise.

Some people pursue spiritual cultivation because they feel that their lives are so miserable and they want their next lives to be better. This is another way of expressing the idea that our futures depend entirely on impermanence. This is similar to getting a new car after our old one has broken down. As humans, how can we expect to attain new bodies without first giving up the ones we have now to old age and death?

Impermanence leads us to cherish our lives and all that we have. Impermanence leads us to cherish causes and conditions, and our relations with others. Impermanence is a central truth of the human realm, but eternal life is also a truth. Though impermanence, suffering, and emptiness are true characteristics of human life, it is also true that humans have within them a true mind that never changes; this mind constitutes their birthless and deathless life. Seen from this point of view, life is fundamentally eternal and "deathless," for death affects only the physical body. I often use this example to illustrate the point: if a teacup is broken, it usually cannot be fixed, but the tea that spilled onto the table and floor can be wiped up and not one drop of it will be lost. Our bodies are like the teacup, for they become old and die, but the life within us is like the tea, for it is eternal and can never be destroyed.

Once there was a couple that had a child when they were quite old. As the couple was very happy about the birth of their child, they held a joyful ceremony in their home to celebrate. Then a monk appeared at the door and burst out crying in front of everyone. The host of the celebration naturally was not happy. He said to the monk: "Monk, if you have come for alms, I can give you some money, but why are you just standing there crying? Don't you know that this is a celebration for the birth of our new son?" In reply, the Chan master said: "I am not here for alms. I am weeping because now your home has yet another dead person."

This tale can really provoke thought, as most people "are happy when someone is born and sad when someone dies." For most, the birth of a son naturally is something to celebrate and be joyful about. Weeping is appropriate only when someone dies. What the Chan master in the story above understood is the inevitable cycle of birth and death—for if there is birth, there must be death. Thus, there is no need to wait until the child actually grows old and dies, for his death is already certain at the time of his birth, and that is why the monk said he was weeping over the couple's addition of yet "another dead person."

The moment of birth predetermines that there will be death one day—it is only a matter of time. Why then should we wait until a person has died before weeping for him or her? Perhaps our view that birth is joyful, and death is sad is misguided. Sometimes death can be very joyful as we may "die wearing a smile" or with our "hearts filled with hope."

There is a man in India who is over ninety years old. One day a visiting Japanese journalist asked him: "Old man, what is your greatest hope now?"

The old man answered: "My greatest hope is that I will die soon!"

"Why?" asked the surprised journalist.

"Why? Because my body is old, my food has no flavor, and I can barely walk. The sooner I die, the sooner I will be able to get a new body!"

Thus, death need not be mourned, for it too can be a time of joy. Only by dying are we able to replace our bodies with new ones. The situation is similar to having a car–periodically, we replace our old cars with new ones.

Birth and death are two sides of the same coin. Birth is but the beginning of death, and death is the beginning of a new life. Life itself exists eternally. Thus, when Christians talk about eternal life, at a basic level, they are not wrong–the problem arises when they say that we gain eternal life only if we believe in God. The truth is that we have eternal life whether we believe in God or not! The material body declines and dies, but the true mind never dies. Similarly, Daoists talk about physical immortality, but truthfully the physical body must age and die. Only the self-nature of thusness that lies within all of us is immortal.

The cycle of life is not dependent on our beliefs, for all things that have form in this world are subject to birth and death, gain and loss, good and bad. Our true mind, however, transcends matter and this world; it is formless, without characteristics, without a beginning or end, and it does not come or go. It puts an end to the false distinction between sentient beings and Buddhas, and goes beyond the duality of non-existence and existence. In this way, it is eternal.

Is life fundamentally eternal or is it immortal? The truth is, it is cyclical. According to the Buddhist perspective, the lives of ordinary sentient beings are demarcated by temporary physical states and forms, i.e., growth within one life, or changes from life to life. This is called the "demarcated cycle of birth and death." Even enlightened arhats and bodhisattvas experience a transformational cycle of birth and death, *transformational* because the "bodies" within this cycle arise from thought alone. due to their extant afflictions; thus, within this cycle they must still practice and gradually purify themselves. That which transcends both the demarcated cycle of birth and death and the transformational cycle of birth and death is eternal life itself. Even if one is unable to attain a state that is fully cognizant of eternal life, one still has it. This is because all human beings have a "self-nature"–that is, their "Buddha Nature."

For this reason, the statement "those who believe in me will attain eternal life" is only half of the truth; the other half is "those who do not believe in me also will never die." If we believe, we know that our lives are eternal; if we do not believe, it is the same–we will continue to live and die within the cycle of birth and death, for all life leads to death and all death leads to life.

Cloning

Due to recent technological developments in the field of biology, there are many examples of cloning–such as cloned sheep and cows–both in China and in foreign countries. What is the Buddhist perspective on cloning? How are we to understand cloning? And is cloning permissible according to the Buddhist tradition?

Since the sheep "Dolly" was cloned in England in 1997, other animals–cows, pigs, and mice–have been cloned as well. In addition, American scientists now claim that they can alter the genes of animals to such a degree that cloned cows may be immune to mad cow disease.

Beyond this, a small, international scientific body that studies human genetics has said that in the future it may actually be easier to clone human beings than to clone animals. For this reason, an Italian scientist has already begun laying plans to clone a human being in order to help couples unable to conceive children on their own, in the hopes of allowing them to enjoy the pleasures of parenthood.

Though it may be possible before long to clone human beings due to advancements in technology, the Buddhist position holds that while it may be possible to clone the physical body, no one will ever be able to clone the mind and spirit. Life can only be cloned from another life, and no part of the process can bypass the Law of Cause and Effect. For example, flowers, grass, and trees cannot provide the basis to clone cows, sheep, and humans. A cow comes from the genes of a cow, while a human comes from the genes of another human. Life cannot be cloned from nothing, and it especially cannot contradict the Law of Cause and Effect.

The Buddhist position on genes is that they are the power or the energy of karma. The content of karma itself is complicated and can be subdivided into several different categories, such as group karma, individual karma, particular karma, general karma, definite karma, indefinite karma, "karma of the three periods of time," "karma of the three types," wholesome, unwholesome, neutral, and "karma of the three natures," another way of reckoning wholesome, unwholesome, and neutral kinds of karma. Genes are the code of life, yet they are not unchangeable. They also embody the relationship between an individual's causes and conditions and karma. There was a report that said that the genes that we inherit from our parents do not remain unchanged forever, for from the moment of conception onward, they constantly respond and adjust to their environment. This means that genes are not a driving force behind our behavior; instead, they are determined by our behavior—and from this we can see that our karma is ultimately in charge of our lives.

The truth is, real life is a function of spirit, which itself is another level of the body. When we describe a person as being without a soul, we are saying that he or she seems like "a walking corpse." If a person's body is empty of spirit or vital energy, it lacks function.

In Buddhism, we have the terms "substance, characteristic, and function." The foundation of life is the "substance," which is made manifest by its "characteristics." Substance here means the "essential substance," which is something that is intrinsic. "Characteristics" are extrinsic shapes and forms–for example, one person has one appearance while another has a different appearance. When the substance and characteristics are united, "spirit" and "matter" are unified, and this union produces the "function" of the person, e.g., physical movement, language, mental functioning, and so on. Due to all of this, we manifest the myriad forms, shapes, and colors of this world.

If we look at the substance of life from the point of view of Buddhist dependent origination, we will see that life is continuous, inherited, orderly, and transformational. For example, the cycle of birth and death within the six realms is a kind of transformation. The evolution of simple forms of life to more complex forms is also a kind of transformation, as is the devolution of complex forms into simpler ones. Understanding transformation helps us understand that life is not a static thing that once formed never changes. And this helps us to understand that all of us have the opportunity to change our lives for the better. If you want to have wholesome conditions and effects, then you must perform wholesome deeds. If you do not perform wholesome deeds, but rather create unwholesome conditions all around you, then naturally you will see nothing but bad results from your behavior.

Since the essential substance of life is its original suchness, something that arises from karmic conditions, it cannot be manufactured by human labor. Thus, no matter how much the world changes, or how much science and the art of cloning develops in the future, the world of the spirit will never be the same as the world of matter, for there are higher realities that transcend everything in this world.

All scientific research and inventions today are developed entirely through worldly knowledge. Though in Buddhism we often say that the supramundane realm cannot be separated from the mundane, it is different in the sense that its substance does not change. Everything in the realm of the mundane changes; that which transcends this world does not. For these reasons, I do not believe that cloning will in any way alter the crucial importance in life of karma, nor will it change the importance of the causes we generate by our words and deeds. All that cloning and science will ever be able to do is manufacture a body and control some of its physical features such as height, weight, and appearance. Cloning, however, will never be able to alter the wholesomeness or unwholesomeness of our karma, for this is something that only we ourselves can control–it is not something any other person will ever be able to determine for us.

So, can life be cloned? True life is not something that can be cloned by scientists, nor is it something created by a deity. The genes that underlie life are made by the forces of karma. Karma is the principal cause that holds life together, and therefore we can be certain that true life–that is, consciousness–is not something that can ever be cloned, much less the Buddha Nature inherent in all sentient beings. In the future, no matter how cutting edge the technology will be for cloning sheep, cows, and humans, or for genetic manipulation, *in vitro* fertilization, and so on, these activities will largely only impact the fields of medicine, biology, psychology, and education. All these advances must be integrated with the teachings of the Buddha as its substance in order to resolve many of humanity's questions.

Living and dying naturally

If there is birth, there must be death, for death is unavoidable. Nonetheless, imaginative people are freezing their bodies after they die in the hope that there will be a means to revitalize them in the future. Is it possible to freeze a body and then bring it back to life?

It seems that all sentient beings instinctively cherish life and fear death. There is a saying: "If even ants cherish their lives, imagine how much more people do." People love life and despise death. As the Chinese people say: "A good death is not as good as a bad life." The English philosopher, Bertrand Russell, once said that he "could give up everything just to live." The Indian poet Tagore wrote: "My existence is an eternal miracle and this is life."

What we call life implies birth and death. Birth is life, but death is also life. Death is not extinguishing, nor is it eternal sleep, oblivion, or without awareness or consciousness. When we die, we walk through one doorway into another, from one environment into another. When we pass through the corridor of death, we have the opportunity to raise ourselves to a higher and brighter spiritual level. Our situation at death is not unlike that of immigrants in this world, and for this reason Buddhist sutras use many positive metaphors to describe dying. For example, they say that death is like being freed from prison, that it is like being born again, graduating, moving to a new residence or changing clothes. It is a kind of complete overhaul.

Death is something that none of us can avoid. Once born, we must die. And once we have died, we must be born again. Birth and death are two sides of the same coin, which turns and revolves as it passes though the river of time. Though life and death are inevitable, people from time immemorial have tried to find ways to achieve immortality. In ancient China, Emperor Qin Shihuang sent Xu Fu overseas to search for elixirs that could make him immortal; Emperor Wudi of the Han Dynasty implored Daoist priests to create a pill that would make him immortal. Today, in this advanced scientific world, people seek ways to freeze their bodies in the hope that one day some advanced technology will be able to revive them.

According to reports, in a French village, there is a man who froze his wife's body after she died in 1984; the body is stored in a freezer in his basement. His dream is that science will advance to the point where his wife will be capable of opening her eyes again. He wants to have his own body frozen after he dies so that one day scientists will be able to revive him as well.

Can someone whose corpse has been frozen be brought back to life? As amazing as modern science is today, the day may indeed come when that can happen. A body is still roughly the same after it has been frozen–it is just that this sort of life extension depends entirely on technology. But the question arises– would anyone be happy after being revived decades after death? Is it possible to become accustomed to the new world around them? Would such a situation be liberation or a troubling problem? This is something we cannot possibly know now, but if this science is perfected, it certainly lead to huge changes. Although cryogenics is dependent on science, it is important to remember that ultimately this kind of breakthrough can only arise from the group karma of the human race.

There is a movie, "*Forever Young*," in which a man decides to allow his friend to experiment with his corpse by freezing it. Fifty years later he is revived, only to discover that all of his relatives and friends are dead and that almost everything else in the world has changed. The world was no longer familiar to him; instead, everything had changed and become so unfamiliar, it was hard to adjust to. Not finding anyone who truly understood him, he felt great loneliness and a deep sense of alienation.

Truthfully, it is not necessary for people to live long lives, for what is far more important is that we live responsible lives filled with joy. Rather than being concerned about whether or not frozen bodies can be revived, it would be far better for us to figure out how to live the lives we have now, radiantly and with a full sense of value and meaning.

People do not live just to eat and sleep, and the meaning of life cannot be found in acts of self-aggrandizement. The value of life is also not found in how great our qualities are in and of themselves, but instead in how useful they are to others. A diamond that costs thousands of dollars is completely useless and worthless to others once one person possesses it; in contrast, a simple pile of stones may be of great use when used to repair a bridge or road. Thus, the meaning of life should be found in how one uses his or her own life to lift up infinite other lives.

To discover meaning in life, we must meld our lives with those of others. The *Diamond Sutra* says: "All sentient beings–be they born of eggs, wombs, moisture or transformation; whether they have form or no form; or whether they are able to perceive, not perceive, cannot perceive or will not perceive–I will lead them to nirvana without remainder and liberate them all." To be a compassionate person who is one in coexistence with all beings, and who is able to treat every sentient being as if it were one of our own six organs, such a life would be eternal and without death. Why then would we ever want to work so hard against the forces of nature to figure out how to save a rotting corpse?

It is important to realize that the great value of life is to be found in expressing the brilliance of human nature and exhibiting such noble aspirations as our spirit, resilience, courage, moral virtue, and care for others. If through our own lives we can inspire others to achieve their goals-even if we only live as briefly as a shooting star–we will undoubtedly become brighter and warmer. There will be no need to worry about how long our lives last. Indeed, is it not more beautiful for us simply to follow the course of nature?

Regarding the course of nature, I am reminded of a time over fifty years ago when I first arrived in Taiwan to teach the Dharma. At that time, because Taiwan was under martial law and people were not allowed to gather in public, I always had to play hide and seek with the police whenever I went to teach the sutras. Frequently, the police would walk up to the stage while I was speaking and tell me "Come down! Come down from there!"

What could I do when in the midst of lecturing to so many people, I was ordered to come down from the stage? Of course I knew that if I did not get off the stage that there would be dire consequences, so I asked someone to lead the group in song while I went to talk with the police.

The policeman said: "How can you have a meeting here? Tell everyone to disperse immediately!"

"No!" I said, standing my ground. "I can't do that. I asked them to come here to listen to a sutra and I cannot now tell them all to go away. If you want them to leave, you had better get up on the stage yourself and tell them to go."

Of course he was unwilling to do that, so he said: "How can you ask me to order them to disperse? That's something you should be doing!"

I replied: "Look, the truth is, there is no need for me to tell them to go either. When I have finished my talk, they will all leave on their own."

So I think that doing things naturally is best. Life is a natural thing, and what is natural is beautiful. The most beautiful things in the world are natural. For people to express their natural beauty, their expressions and mannerisms should be graceful and poised, and their speech should be humorous and flowing. In dealing with others, we must learn to be both reasonable and considerate, knowing the appropriate time to advance and when to retreat. If we can be like this, we will come close to attaining the beauty of what is natural.

Our true mind–our "original face"–is a very natural thing; there is nothing false about it. To freeze someone who is not yet dead through cryonics and then revive them decades later is unnecessary. Not only will it lead to many problems, but it also won't necessarily bring happiness. People use their imaginations and often get carried away for a time, but these sorts of fantasies offer very little to the true meaning and value of life.

Our beliefs

What is the difference between believing in the teachings of the Buddha and not believing? Is it true that if we believe in Buddhism that we will be relieved of the problem of birth and death?

As mentioned above, Christians hold that if one believes in God, one will attain eternal life. In Buddhism, however, we do not say that one will be relieved of the problem of birth and death simply because one believes the teachings of the Buddha, for those teachings are intended to help us to see beyond birth and death! Birth and death are to each other like shadow is to form. Whoever is born must die, and having died, they will be born again. Birth and death, death and birth—the cycle never stops. Even the Buddha is subject to these imperatives for: "The Buddha was born when the conditions were right and passed away when the conditions no longer existed. The Buddha came for the benefit of sentient beings and departed for their sake, too." From this we can see that there is nothing more natural than the cycle of birth and death.

Upon hearing this, though, someone is usually compelled to ask: "If I am going to die anyway, even if I believe in Buddhism, why should I bother to believe in it at all? Since I will die regardless of whether or not I believe, it makes no difference one way or the other."

Belief is very important! If we have belief—or faith—our lives are strengthened, we gain new hope, and we learn to fashion new goals for ourselves. People who have faith in the teachings of the Buddha are better able to understand the true nature of life and with this understanding are also better able to face the questions of birth and death, though they still feel happiness and sadness and must face the cycle of birth and death. Their belief will spare them from the suffering of "the second arrow."

The "second arrow" is a metaphor used in Buddhist sutras to illustrate how both believers and non-believers will be affected by the joy and pain they encounter in life. However, a person without the Buddha's teachings in mind is more likely to become despondent or confused when confronted with adversity, and will not know how to find peace. This is like being struck by a second arrow after the first and having to bear the insufferable pain it brings.

When a person who believes in the Buddha's teachings encounters adversity, he or she knows how to examine the situation from the standpoint of "causes" and uses adversity to self-reflect and improve, instead of focusing only on the "result" and using it to blame the heavens or other people and becoming despondent. The believer will thus naturally be spared the pain of the second arrow. Likewise, when such a person encounters more pleasant circumstances, he or she will not live with abandon, because allowing one's body and mind to indulge in reckless behaviors will only bring more pain through the second arrow.

Thus, even though neither believers nor non-believers can ultimately escape death, when the moment of death comes, the non-believer will experience dread, confusion, ignorance, and even regret. In contrast, for people with faith in the Buddha's teachings, just as for Christians and Catholics who believe that "God will call them home" at the time of death, death is like a form of emigration where we move from one country to another—or to employ a Buddhist phrase commonly used, "rebirth in the Buddha realm." Naturally believers will not feel the same pain and fear.

Therefore, belief does not keep us from dying, but it does help us face death with clear understanding and the full knowledge that death is not an absolute ending, but rather the beginning of a new life. Life and death go hand in hand; the one always entails the other and thus there is no reason to feel great joy at a new birth or to feel great sadness when someone dies. If we can both live and die without fear, we will have much more strength when the time comes for us to face death, and we will be able to view it quite differently.

I have been a monastic for more than sixty years, and I do not dare claim that I have attained any great spiritual practice, but I am deeply aware that there are many benefits from having religious faith. The subject of birth and death reminds me of a story: Some years ago I went to the Veterans General Hospital in Taiwan for a check-up. The doctor spent an entire day examining me meticulously, but he still did not feel reassured. So he asked me to return the next day for more tests. I said: "Sorry, I cannot come tomorrow as I have to attend a nun's funeral."

He replied: "Isn't your own life important to you?"

"I go along with whatever conditions may prevail," I

responded. "It's hard for me to say if my life is important or not."

The doctor asked: "Aren't you afraid of death?"

Now, this is a question I had some difficulty answering. If I said that I feared death, the doctor would have laughed at me and thought that I was a useless monk. But if I said that I did not fear death, I might have sounded pompous, since if even ants fear death, how can a human being be expected not to? So I said: "I don't fear death. I just fear pain." I said this because there is a threshold as to how much pain anyone can take. If it is exceeded, even someone who at first felt like a hero will end up more cowardly than a puppy.

Several years after that incident, I went to stay at the Veterans General Hospital again to have heart surgery. The operation took eight hours, and from the time I awoke in the recovery room until the time I was placed in the intensive care unit, my doctor kept asking me if I felt any pain. Again I had to think of an artful way to answer him. I told him: "I feel so comfortable!"

He was somewhat surprised by my response and said: "It is one thing to feel no pain, but how can you say you are comfortable?"

I realized that the doctor really did not understand me. I am so busy carrying so many responsibilities every day that it is rare for me to have time to lie down and rest so leisurely. So, for me, it was comfortable.

But was I in pain from the operation? After all the drugs they gave me, I felt no pain whatsoever. Was I suffering in any way? Not at all, for all I had to do was lie in bed. Normally I spend so much time talking to people and inquiring after their needs, but after my operation people were coming to me and asking: Are you well? Would you like some water? Do you like it like this? Would you like it like that? All day long there were people coming around to care for me—it was great and I truly felt quite happy!

I think that this story shows what the greatest distinction is between a person who has religious faith and one who does not, for a person with faith is, at the very least, able to view death more lightly and naturally. A person who can face death without feeling terrified is more likely to live life with a deeper sense of meaning. To have faith is to have strength and confidence. A person who has faith–even if he or she is wronged or humiliated–will not lose heart for he is well aware that there will be another chance.

Where there is faith, there is light. Buddhist sutras say that faith is like a hand, a staff, a root, a boat, strength, and also wealth. When we have faith, it is as if our hands were holding onto something for the feeling is very real. When we do not have faith, it is as if we had nothing, and this situation is quite pitiable. Often people claim that they do not have faith in any religion or the cycle of life and death, or that life will be reborn.

But if you have no faith, you will end up with nothing at all. Wouldn't this be a problem of your own making? This is why I feel that people who have religious faith–whether it is based on Christianity, Catholicism, folk religions, or even superstition–are always better off than people who have no faith at all, for if there is no faith, life seems empty, without purpose, and without any future.

This having been said, I must add that I also believe that the most important thing about religious belief is that it be proper and correct. By this I mean that it should include morality, truth, purity, and have a history. Our belief must have the means to liberate us from suffering. It is not good to believe in things that are false, for once we pursue a deviant belief, it is quite difficult to turn back.

Nowadays there are many false religions being practiced in Taiwan, and yet every time we hold a "Taking Refuge Ceremony" at Fo Guang Shan, thousands–even tens of thousands–of people show up. The reason so many come is that they know they must quickly take refuge in the correct beliefs of Buddhism to avoid embarking on the wrong path. Who would have thought that even the presence of erroneous religious beliefs could also be a factor in promoting the spread of the Dharma?

In the past, most people who studied Buddhism were looking for a way to "see through life and liberate themselves from death." From the point of view of life, this sort of liberation means that one learns to see the "true characteristic" of human life, that one understands the meaning and significance of life, and that as a result of this one is able to live carefree and in the moment. From the point of view of death, this sort of liberation means that one understands what follows death, that one has hope for the future and does not fear either life or death, and that due to this one is able to transcend the duality of birth and death. If one can go beyond even this and help others see these truths–if one can awaken oneself and others at the same time–then one will be actualizing the Mahayana bodhisattva path and thus completing the highest level of practice in this human realm.

There is a saying: "To be a fully accomplished human being is to be a Buddha." This means that if we want to live fulfilling, liberated and carefree lives, we cannot do it without Buddhist teachings to guide our conduct and understanding of life; for if we do not rely on the wisdom of the Dharma, we will not be able to solve many of life's questions. A person who relies on the teachings of the Buddha in life is one that can attain liberation from the cycle of birth and death, and be whole and carefree.

The cycle of birth and death

The Buddhist tradition often talks about the cycle of birth and death. What is this cycle of birth and death, and how are we to truly know that our lives cycle in this way?

We now live in the 21st century at a time of great scientific advancements. There are surely many people today who do not believe in the cycle of birth and death and feel that this belief only belongs within the religious sphere. They think that this belief is merely concerned with where the soul goes after death and that it is not a practical belief with any impact on daily life. For these reasons, people are not terribly concerned about the cycle of birth and death.

The truth is, though, that there is not a single phenomenon

anywhere in this world that is unaffected by the cycle of birth and death. The four seasons come and go, replacing each other as they cycle through the year. Time passes and the past and present are transformed into the future, while night and day constantly change places with each other. These are all signs of the cyclical nature of time. And in space, we see cycles as well, for as our positions change, so do our relations to other places and to the four directions.

The principle of the cycle of birth and death is no different from that of the saying: "If you plant a melon seed, you will reap a melon; and it if you plant a bean, you will reap a bean plant." If we scatter beans in a field, beans will later grow in that field. If we scatter melon seeds, melons will grow. Is this not a cycle of birth and death? When we go to sleep at night, we know that we will wake in the morning–is that not a cycle? The sun sets in the evening and then rises in the morning–is that not a cycle? Leaves may wither in the fall, and grass and trees may become dry and brittle in the winter. But once spring arrives, flowers will bloom like flames, while the same grass and trees will revive–is that not a cycle?

Life transforms itself through cycles. In human life, we have birth, old age, sickness, and death. Death does not mean nothingness, for following death there is another life. When Buddhists speak about life being part of the "cycle of the three periods of time," they essentially mean that from "beginningless time," human beings have been generating karma through acts of body, speech, and mind; and that this karma continuously transforms life through a sequence of causes and effects. Life itself flows through a sort of time that has neither a beginning nor an end, and out of this arises the various realms into which sentient beings may be born–such as that of devas, humans, ghosts, and animals. In all, there are six realms into which a vast variety of lives may manifest and take form. In the Buddhist tradition, we call this immense cycle "the cycle of birth and death within the six realms."

Since there is a cycle of birth and death, there is a future life. Since there is a future life, we can have hope for the future. There are some young people who become spiritually numb, and end up committing serious crimes for which they are executed. Before their sentences are carried out, though, they sometimes say things like: "Twenty years from now, this guy you see here will be a hero!" Though people like that may be bad, even they have hope for the future. If they can feel hope, then how is it that people who lead good lives cannot feel hope for their own futures? How can they believe that there is nothing after death? A life without hope is truly pitiable, boring, and without value; thus, we must believe in the cycle of birth and death.

How the cycle of birth and death manifests itself is not set in stone. Just as a mango tree can be grafted into an apple tree to produce a new kind of fruit, so a person's conditions will change from life to life. Just as the genes of some animals can be altered and some of them can be cloned, the cycle of birth and death can also undergo beneficial changes. Therefore, it is very important for people to realize that no matter what they have done—even if they have committed a serious crime—their futures can be changed for the better if they are willing to repent their misdeeds and vow never to commit them again. Furthermore, if they are willing to make vows to benefit others, they can use merits to mitigate unwholesome deeds and transform the effects of their causes and conditions within the cycle of birth and death. This shows how our beliefs can change the way we live and our destiny, prospects, and future.

Some people do not believe in the cycle of birth and death, and though they may think that makes them appear sophisticated in some way, in truth they are only revealing the shallowness of their thinking. Denying the cycle of birth and death is not about being contrary; it is about limiting the potential growth of one's own life. The American automaker Henry Ford once said that the significance of life can be found in its cycles, and that since there are cycles, the knowledge and understanding of one generation can be passed on to the next. He believed that if we were not able to pass our life experiences on to others that our work would become nothing but drudgery. If the accumulated storehouse of knowledge acquired by our society cannot be passed on to future generations, then the course of history itself will be limited.

The modern writer Shu Shuilin, in his work *Cycles of the Universe*, introduced many theories of cyclical existence from all over the world that are well worth studying. For example, ancient Mayan culture held that this world would be completely destroyed in 470,000 years and that following its destruction, it would regenerate anew again. This belief is similar to the Buddhist notion of all things being "born, abiding, declining, and returning to emptiness."

Native Americans said that they are a people who have escaped doomsday three times, and that the fourth doomsday for the human race is not far off. They also say that the conditions for each doomsday are different. The first was caused by a volcano, which spread lava over the surface of the earth. An earthquake caused the second. And warfare caused the third. Is this not similar to the Buddhist prediction that the world will end "in the first instance by fire, in the second by wind, and in the third by water?"

We also know from history that there have been many wise and visionary literary people whose writings attest to the reality of the cycle of birth and death in the six realms, some of which are hard to refute. For example, there is the story of the Ming Dynasty Confucian, Wang Yangming, who upon visiting Jinshan (Gold Mountain) Temple for morning worship noticed that everything seemed extraordinarily familiar to him. He felt that he was able to recognize every tree and blade of grass. As he strolled the grounds of the temple, he came upon a room whose entrance had been sealed with a strip of paper. Upon closer examination, he felt he had lived there before. Unable to control his curiosity, he asked the reception monk to open the room for him, but the monk replied apologetically:

"Sorry, this is where one of our older monks died some fifty years ago. Inside, remains the relic of his whole body. On his deathbed he made us promise never to open the room again. Please understand and forgive me."

"Since this room has doors and windows, is there really a good reason never to open it again? Please, I kindly beg you to open the room today for me to take a look!"

Since he kept pleading and the monk did not want to hurt his feelings, he very reluctantly opened the room and let Wang Yangming go inside. The room was dark and hazy inside, but Wang could still see the form of the old monk seated in the lotus position on his bed. Taking a closer look, Wang was astonished to discover that the old monk's face exactly resembled his. As he looked up, he noticed a poem written on the wall. It said:

> Wang Yangming, fifty years later,
> The person who opens the door is the one who closed it.
> When the consciousness that once left returns,
> It then believes in the Chan teaching of indestructible being.

With this he understood that in his previous life he had been this old monk. Years ago, he had shut this door himself and now he had returned to open it again to prove to future generations that rebirth is real. To commemorate this experience, Wang Yangming left a poem at Jinshan Temple:

> The Gold Mountain awakened me like the strike of a fist;
> I see through the sky under Weiyang Lake.
> While enjoying the moon above the balcony,
> The playing of the flute awakens the dragon within me.

There are many Buddhists, who though they have studied the Dharma for years, still have trouble believing in the cycle of life and death. This belief is not some mere Buddhist credo or an idea whose sole purpose is to comfort us at death. It is a precise science for explaining where we have come from and where we go after we die. If in life there is no such thing as the cycle of life and death, then where do we go and where did we come from? And in which direction does hope for the future lie? If there is no cycle of birth and death, then life is truly brief and our futures so vague and empty. Once we understand that there is rebirth, then our lives will have ground for transformation. There will be another bus to board in life, which will continue to move us toward a world of infinite hope and light.

The question is not whether we believe in the cycle of birth and death. Even those who do not believe in its truth only have to open their eyes to all the manifestations in the universe, such as the natural world, in human life, in physics, and even in our relations with other people, to see that everything revolves within cyclical existence. It takes wisdom, though, to understand the deep principles that underlie the cycle of birth and death, and to overcome and transcend this cycle, turning it into the path of liberation of the Buddhas and bodhisattvas.

Understanding genetics

With modern medicine and continuing advances in scientific research, it is now possible to alter genes. Can genes be truly altered? And is there really any difference between the genes of saints and criminals?

Genetic alteration and gene reorganization are major developments in biology. Using scientific methods—either through direct alteration of genes or traditional breeding practices—the genes of plants, animals, and micro-organisms can now be altered; these changes are capable of producing entirely new life-forms. These methods can change the speed at which plants and animals grow, boost their immune systems, increase their nutritional value, and give plants longer shelf life after they have been picked. The "Genetically Modified Organism" [GMO products] that we now find on market shelves are simply produce that have undergone a process that alters their genes.

If we want to talk about genetic alteration—or genetic modification-we must first be clear about what genes really are. A gene is simply a "cause" that has been inherited and it is made up of many strands of DNA. Genes are the vehicles that allow one generation to pass its traits on to the next generation. Genes determine traits such as the color of flowers, the height of plants, and the amount of body fat a human being has. There is a Chinese folk saying that expresses this truth quite well: "Dragons give birth to dragons, phoenixes give birth to phoenixes, and the offspring of rats all know how to burrow holes."

Genes are the causes of what we inherit. Some people also say that they are the code of life. Each one of us has a different genetic make-up and, for this reason, also a different appearance and a different destiny. Some people are tall and handsome, while others are short, thin, and weak. Some are very lucky, while others suffer often. These differences are all due to differences between people's genetic causes.

In Buddhist terms, genes are nothing other than the power of karma. Nevertheless, for all the questions that genetic makeup cannot answer, we still need to rely on our understanding of karma. In the medical report *A Discussion of Genes and Karma*, the researcher, Li Zi, clearly shows that "Genetic deficiencies often have a cause-and-effect relationship with diseases and their symptoms." He adds, however, that: "Medical science has not been able to prove that each and every individual with the same genetic deficiency will be affected the same way by disease. Nor has science been able to prove that every person who contracts a certain disease has the same genetic deficiency." The reason, he says, is that "the true cause of disease is karma itself."

He gives this example: "Why is it that two different people may contract the same illness, yet respond quite differently to whatever medicine is given them as a cure? And why is it that the same person will have very different reactions to the same treatment under different conditions?" The reason for this he concludes is: "The degree of effectiveness of medical treatment is dependent on the extent of the patient's karma."

Li Zi offers some medical records as illustration: "Through strict ascetic practice, a patient with a basic genetic deficiency was able to completely eradicate a disease associated with it, even though he was not able to change his genetic makeup. There are examples of rigorous practitioners who completely overcame the symptoms of diabetes, even though their blood sugar levels remained high. This is because they were able to eradicate their karma at a fundamental level, which allowed them to overcome their ailment."

In the Buddhist tradition, karma is often metaphorically described as a "seed." The type of seed we sow will determine what flower will bloom and what fruit will ripen. This is why we say that if people want to change their destiny, they must begin by sowing wholesome seeds. Only by doing so can they be assured of a good harvest in their rebirth.

As for whether the genes of a saint and a criminal are different, according to the Buddhist tradition all people have Buddha Nature, and all of them can become Buddhas. Since this theory of Buddha Nature says that all people will one day become Buddhas, the innate basic causal makeup–genetic or otherwise–is the same for all of us. What is different then are the conditions that support the cause. When the same cause meets different conditions, there will always be different results. Medical science speaks of genetic alteration, whereas the Buddhist tradition asks us to alter our own genes by doing wholesome deeds and not unwholesome ones.

Technological advancements in genetic alteration applied to medical treatments today will most definitely have a huge impact on the future of the entire human race. According to reports, it is almost possible now to insert genes for human proteins into organisms and to later extract from them proteins that will provide an endless supply of human plasma needed for medical treatments.

The concept of an Aryan race in Germany, the old stereotype of the refinement of gentlemen and fair ladies of the British Empire, and even the arrogance of some Americans who see themselves as part of a distinguished culture based on technological accomplishments all assume a relationship between culture and racial-genetic makeup. Chinese claim that they are descendents of the dragon and that they are one of the four great ancient cultures in the world, endowed with a rich history and culture. However, since people today no longer place much emphasis on virtue or on dealing reasonably with each other, our society has naturally declined as each generation becomes worse than the one that preceded it.

When a man and women give birth to a child, prenatal care clearly is very important, as is rearing children with an emphasis on compassion, virtue, good character, and personal integrity, thus allowing parents to influence the next generation. In addition to these influences, people are also shaped by the education they receive at home and at school as well as by their friends, for all of us are subject to the truth that "if we draw close to vermilion, we will be stained red; if we draw close to ink, we will be stained black."

Nonetheless, though each of us is influenced by parents and teachers, our destinies will always be largely of our own making, for we generate the causes that set in motion the karmic forces that will shape our lives the most. The conditions that affect our lives will never be as influential as the karmic causes that we have generated ourselves. For example, if we sow a good seed and care for it well by giving it plenty of sunshine and water, a fine plant will grow from it. And yet, if the original cause of the seed is unwholesome, no matter how conducive to growth the conditions are, such as ample rain and gentle breezes, there is no guarantee that one day it too will produce a good result.

This is why it is important to realize that no one else–be it divinity or a Buddha–can really help us all that much in life. We are responsible for helping ourselves because only we can alter our genes and the karmic causes that shape our destiny. Karma can be either the wholesome, unwholesome, or neutral karma generated through the conduct of our body, speech, or thought.

There is a saying: "Even if it takes eons, our karma is never lost. For once conditions are right, we will receive our just reward." The karma that we generate through our acts of body, speech, and mind is saved as if on the hard drive of a computer—when conditions are right, the file will be called up and we will have to face the consequences of what we have done, be it pleasant or unpleasant. There is no escaping the ironclad Law of Cause and Effect.

Karma was one of the Buddha's great discoveries. What happened in former lives affects us in this life. What we do in this life will have an effect on our future lives, because everything is bound together by karma. Chaining together life after life, or the segments of life and death, nothing is ever lost or missing. Thus the reason our lives are eternal is related to the presence of karma.

It is just as Li Zi said: "Though we cannot actually see the power of karma in this realm, and cannot as yet prove its existence scientifically, nonetheless, the notion of karma can explain many phenomena that are otherwise most difficult to comprehend." Though it is true that modern genetic research will have a great influence on the human race, it can only explain the factors underlying an individual organism. In contrast, the Buddhist concept of karma includes both the factors that comprise the individual—individual karma—as well as those factors that generate what is known as group karma.

For example, why are some people born into the same family, the same village, and the same ethnic group? This is explained by the concept of group karma. A group of people may all be traveling on the same ship or airplane, but if an accident occurs, only some of them will die while others will live. The reason this happens is that while their group karma is the same, their individual karma is not. Thus, one hopes that scientific understanding of the code of life for individuals—genes—will one day lead to the discovery of a group genetic code that will explain our fundamental relationship to one another.

The basic Buddhist teachings on karma and cause and

effect are truths that are unshakeable, for they are ineluctable, eternal, and universally applicable. The genes discovered by science simply deepen our understanding of karma and how it operates and nothing more!

Understanding the intermediate body

According to Buddhism, there is an "intermediate body," which has no choice but to be reborn and, once it is reborn, it has no choice but to grow old. What exactly is the intermediate body, and what affect does it have on our lives?

After a person dies, the spirit that exists prior to the next rebirth is called the "intermediate body." This is what most people are referring to when they speak of a spirit or soul. In the Buddhist tradition, however, we do not use those words; instead we call this entity a "middle yin body."

This yin body is the karmic body that is held together by the five skandhas—form, sensation, perception, activity, and consciousness. When a person dies, the physical "form" ceases to function. The three skandhas of sensation, perception, and activity cease to function as well. Thus, only the skandha of consciousness is left, and it floats around looking for a future place to reside. Does the future hold a life in the deva realm? Will that consciousness continue in the human realm? Or will it fall into one of the hell realms, the ghostly realm, or the realm of animals? None of this is definite, and so this stage is called the intermediate body or the body of intermediate existence.

The middle yin body can be said to be both the dividing point between two lives and the point that unites them. It lies between life and death, and can be thought of as a process that takes place between two lives. The stage between lives is the intermediate existence. Thus, after living a full life, a person dies and moves on to another life much as one leaves one place of residence and moves to another. The intermediate stage of being simply corresponds to the period of time when one is between places of residence.

The intermediate body is not produced by sexual union, and it is not a physical body in any sense of the word. Rather, it is a sort of shadowy light being that floats in space like a mayfly. Where it flies to is determined by its karma or by its memories and the habits of its former life. This is why the Pure Land teachings stress that "a single thought of Amitabha Buddha at the time of death" will lead to rebirth in Amitabha's Pure Land. What is important is that the thoughts just before death have a great influence on where a person will be reborn.

The intermediate state of existence depends on the consciousness of the individual in question. It consumes scents, and its main purpose is to find the place where it will take rebirth. The sutras say: "It is well suited to finding the place it will be (re)born." Whether or not it easily finds the place of rebirth depends on its roots. The *Mahaparinirvana Sutra* says:

> *Those with superior roots will be reborn in the midst of a single thought.*
> *Those with average roots will be reborn in fifteen days.*
> *Those with inferior roots will be reborn in seven times seven, or forty-nine, days.*

This is the reason that Buddhist devotees have become accustomed to temples holding ceremonies for the dead at several different intervals—immediately after someone's death, seven days after, twenty-one days after, and forty-nine days after.

As for the practice of chanting for the deceased who are in the middle body stage, there are many who wonder if it really does any good at all. According to the *Ksitigarbha Sutra*, six-sevenths of the merit gained by such chanting goes to the living, while only one-seventh goes to the deceased. This is why it is so important to use the time that we are alive to do good things. No one can get through an entire life without doing some harmful things; the bad karma we generate by our mistakes can be compared to heavy stones—if we throw a stone into the water, it will sink. However, through the merits we earn by chanting the sutras or doing other good deeds in life, we can generate positive karma to offset the bad things we have done, like using the Dharma as a boat to keep the "stones" of our karma from sinking and carrying it across to the other shore of life and death.

But can chanting sutras really help us overcome bad karma? Here's one example to consider: Some decades ago in Taiwan, during the period of "white terror," if you were frequently heard saying "Long live the Three Principles of the People!" or "Long live Chiang Kai-shek!" you would have found it easier to get a job or a passport to go abroad. If simply saying "Long live the Three Principles of the People!" or "Long live Chiang Kai-shek!" could be so useful, wouldn't chanting Buddhist sutras be even more efficacious?

There is a joke about a monk who while teaching the sutras repeatedly emphasized how good it was to chant Amitabha Buddha's name, how it would prevent calamities, extend the lifespan, and bring about all manner of good fortune¡K A young person who was listening thought that what the monk was saying did not seem quite right, so he said: "Hey, you are being too mysterious! Can a single phrase 'Amitabha Buddha' really have that much good effect? I simply don't believe it!"

The monk thought that the young person would not understand even if he tried to explain the idea more thoroughly, so he replied rather rudely: "What are you trying to say, you jerk?"

The young person exclaimed: "How can a monk speak to me like that?" And with that he rolled up his sleeves and prepared to fight.

The monk answered calmly: "Now look at you! All I said was 'you jerk,' and look at the great effect it produced on you. Imagine how much greater the effect would be if you say Amitabha Buddha!"

Though the intermediate body has no form or characteristics, and though it cannot be seen with the physical eye, it still possesses the full six roots and somewhat resembles a young child that is about three-feet tall. It has psychic powers and can pass through all manner of solid objects, including steel and iron walls. It moves very quickly and can be stopped by nothing, except the womb of a woman or the diamond seat of a Buddha.

When an intermediate body sees a man and woman having intercourse, if it develops a strong feeling of love for the woman, it will be born as a boy. If it develops a strong feeling of love for the man, it will be born as a girl. Whether it is to be a boy or girl, the process of the intermediate body entering and leaving the womb depends on this. If in falling toward the hell realm, the middle yin body experiences oppressive sensations of cold and wind such that when it at last glimpses the fires of the hell realm, it will be strongly attracted to the heat and throw itself toward it; in this way it will enter into one of the eight hot hells. If on its way to the hell realm, it experiences oppressive sensations of extreme heat such that when it feels the cold air of some of the other hell realms, it will be attracted to the coolness and throw itself toward that; in this way it will enter one of the eight cold hells.

If there is really a cycle of birth and death, then why is it that we don't remember anything from our former lives after we die? The sutras say: "Human life truly is full of suffering. Grandchildren marry their grandmothers; cattle and sheep spread on the banquet table, their kin cooked in pots." What is it that makes us pass without memory from one life to the next, to forget everything through our ignorance, even something like taking as our wife the woman who was our grandmother in a former existence?

According to the Chinese folk text *Yu Li Bao Chao*, just before a person takes rebirth, they drink "soup of the goddess of the wind," which causes them to entirely forget all that has happened to them. The Western philosopher Plato believed that prior to taking a new birth, the soul has to travel across a blazing hot desert. The journey makes the soul extremely thirsty, so it drinks cool water from the "River of Lethe," after which it is reborn. The problem is that the water from the "River of Lethe" completely erases the soul's memories. The Romans believed that when a person is between one life and the next, they must cross this "River of Lethe." Once they drink water from the river, though, they forget everything that has happened to them to that point.

In the Buddhist tradition, our lack of memory of past lives is caused by the confusion of birth. The *yin realm* here indicates the intermediate body. Due to the nature of this middle yin body, we forget all that happened in our previous life and do not even know which realm we will be born into next.

Some say with great sincerity that it is truly a pity we are subject to the confusion of birth and not able to remember our former lives, for if we could remember everything that happened to us we would be much happier and more self-aware. Is it true that we would be happier if we had this sort of psychic power?

Probably not, for if we could remember all of our past lives we would also be able to recall those lives in which we were pigs, horses, cows, sheep, or other animals—and would it really feel good to remember such things? Similarly, if our powers allowed us to know we are going to die in three years, would we really be all that carefree and leisurely in how we live the rest of our lives? Some people who have psychic powers are able to see through the surface truths of a smiling, beautiful face; they can see that behind that face is a dark heart filled with malice and danger—wouldn't it be possible not to feel tremendous pain or hatred? Without psychic powers, every day is a good day, and every place is a good place. Then we are truly carefree and unattached!

Human life within this universe has its own natural course of development, and it is only by respecting and understanding the process of change that we are able to achieve true happiness and contentment in this life. By passing through the confusion of birth, gaining a new body, and forgetting all of the bad things that happened in the past, how can we not see everything as wonderful?

Our future lives

The Buddhist tradition calls human death "future life."

Where, then, do we go in our future lives? And is it true that we must become ghosts?

In the Chinese folk tradition, it is believed that we should burn paper money for someone who has just died. This is a traditional Chinese custom based on the belief that after a person dies he or she will go to the nether world and become a ghost. As people believe that the newly deceased will need money for their journey to the "yellow springs," they burn paper money so that their ancestors will live more comfortably in the nether world.

The Buddhist tradition holds a different view of these matters. Buddhists believe that after people die, their karma determines into which of the six realms they will be reborn. The six realms are the realms of devas, humans, asuras, animals, hungry ghosts, and hell. So, when a person dies, it is not certain that he or she will become a ghost. But even if someone is reborn as a ghost, the kind of resources he or she will enjoy will still be determined by the extent of his or her merits. If a ghost has not accrued any merits, it does not matter how much paper money you burn for the person. If the ghost has accrued merits, then even if no one burns money, the person will still be quite comfortable. Of course, if the practice of burning money for the deceased makes the living feel better, then there is nothing wrong with doing it. However, it is actually rather disrespectful to assume that our ancestors will be reborn as ghosts, is it not?

Based on the theory of karma, a person's next rebirth is contingent on the relative weight of his or her karma, habits, and predominant thoughts at the time of death. The most important factor in determining a person's next life is the relative weight of his or her karma; the second most important factor is the karma of his or her predominant thoughts at the time of death; and the third most important factor is the karma of his or her habits during the life that has just ended. More specifically:

1) The relative weight of karma: This means that a person's heaviest karma–be it good or bad–will be manifested first.

2) The karma of predominant thoughts at the time of death: This means that people tend to be reborn in conditions that resemble what they were most nostalgic for or what they were thinking about the most. For example, if a person comes to an intersection while out for a stroll, he might wonder which way to go. If he suddenly thinks of a friend over to the west, then he will simply head that way. When a person dies, his last thoughts and memories may similarly direct his rebirth.

3) The karma of the habits formed during the previous life: This means that rebirth is determined by our daily habits. For example, people who have dedicated themselves to the Pure Land practice spend a great deal of time chanting the name of Amitabha Buddha. The purpose of this sort of concentration is to establish a habit that will help them earn a response from Amitabha Buddha with just one recitation of his name and ensure that they will be reborn in the Pure Land of Ultimate Bliss.

The Western Pure Land of Ultimate Bliss is an ideal state, filled with joy, purity, tranquility, and beauty. It is the perfect place for peaceful nurturing. Thus, this Land of Ultimate Bliss is also called the "Land of Peaceful Nurturing." The Amitabha Buddha has fashioned this world in such a way that there are never any conflicts between men and women, never economic problems, never bad people who seek to do harm, no fear of evil, no traffic accidents, and no treachery among people. In the Pure Land, one can just think of clothes and they appear, or think of food and it appears. The land is covered with gold and pleasant breezes waft the air. Rows of trees covered with the seven precious stones, while the water is replete with the eight merits. It is truly a wonderful and perfect place.

Some people wonder if such a place really exists. But think about it–if you had lived a few hundred years ago and someone had told you that it is possible to pave roads with asphalt, would you have believed them? That the Pure Land is covered with gold is not all that different from using asphalt on our roads today, or covering the floor with carpets. If we can do that, why should it not be possible for the Pure Land to be covered in gold?

Pure Land sutras describe pleasant breezes wafting in the air; is this so different from modern air-conditioning? They describe water replete with the eight merits; is this so different from the hot and cold tap water that is available even on the top floors of great skyscrapers?

The Pure Land is as beautiful as a park, and the trees, made of the seven precious stones, that grow there are stand in orderly lines that encircle the seven kinds of pagodas that have been erected there. Thus, the Pure Land is also described as "curved corridors turning gently, the tiles on the eaves projecting nobly."

Can there really be such a beautiful place? Is it real or is it make-believe? Since it is recorded in the sutras and comes directly from the words of Buddhist sages, it cannot be false. Then where is this world? It exists both in the Pure Land of Ultimate Bliss and within our own minds! There is the saying: "If our minds are pure, whatever land we are in will be pure as well." If the space of our minds is bright and wholesome, the ground of our minds kind and sincere, and the center of our minds joyful and carefree, then wherever we are in the moment is the Land of Ultimate Bliss, the Western Pure Land. This is why we say that one need not die to experience the Pure Land, for a pure land can be found right here in this world.

In my life I have seen many devotees come into Buddhist temples to burn incense, make donations, show their respect to the Buddha, or do other wholesome chores. Monastics in the temples often assure them: "Your good intentions surely will cause Amitabha to protect you and take you to his Pure Land some day in the future." I feel that that sort of response is very irresponsible, for the monastics are basically saying that the generosity and positive connection of the devotees are not something that they themselves are going to repay, but that Amitabha Buddha will repay it instead. This seems to be shedding responsibility and is thus quite indefensible.

This is why, when we built Fo Guang Shan in 1967, I also

established facilities and resources for caring for the elderly and youths, and for education and cultural enrichment. My goal was to make Fo Guang Shan serve devotees their entire lives. I hoped that people would be able to be "reborn" at Fo Guang Shan, and not have to wait to go to the Pure Land in the future. To me, this was the only way to repay devotees for their support and the vows they make.

In addition, I feel that there are some problems with the way that so many devotees devote themselves to chanting Amitabha's name. For example, when I ask some people where they are going, they answer: "I am going to the temple to chant Amitabha's name with other devotees." And then when I ask them why they do that, they said it is because chanting his name will allow them to grow closer to the Amitabha Buddha and be reborn in his Western Pure Land of Ultimate Bliss. They say: "I will transform my life like a lotus flower and never regress in my practice..." But the thing is, if Amitabha Buddha actually came to these people to take them to his Pureland, most of them would respond: "No, not now. This is not a good time as my son has not yet gotten married, my daughter has not yet found a husband, my grandchildren are still very small, my husband still needs me to take care of him... "

From this we can see that such pleading to go to the Pure Land is false and insincere. It would be better if people simply said that they "are practicing self-discipline in the hope of generating enough good causes to accrue merits." There is no need for them to sound so lofty and high-minded. We must learn to be honest in our practice of Buddhism and avoid hypocrisy. Sometimes it is possible for a person of small virtue to exaggerate his or her morality, but in practicing Buddhism, what we accomplish is exactly what it is—no more and no less. The energy we put into Buddhist practice, similarly, is not something that should be faked or exaggerated. A true, honest, and straightforward mind is the key to successful Buddhist practice. Indeed, that sort of mind is our true temple.

In sum, we all think often of departed loved ones as we do not know what has become of them. And this is the basic reason that we chant sutras for them at New Year's or on other festival days, hoping that our prayers will free them from suffering and bring them peace. If this sort of behavior springs from a deep sense of filial piety and honor for the dead, it naturally is a very good thing. But if it springs from the erroneous belief that our loved ones will descend into the hell realm unless a monastic chants for them, or that only by repeatedly chanting the name of Amitabha Buddha they will find liberation from suffering–well, this sort of thinking is completely wrong and actually dishonors our parents and ancestors.

We are dishonoring them because we are assuming that they have done so many terrible things in life that they have earned themselves a stay in the hell realm, for only people who have committed very serious transgressions are reborn there. Now, can it really be that we have such a low opinion of our own parents? Why is it that we do not think of our parents as having been wonderful people who were reborn in a blissful deva realm or in Amitabha's Pure Land?

It is therefore a profound mistake to believe that our relatives will surely become ghosts or denizens of the hell realm after death. Though the Buddhist tradition recognizes the existence of ghosts, it does not hold that every person who dies will turn into a ghost who will come and frighten people. When people leave this world, the hell realm is not the only place they will end up. They might also be reborn in the Pure Land, in the deva realm, or once again in the human realm.

The important thing is to do good deeds prior to taking rebirth. Good people do not just become ordinary people in their next lives, for some of them can become saints, bodhisattvas, and even Buddhas. Many may even end up in the Pure Land in accordance with the vows they took while in this realm. However or wherever we end up is ultimately determined by what we do in this life, so the most important thing is to pay close attention to the karma we generate through acts of body, speech, or mind.

Where is the Buddha?

Where do the sages of the past–such as the Buddha, Confucius, Jesus, and Muhammad–live now? If they are alive, how tall are they? What do they eat, what do they use, and how do they live?

Before discussing these questions, I want to share a koan. The Tang Dynasty emperor Shunzong once asked the Buddhist monk Ruman: "Where did the Buddha come from and where did he go after he died? If you say that he is eternally present in this world, then where is he right now?"

Ruman answered: "The Buddha comes from the unconditioned, and he returned to the unconditioned when he departed. His Dharma body is emptiness itself, and he resides in the state of no-mind. All thoughts return to non-thought. All that abides returns to the non-abiding. He came for the benefit of all sentient beings, and he departed for their benefit as well. The pure ocean of the bhutatathata (that which is always true) is the profound place of his abiding. When the wise contemplate this, they discover that they have no doubts."

Emperor Shunzong had some trouble accepting this, so he asked: "The Buddha was born in the palace of a king and died between two trees. He lived in this world for forty-nine years, and claimed that he had no Dharma to teach. Mountains, rivers and the ocean, heaven and earth, the sun and the moon, will in time all reach their end, so how can anyone say there's no birth and no extinguishing? With questions like these, wise one, please kindly explain."

Ruman tried explaining further: "The Buddha's body is fundamentally unconditioned, and it is a delusion to see it as a discreet thing. His Dharma body is emptiness itself; it was never born and it does not become extinguished. When conditions are right, a Buddha appears in the world; when conditions change, he enters nirvana. Everywhere he transforms people. He is like the moon reflected in water, for it is neither constant nor inconstant, and neither born nor extinguished. It is born though it is never born, and extinguished though it is never extinguished. If you can understand the place of no-mind, then you will understand that there is no Dharma to be taught."

At this point, the emperor had a small awakening and from that time on he showed great respect to the monk.

People often ask who is the greatest: Sakyamuni Buddha, the Medicine Buddha, or Amitabha Buddha. The Buddhist tradition holds that all Buddhas are equal. Neither Buddhas nor bodhisattvas are ever distinguished by rank, amount of merit, or level of importance. All Buddhas are "pure light without obstruction" and in this they are exactly the same. As for Confucius, Jesus, and Mohammad–each of these is a "founding sage" for the followers of their teachings. Though their names are different, their basic significance is the same.

People sometimes ask the question: If Amitabha Buddha is in the Western Pure Land and the Medicine Buddha is in the Eastern Pure Land, then where is Sakyamuni Buddha? If Sakyamuni Buddha lives in the eternal and tranquil world of light, then where is this tranquil and eternal world of light?

This sort of question often leads to very creative answers from Buddhist masters. If our minds are focused on this world, we will see the "transformational" body of the Buddha that was born and later died. But if our minds transcend this world–if we can attain a state of no–mind-then we see the Buddha's Dharma body, which is subject to neither birth nor death in this world. No-mind indicates the Chan mind. Only if we can attain this state of mind, will we truly know where the Buddha is.

"When conditions are right the Buddha appears in this world. When conditions have changed, he enters nirvana." The *extinction* referred to here is not the extinction of something that has arisen, but rather nirvana. Right now the Buddha is in the realm of nirvana. And where is the realm of nirvana? This realm is omnipresent, permeating all things. When a person has accomplished a high level of Buddhist practice and his life is over, he will enter into the great transformation of the universe and join the Buddha.

But how are we to know if we have really joined the Buddha? When we eat, he is beside our mouths. When we sleep, he is near our pillows. He is beside us twenty-four hours a day, whether we are walking, standing, sitting, or lying down. It is as the poet Su Dongpo said: "The sound of the stream is the broad long tongue; the form of the mountain is nothing but the pure body." If you can understand this, then the babbling brook will become his [Buddha's] transformational body, and the calls of birds will become the sounds of his teachings. In this way, we can all rise in the morning with the Buddha and embrace him as we sleep at night.

Then where are all of the Buddhas? They are in our minds, for when the Buddha is in our mind, all that we see will be his realm. If the Buddha is in our mind, then all that we hear will be the sound of his voice. If the Buddha is in our mind, then all that we say will be his words. If the Buddha is in our mind, then all that we do will be his deeds. If the Buddha is in our mind, then all Buddhas of all periods of time will be with us in the most wonderful way.

The Buddhist tradition never compels us to believe in the Buddha, for what difference would it make to him whether we have faith in him or not? He does not want us to worship him, for what good would that do him? Shall we call on him? It is hard to know whether he will respond to our calls. No, what the Buddha wants from us is for us to follow what he practices–for us to do what he did. Since the Buddha was compassionate, we should be compassionate as well. Since the Buddha brought joy to others, we too should bring others joy. Since the Buddha exhibited great patience and courageous perseverance, we too should do our best to be patient and to persevere. If we have the Buddha in our minds, then we will be able to do whatever he did. If we practice in this way–even though we may never call on him directly–we will gain incredible merits, as numerous as the grains of sand in the Ganges River.

Whenever I give a ceremony for people taking refuge in Buddhism, I always end by asking everyone to say "I am a Buddha!" Do you dare say that? Do you dare say "I am a Buddha!" It is good to say it. And once you have, remember that you can no longer argue with your wife or husband. Instead you must stop yourself and realize that since you are now a Buddha yourself, you can no longer scold and argue with others. This way, you might stop fighting all together.

If you enjoy smoking or drinking, you must now stop yourself the next time you crave a cigarette or a drink. You must ask yourself: "Since I said that I am a Buddha, does a Buddha smoke or drink?" If you can learn to think like this, then you might be able to kick both of those habits. So you see, the moment you recognize that you are a Buddha, your whole life begins to change.

Where is the Buddha? The Buddha is in our minds. He is with us at all times. When he is with us, it is an incomparable wonder. A person may have great wealth, an illustrious family name, an excellent education, and much power and influence¡K but none of these things can last forever, and not one of them can give us peace of mind. It is only through understanding that the Buddha is within us that we can learn to see this world in an entirely different way.

The Buddha cannot be understood by looking only at his form, for it is as the *Diamond Sutra* says: "If you try to see me as a form, or if you try to call on me with sound, then you will be practicing the wrong path and will never be able to perceive the Tathagata." The *Flower Garland Sutra* states: "If someone wants to understand the realm of the Buddhas, he must purify his awareness to the point that it is like emptiness." Do you want to know what the realm of the Buddhas is like? Then first you must purify your mind until it is as clear as space itself, for then you will be able understand the world of the Buddha.

Living a satisfying life

In life there are many things that are unsatisfying and imperfect. How can we find satisfaction and live in a way that we do not experience regret?

Life does not necessarily have to be perfect, for deficiency can also be seen as a sort of beauty. This is what is known as the "beauty of deficiency," which is not all that bad. For example, the moon is quite beautiful even when it is not full. In life, if we can learn not to feel bitter about deficiencies, but instead understand how to appreciate the beauty of deficiencies; then we will always feel satisfied.

Normally, we seek perfection in life, but what does perfection really mean? Is beauty that is fragile perfection? When a brave man dies on the battlefield, is that satisfying? Those that are killed are often good fighters, those that drown are often good swimmers–were they perfect? Wealthy people go bankrupt and talented ones often meet with misfortune–are their lives perfect?

Nothing is perfect in this world. We can often only attain half of what we want instead of everything. For example, one person may be very wealthy, but physically unhealthy. Another may have perfect love, but lack money. Others have a lot of property, but no children. Still others are wise and well-educated, yet they cannot find satisfying work. This is why we say: "human life arises out of many deficiencies."

Since human life is essentially replete with deficiencies, it is best that we seek satisfaction in the realm of the spirit, the enlightened path, and religious faith. If you know yourself, you will feel satisfied. If you feel content with what you have, you will be satisfied. If you are able to accept whatever comes your way, you will always feel satisfied. And if you are tolerant of others, you will know how to be satisfied. Beyond this, if we recognize our oneness with others, and learn to respect them and treat them as friends so that everyone is happy, then we will have gone a long way toward making this life into something that is deeply satisfying.

In addition, practicing the Buddha's teaching of "enlightening, liberating, and benefiting oneself and others at the same time" will also lead to great satisfaction.

A satisfying world is not something that someone else can create for us. Rather satisfaction in life is built step by step through learning how to conduct ourselves and handling matters on a daily basis. For example, some people are extreme in everything that they do; if they are not way over to the left, then they are way over to the right. Some people are very rigid about rank and status. Some people are particular about everything, and they cannot stand it if anything is vague or left unplanned. People like that are not accommodating enough. In contrast, other people are good at walking the middle path–if something is done honestly and to the benefit and happiness of all, they will feel satisfied. It does not matter to them if a few details are changed, for they are good at following whatever conditions prevail. This is being accommodating; this is being content.

If you will notice, in this universe, the sun, moon, and earth are all round. But among the things of this world, many of them are square, rectangular, quadrangular, or hexagonal–they all have edges and angles, features that cause so much friction! In contrast, if we can find roundness within ourselves–be it a circle, an ovoid, or an ellipse–we will find that people will be more likely to accept us. If we are not "round" in some sense of the word, then others will see us as having deficiencies and find it difficult to get along with us.

What are the best things in life? Truth, goodness, beauty, and purity! If we wish to live a life filled with truth, goodness, and beauty, we must start with being accommodating and gracious. When we interact with our parents, family members, and friends, we must try our best to be accommodating and harmonious. When we do things, we must remember to be considerate. When we speak, we must remember to be gracious. If we can do these things, we will be satisfied with our lives.

It takes great effort to find satisfaction in life. Why else would Buddhist practitioners put up with so much hardship in their practice? Because they feel that a world of complete satisfaction is possible. People who practice Chan seek enlightenment through practice, but why do they want to be enlightened? So what if they are enlightened? They pursue these ends because they realize that there is a world that is pure, carefree, liberating, and satisfying. Thus, in our relentless pursuit for the perfect world, what is most important is for us to look within our own minds, for once our minds are open, clear, expansive, and elevated we will know complete satisfaction in this world.

Today, the whole world esteems freedom and democracy, but having democracy alone is never enough, for people also need to be happy to feel fully satisfied. Facing a practical world, we do not need to seek great wealth or fame. As long as we can feel content with what we have, we will be satisfied. The truth is that this world is quite complete and perfect; it is simply because we do not understand this that we feel that we are lacking something.

Some people ask: "Where do we come from?" The answer is that "people arise from birth, and birth arises from death, and death arises from birth." Someone else might ask: "What comes first, the chicken or the egg?" The answer is that "the egg arises because the chicken exists, and the chicken arises because the egg exists." Everything moves in beginningless and endless cycles that are themselves perfect in every detail. The problem is that so many people do not understand these truths; they are ignorant and unenlightened, so they suffer pain and afflictions, while sinking ever more deeply into the cycle of birth and death.

To study Buddhism is to develop wisdom. Through our study of the Buddha's teachings, we learn to turn pain and suffering into valuable experiences that lead to wisdom and an expanded and elevated consciousness. This is the way to find complete satisfaction. In times of deficiency and unhappiness such as these, we must learn to have faith in the Buddha, to study his teachings, and to practice them, for when our minds are filled with the Buddha we will be perfectly satisfied.

Physical and Mental Illness

Technological progress and advances in modern science have led to material improvements that have enhanced people's quality of life on many levels. Yet no matter how much we have progressed or how advanced our technology is, there still remain fundamental problems of life that science will never be able to solve.

Two of the greatest problems that people face are birth and death. No sooner are we born than we must begin to face the problems of sickness and aging, both of which are now being intensively studied by medical researchers and social scientists. Religions, such as Catholicism and Christianity, have yet to offer anything substantive to help solve these problems. Even in the case of Buddhism, if we continue to employ Vinaya rules in our exploration of human life, we will find that many of them no longer are suitable to the modern age and that as a whole they leave open many of the most pressing questions of our time.

Fortunately, however, the basic principles of Buddhism teach us to constantly renew our understanding of the Dharma. The principles never change, and yet their applications to the problems people face today—such as physical and mental illness and death—allow us to see many things in new ways, and thus to find answers to the sorts of questions that we must face now. The Buddha was a great doctor and teacher of all humanity, and the Dharma is like *agada* medicine that can cure both physical and mental problems, while monastics are like nurses that protect all sentient beings. Thus, the Triple Gem is often referred to metaphorically as the doctor, the medicine, and the caregivers. If we use Buddhism to solve the problems faced by people today, we will discover a prescription with great efficacy.

On June 19, 2003, Master Hsing Yun gave a seminar about Buddhist views on physical and mental ailments at the Cloud Residence Hall at Fo Guang Shan, with over 160 people in attendance. The content of this seminar follows below.

Healing ourselves

Due to the various foods people eat, it is difficult to prevent the physical body from becoming ill. Is there a way to heal our bodies according to Buddhism, without using medicine?

The ancients used to say: "A serious practitioner should have a few ailments for these are what teach us to commit to the way." Basically, people become Buddhists for the most part due to certain causes and conditions. For example, some people, after experiencing difficulties and setbacks in their lives, want to have something to rely on and so they become Buddhists. Other people become Buddhists because, while they are deeply despondent or saddened, they hear some Buddhist teachings and feel comforted by them, and thus commit themselves to the Dharma. Still others are confused by life and hope to find answers in the Dharma, which leads them to practice Buddhism. And then there are those who become ill and discover that life truly is impermanent and filled with suffering, and so take on the Dharma.

Therefore, we can see that it is not necessarily a bad thing for someone to become physically ill, for illness is one way for people to discover the Dharma, and sometimes the only reason that they commit themselves to it and overcome their fixations on worldly matters. Though physical ailments do have a negative impact on people's lives, they also can bring positive meaning to life.

As for illness itself, who among us with a physical body that arose out of the four elements and the five skandhas will never become ill? Birth, sickness, old age, and death are processes that we all must experience in life. Thus, if we want to know how to cure diseases, we must first establish a correct perspective. We must understand how to prevent disease by distancing ourselves from it. If we become sick, we must know how to befriend our illness. It is especially important that we come to some realization of the deeper significance of life itself. Only by facing illness and death without any sense of attachment or clinging can we face our illnesses calmly, instead of letting our minds be filled with denial, dread, and anxiety. This is quite important, as a perturbed mind can only worsen physical conditions.

When we think about physical illness, we realize that there are so many kinds of ailments. For example, there are many branches of medical practice that deal exclusively with a particular area of the body, such as the eyes, ears, nose, tongue, mouth, throat, teeth, skin, heart, liver, kidney, or lungs. Beyond these, there are also specialists who work mainly with pregnant women, children, and those with mental or psychological problems. There are professionals who work in the fields of urology or family medicine, or with brain diseases, bone diseases, tumors, transplants, cosmetic surgery, external medicine, internal medicine, recuperation, the immune system, allergies, contagious diseases, diseases that are quick in developing and those that are slow, and so on.

The *Sutra of the Supreme Dharani* says: "Goiter, nervous diseases, those that produce excessive phlegm, diseases of the eyes, headaches, abdominal pains, hemorrhoids... skin funguses, or leprosy are rampant throughout the world and cause extreme suffering among sentient beings."

When we are sick, we of course must consult with a bona fide medical doctor and listen to his or her advice, and from this select the best cure that we can. The cure we use may be based on medicine, diet, physical therapy, psychotherapy, or even folk remedies or music therapy. For some illnesses, all that is required is extra rest, for they are best healed by the passage of time. For example, most doctors say that the flu is essentially incurable as there are over one hundred types, and medicines that target each type are simply too difficult to produce. So in the case of a disease like this, the best the medical profession can offer is a little sympathy and comfort, because those that truly understand the condition know that if they get the flu, the best thing to do is rest, drink a lot of fluids, and stay inside in order to overcome it.

Sometimes there is nothing wrong with our bodies at all, but as we suspect that there may be something wrong, we begin to feel ill and suffer from a sort of hypochondria. I have had this experience myself. When I was around twenty years old, one of my teachers said, "People often become ill because of paranoia; tuberculosis is an example of this." Upon hearing this I began to doubt the health of my own lungs and actually spent quite a lot of time under the shadow of that fear. I controlled my anxiety by reminding myself: "My health is so good, how could I possibly have tuberculosis?" Still, I could not help being affected somewhat by those words.

Years later I arrived in Taiwan and, while I was living in Chungli, someone told me that tuberculosis could be cured by eating tomatoes. Since tomatoes were not expensive back then, I bought a bushel of them. After finishing all of the tomatoes, I convinced myself that that many tomatoes ought to be able to completely cure my ailment, and from that time on I ceased to worry about the possibility of having tuberculosis.

Thus, we can see that sometimes our physical problems are caused by the mind's fears, such that mental illnesses require mental cures. Some physical illnesses often require nothing more than having faith in ourselves, being optimistic, getting enough exercise, and eating the proper foods. We can naturally overcome such illnesses without medication.

Beyond this, "an ounce of prevention is worth a pound of cure" when it comes to diseases of the body. Strengthening our immune systems is the best way to maintain our health. According to research, over ninety percent of human diseases have something to do with problems in the immune system. A working immune system is like having an army of experts capable of fighting off infections, cleaning out waste materials, and repairing damaged organs or systems.

Stated more simply, the immune system fights diseases and prevents foreign matter from entering the system. In a normal immune system, there are many beneficial bacteria that kill harmful germs. For example, some people catch a cold easily after being exposed to low temperatures, while others who have healthier immune systems do not become ill under the same circumstances. This is also true in the case of other contagious diseases, such as tuberculosis, hepatitis, or malaria, which can be easily contracted by those with weak immune systems. A person with the right antibodies in his or her immune system will not easily contract these diseases even with the same exposure.

In most hospitals, doctors do whatever they can to boost the strength of their patients' immune systems, and often spend a lot of time teaching people better ways to care for themselves. For example, they advise getting enough sleep at night, exercising at least thirty minutes every day, getting massages, laughing more often, relaxing, adopting better hygienic practices, and so on. They teach this because these techniques strengthen our immune systems. In addition, a study done at the Harvard Medical School clearly shows that people who have religious faith are generally healthier than those who do not. From this we can see that the best cures involve fixing our perspective and curing the mind, for if the mind is healthy and imbued with the right perspective, it is the most effective cure for physical diseases.

As for illnesses, they usually cannot be considered apart from pain. If you ask people whether they are afraid of becoming ill, they will reply that they are not. If you ask them if they are afraid of death, they will also reply that they are not. The truth is death is no different than moving from one home to another, changing clothes, replacing the old with the new, having a lamp run out of oil, or going to sleep-it is not really anything to be afraid of. Buddhists believe that life itself never dies and that it is simply part of a cycle of birth and death, much like the seasons of the year. Everything that is born must die and everything that dies is born again—there is nothing frightening in this. What is frightening is pain, for pain is difficult to endure. If there is illness without pain, then it is not a serious matter.

Nonetheless, most of us must become ill before we can

understand the suffering of having a body. It is said that "the hero fears only the torment of illness," for a serious disease can make even a brave man crawl like a dog. When we are healthy, few of us appreciate how precious that state is; but once we become sick, we realize how truly difficult suffering can be. But sometimes having to overcome an illness can in turn strengthen the immune system. So illness may actually be beneficial to our health in the long run.

The most dangerous thing with the onset of an illness is the confusion it can generate. Some people, upon first learning that they have a disease, will panic and search recklessly for an unconventional remedy. In Taiwan, there is a strange phenomenon in that suddenly everyone claims to be an expert the moment they learn that you are unwell. They say things like "You should take this kind of medicine," or "This kind of disease should be treated in such and such a way." It is all just reckless banter, but if you are without your own opinion, you will either follow one person's advice and go to that doctor, or you will follow someone else's advice and go to a different doctor. Then there are those who try to hide their illness out of fear or embarrassment of getting treatment.

Honestly, you should not look upon illness as something frightening. Once a group of us went to visit someone who had tuberculosis. One person in our group was afraid that the patient's illness would be contagious, but a member of the nursing staff said that it was a good thing to be exposed to contagions once in a while as such exposure can strengthen the immune system. He said that if you never exposed yourself to any germs at all, you would have a very weak immune system. Remember when everyone was afraid of catching SARS? Actually, the situation was never so bad, for an illness is much like a demon—the more you fear it, the more formidable it becomes and the more it can harm you.

For these reasons, I hope that everyone will develop a good attitude toward their health and learn to be their own best doctor. We say, "When the enemy comes, use the generals to block them; when floods come, use the earth to block it." If we get sick, there is no need to panic. Of course, we need to find medical treatment for our illness, but what is most important is knowing how best to treat ourselves and being our own best physician. If our minds are healthy and strong, we will be able to overcome any difficulty. If our willpower is strong, we will be able to overcome the suffering of any disease. If our minds are free of suffering, our bodies will likewise become free of pain. Then, what disease is there anywhere that can cause us consternation? The secret lies in practicing the three trainings–morality, meditation, and wisdom– and using these methods to erase from our minds all traces of greed, anger, and ignorance.

Healing the mind

In addition to physical diseases, people suffer from a variety of diseases of the mind, such as greed, anger, and being judgmental. Does Buddhism advocate some form of counseling that will help to solve these sorts of problems?

The *Great Prajna Sutra* says, "There are four kinds of diseases of the body, which are due to excessive wind, heat, phlegm, or other causes. There are also four kinds of diseases of the mind, which are greed, anger, ignorance, and pride." To tell the truth, it is much easier to cure physical ailments than mental ones. Nonetheless, just as the body is ours to have and understand, so also is the mind something that each of us has and should come to know well. If we know both our bodies and minds well, then whether it is a disease of the body or mind, we will be able to cure it more naturally.

Previously I mentioned that "mental illnesses require mental cures." There are many kinds of mental illness, including worry, fear, anxiety, depression, jealousy, confusion, delusion, hallucinations, irrational thoughts, depravity, sloth, indolence, and being anti-social.

Mental sickness is like a demon. Each of us has many demons living in our bodies or entrenched within our minds that may appear at the slightest opportunity to wreak havoc on our lives. According to the Buddhist tradition, there are 84,000 kinds of afflictions, which are nothing more than 84,000 kinds of illnesses. At the vanguard of all of those afflictions is greed. The next battalion is anger, the third is ignorance, the fourth is pride, the fifth is suspicion, and the sixth is wrong views. In the *One Hundred Dharmas* analysis of the Mind Only School of Buddhism, these six afflictions are known as the six most basic defilements.

The truth is that there are many demon armies of afflictions residing in our minds, but in the end, there is only one affliction that commands them all. It is ourselves–otherwise known as "clinging to the self." The affliction of clinging to the self unites and controls all other demon armies of greed, anger, ignorance, pride, and doubt. Most of the time when our minds are healthy and strong, our views correct, and our thoughts appropriate and filled with compassion and wisdom, we can very easily control our minds. As the *Flower Garland Sutra* says, "A single shot of the arrow of wisdom can destroy an army of demons, while one swing of the sword of sagacity can slash through the nets of suspicion." The moment we become careless and forget to protect ourselves, we will be beset again by the demons of our minds, which in the *Sutra of Bequeathed Teachings* are compared to thieves, wild horses, and enraged elephants.

If we look for the deep reasons why there are so many troublesome demons in our minds, we will find that it all comes down to ignorance and distorted views. For example, as soon as you become suspicious, you give your demons a chance to rise up. If you become arrogant, extreme in your opinions, stubborn, selfish, gullible, and if you enjoy seeing people argue, have no sense of what you believe in, and have low self-esteem, you will easily be led and become a ready victim of the demon king and his armies.

Then, how do we cure the problems of the mind? In the Buddhist tradition, it is said that the secret lies in practicing the three trainings–morality, meditation, and wisdom–and through them, erase all traces of greed, anger, and ignorance. Greed, anger, and ignorance are sometimes called the three poisons for they are the enemies most profoundly deleterious to the body and mind. Let me use a few metaphors to describe them more clearly: Greed can be compared to a stomach ailment, since so many stomach problems are the result of gluttony. Anger can be compared to lung disease, since diseased lungs gradually ruin the body just as anger ruins all that it touches. Ignorance can be compared to a nervous disorder, since nervous disorders are characterized by a loss of control over speech and motor functions, just as ignorance is the source of mishaps.

We can view the three poisons—greed, anger, and ignorance—separately. People all harbor some degree of selfishness in their minds. They always think of themselves first. When they see something they like, they want to possess it; as long as they can get what they want, they do not care if others live or die. As a result, the disease of greed naturally arises. Wouldn't it be better if we could learn to be like candles that sacrifice themselves so that others may have light; or like the dew that though it appears but briefly, gives of itself to nourish other living things; or like the sun that selflessly shines across the earth providing warmth and light? People who are able to give of themselves and who know how to help others feel happiness and joy are people who have learned to overcome greed, for generosity is the best cure for selfishness.

Anger is another common illness that troubles people's minds. People who become angry quickly have not spent enough time cultivating their character. The moment something that they do not like happens, they become angry; in a moment of anger, a friend may become an enemy, while a spouse may become a foe. When a thought of anger arises, all things may appear so loathsome and hateful that he or she may wish to smash the entire world with one blow. The *Dhammapada* says, "If one tries to end disputes with more disputes, they will never end, for it is only through patience that one can end disputes." Anger never solves problems. If we practice patience at crucial moments, and realize that all things in the world are essentially equal, and that there is no real difference between good and bad, self and others, then the disease of anger will not easily arise.

The third great mental illness is ignorance. People have this illness because they are confused and lack awareness. Ignorance exacerbates the problems of greed and anger. Moreover, all our afflictions and the main reason we remain trapped within the cycle of birth and death can be traced to ignorance. Ignorance leads to wrong views, and wrong views all too often lead to the creation of unwholesome karma, which in turn may lead to being reborn in one of the lower three realms, the hell realm, the ghostly realm, or the realm of animals. If we can spark a bit of awareness in our minds and realize that an ocean of wisdom resides within us, then we will be less susceptible to the harsh winds and roiling waves that are generated by ignorance.

Thus, the way to overcome the three poisons is threefold: generosity cures greed, patience cures anger, and awareness cures ignorance. Beyond these methods, Buddhism also teaches another five methods, which are called the "five contemplations that still the mind." The *Commentary on the New Flower Garland Sutra* says, "Wholesome methods for curing illnesses are: for illnesses that arise out of the four elements of this world, herbal medicines are the cure; for mental afflictions, the five contemplations that still the mind and the ten paramitas are the cure." The five contemplations that still the mind are used to address five kinds of harmful mental afflictions. They are:

1) The contemplation of defilement is used to cure greed and lust.

Sentient beings often confuse defilement with purity. A flower that appears beautiful may arouse desire in some people, just as a handsome man or attractive woman may arouse passion in others. These sorts of reactions create all sorts of clinging and afflictions in the mind. The contemplation of defilement teaches us to see that the things we desire have another side to them–in addition to being beautiful, they can also be filthy and defiled. For example, a flower may appear attractive, but when you remember that it grows in dirt and that its petals and leaves may hold many parasites and germs, you may no longer be attached to it. Or you might see a person who you think is very attractive and beautiful; if you contemplate that his or her body is a rancid skin bag put together by many causes and conditions and that it is merely an unclean bundle of flesh and bones, then naturally the mind will be rid of its lust.

2) The contemplation of compassion is used to cure anger.

Some people often lose their temper for no reason and aggravate others. Some people feel no joy when they see others do good, yet feel spiteful when they notice someone doing something bad. Some people tend to always point out how much they dislike someone, someplace, or even a time schedule. Still others think that they are always right about everything and that others are always wrong. These kinds of people tend to argue a lot and are easily angered.

The contemplation of compassion is sometimes called "the contemplation of the compassionate mind" or "the contemplation of sympathetic compassion." This contemplation can be used to cure a mind of anger and spite. Most people are familiar with the adage that Buddhism embraces compassion as its core. The definition of compassion is to remove the suffering of others while giving them joy. Any Buddhist teaching that departs from the spirit of compassion is nothing more than deluded teaching. After all, compassion is Buddha Nature; compassion is wisdom itself.

Compassion means that our minds have a correct view of the importance of helping others; it is based upon benefiting other sentient beings selflessly and altruistically. Compassion is purified love; it is generosity that does not seek rewards. If you have a truly compassionate mind, why would you cling to notions of what you like or dislike? Compassion is not confined to the purview of Buddhist practitioners; it is a gift that belongs to all sentient beings. When there is compassion among people, life will be filled with infinite meaning. In China there is a saying: "A humane person has no enemies." If we capture this sensibility in Buddhist terms, it means that compassion has no adversaries and that it can overcome all kinds of problems. Compassion is virtue implemented through our actions and not a ruler to measure the worth of others. True compassion is not always expressed through pleasant praise and gentle encouragement. Sometimes, using its diamond-like toughness to succumb demons is the more difficult and nobler manifestation of great compassion.

3) The contemplation of causes and conditions is used to cure ignorance.

Some people believe that the self and everything in this world are either truly existent or truly non-existent. This is ignorance based on clinging on to a one-sided view of reality. People who contend that there is nothing after death are ignorant in that they are clinging to a type of nihilism. People who believe that they will be reborn as humans after they die are ignorant in that they are clinging to a type of eternalism. Some people believe that Buddhist practice must be very austere, depriving oneself of food and sleep. This sort of person is ignorant in that they are clinging to extreme asceticism. Others think that Buddhist practice should always be completely joyful, which is another sort of ignorance in that they are clinging to the feeling of joy.

Ignorance can be overcome by using the contemplation of causes and conditions, since ignorance exists essentially due to a failure to understand the truth. What is the truth? It is causes and conditions. The Buddha's explanation of the three periods of time and the twelve links of dependent origination teaches us how to understand the interconnectedness of the past, present, and future. There is nothing in this world that arose alone or stands alone, for each thing depends on many causes and conditions. For example, a building consists of steel framework, cement, and wood, and it depends on human labor for its construction; thus, it is formed by many causes and conditions. Take a grain of rice, which is the result of such causes and conditions as a seedling, a rice paddy, sunlight, water, and a farmer's labor planting, irrigating, and tending the rice. From the contemplation on causes and conditions, we learn that all things in the universe are the conditions on which our lives are based–all things in the universe have led to arising and development. They are wholesome causes and conditions that have supported us, so we must always show our gratitude by being kind to all people. If we can truly understand the profound and wondrous causes and conditions that underlie all being, we will transform ignorance into wisdom.

4) The contemplation on the Buddha is used to overcome karmic obstruction.

Due to bad karma generated by unwholesome actions, speech, and intentions in former lives, some people experience many difficulties in life. Nothing they do seems to go right: when they try to make money, someone always swindles them; when they try to do good things, someone always slanders them; and when they go out, they often have accidents. Indeed, no matter what they do, they always tend to incur resentment and criticism. The contemplation on the Buddha can cure such problems of karmic obstruction. This contemplation asks us, first, to reflect on the emptiness and non-action of the Buddha's Dharma body, using it to combat the karmic obstacles that arise due to pressures around us. Second, this contemplation may also be used to consider the enormous virtues of the Buddha's reward body, as the mental states produced by this tend to lessen the negative karmic obstructions that arise within the mind. Lastly, this contemplation may be used to consider the noble and radiant features of the Buddha's transformation body, as the mental states produced by this tend to lessen the negative karmic obstructions of sloth and pessimism.

5) The contemplation on the breath is used to cure confusion and anxiety.

Our thoughts are everywhere. Sometimes they are focused on a daughter in the U.S.; other times they drift to a son living in

China. One moment they are in heaven, the next they are in hell. Our minds constantly fly between wholesome and unwholesome thoughts and back again. The contemplation on the breath can cure a confused and chaotic mind. Contemplation on the breath is called "*anapana*" in Sanskrit, a practice that entails counting each inhaled and exhaled breath to allow the confused mind to settle.

Beyond the five contemplations, there is the Buddhist practice of simultaneously cultivating both Chan and Pure Land techniques. Chan practices are good for gathering oneself, not allowing our thoughts to run wild, and keeping the demonic forces of delusion at bay. Pure Land practices are helpful for purifying the spirit and focusing the mind. When we can recite the Buddha's name with total concentration, we can also subdue delusions and keep the disease of stray thoughts from unsettling us.

There are many other forms of practice in Buddhism such as bowing to the Buddha and taking vows. Vows provide us with the strength to resist the demons of delusion. Buddhist practice emphasizes the importance of making vows of compassion, of repentance, and of cultivating *bodhicitta*, because such vows can endow us with incomparable strength. Additionally, we can learn how to shoulder that which we must and to let go of other things when we need to. We can also cultivate prajna-wisdom and sound reasoning. All of these practices are unsurpassed remedies for treating illnesses of the mind.

Today, many of the counseling techniques used by psychologists are similar to the practices taught within the Buddhist tradition. This is especially evident when we consider that Buddhism clearly teaches that virtually all mental problems spring from clinging to the self. The *Heart Sutra* says: "If we can clearly see that the five skandhas are empty, we will overcome all suffering." Similarly, once we can understand that the self is empty, we will overcome all confusion and mental turmoil.

Nonetheless, although it is somewhat easy to overcome clinging to the self, clinging to the Dharma is another matter.

Buddhist practice entails doing battle with 84,000 kinds of demonic forces of affliction mentioned by the Buddha. If we allow ourselves to be careless, we can easily be defeated by any of those afflictions. For this reason, curing illnesses of the body and mind require us to reinforce our strength with wisdom, compassion, and sound reasoning. A martial artist must know eighteen martial forms; similarly, Buddhist practitioners need to shore up their defenses with positive forces, such as the Six Paramitas, the four means of embracing, the Noble Eightfold Path, and so on. Only by being prepared can we expect to subdue the demonic armies that can do harm to our mental health.

In conclusion, if we want to cure mental illness, we have to rely on our own efforts. A doctor can prescribe medication to a patient, but no one can force the patient to take it. If the patient does not take it, he or she may never recover. In the same way, even though Buddhist practices can cure illnesses of the mind, if one refuses to follow them diligently, his or her disease may never be cured. Learning from the Buddha is nothing more than studying his teachings and putting them into practice. It is much more important to practice the teachings prescribed by the Buddha than just to believe in them. For if we merely believe but do nothing, it is like talking about food or counting someone else's money without enjoying any real benefits. You may exclaim how wonderful Buddhism is, but if you don't actually practice it, it will be completely useless to you!

Overcoming Moodiness

When some people become moody, they become volatile and may easily anger or act on impulse. What can people do to help control their emotions better?

When our moods are unstable, we are like a table with only three legs. With one leg missing, the table will lack adequate support and foundation. Naturally, it will be unstable. People are the same. When their state of mind is weak and unstable, they may feel that everything in the world is unfair. As a result, they will feel resentful toward others, or depressed, spiteful, and even jealous. Due to such misguided feelings of dissatisfaction and unfairness, their minds become unbalanced and given to abnormal mood swings, which further causes them to be violent, unreasonable, irrational, and skewed in their behavior and speech.

Unstable moods result largely from people's lack of self-control and their consequent inability to deal with the world in a proper manner. We often hear people say things like: "I can't help it! I have to be angry!" or "I cannot control myself! I want to hit someone!" Due to people's lack of self-control, greed and anger frequently rise in their minds, unsettling them and impairing their judgment and ability to reason. All of this is a result of an immature and vulnerable mental state. When we are prone to mood swings, our judgments are distorted and we cannot tell right from wrong, or good from bad; then we become willful and contrary. History tells us that the majority of emperors and leaders who became tyrannical and ruthless were people who could not control their moods. As a result, countries were destroyed and families broken, as well as lives lost and reputations shattered.

When people lose control of their moods and feel at a loss as to what to do, they must seek help from others! But from whom? Bow to the Buddha, for the Buddha will always help you! Chant the Buddha's name, for he will always empower you! If you want to hit or yell at someone, say the Buddha's name instead, for perhaps just this one word will help quell your anger and allow you to put down your fists.

If we want to control our moods, it is good to read often, for reading strengthens our ability to reason; it also helps us treat others more reasonably and respectfully. As the saying goes: "Those who treat others with respect will always be treated respectfully in return." This is a very natural thing. Furthermore, we may also copy sutras, meditate, paint, chant, and self-reflect, in order to appreciate the need for repentance and the source of suffering. When we often feel moved and inspired, our minds will naturally be gentle and calm and less prone to mood swings. In contrast, those who spend a great deal of time blaming heaven and others will gain little control over their moods and will instead create afflictions through their ignorance.

The *Hongming Ji* says: "Those who are bound by many afflictions are called ignorant." It is disconcerting when a Buddhist practitioner has no control over his or her moods and spends a great deal of time behaving in an ignorant way, for if such a person cannot even control himself, how can he or she be expected to aid others? For this reason, each of us must very carefully scrutinize ourselves and ask what fundamental problems we may have. Are they physical in nature? Or psychological? Do they stem from our perspective or interpretation of things? Or are they related to our moods? Whatever the problems might be, everyone ultimately needs to have a method for addressing them. If you always expect others to help you in situations like these, you will eventually run into problems for very few of us have such good causes and conditions that we will always have a wise and good friend around to help us out. Therefore, it is very important to learn to be a wise and good friend to yourself and solve problems on your own.

There is a folk saying: "Those who start trouble must also end it." Our moods belong to us, and so ultimately we are responsible for correcting them. If we feel lazy, we must work to become more industrious. If we feel despondent, we must rouse our spirits. To correct untoward moods, we must also learn to be content, grateful, repentant, self-reflective, optimistic, reasonable, empathetic, and willing to make vows. We must also learn to criticize ourselves rather than others, and we must understand how to improve our minds and transform our nature, to turn around and move forward. The most important thing in life is to understand how to change: how to turn delusion into enlightenment, weakness into strength, darkness into light, and ignorance into wisdom. If we can learn how to transform ourselves, a new venue of life will open up for us.

In conclusion, we want to avoid moodiness whenever we can for moodiness is nothing more than a karmic wind of ignorance. The *Explication of the Significance of Guanyin* says: "The winds of karma can destroy the boats of the five precepts and the ten wholesome deeds and cause us to fall into one of the three suffering realms or into the realm of desire." Thus, by upholding the precepts, meditating, and being compassionate, we will be able to protect ourselves from the winds of karma. Otherwise, when the winds of karma begin to blow, the great seas will roil and surge, and the world will seem gloomy and dark; our nature will be shrouded in clouds, while the truth will be skewed and distorted. The harm caused by moodiness can indeed be enormous if left uncontrolled!

Overcoming Afflictions

What are people to do when they are troubled by afflictions? For example, some people are troubled by a single word or issue; others encounter poverty or have poor relations with other people. When afflictions of these sorts occur, what is one to do?

Most people become disturbed the moment they hear even the slightest comment that they do not like, or they become angry when they see someone doing something they do not approve of. Actually, this sort of reaction only cheats the person who feels it. Someone else says something, but I am the one who becomes angry; someone else does something, but I am the one who loses my appetite. Someone looks at me a certain way, but I am the one who loses sleep over it. If we allow ourselves to be so easily affected or unsettled by others, it means we lack resolve and resilience.

Most people today lack inner strength and are unable to withstand even one comment they do not like. Anything that has worth must have endurance. For example, at one time Taiwan tried exporting lumber to the United States (U.S.), but due to the dry climate in the U.S., the wood cracked and no one wanted to buy it.

When Hsi Lai Temple was built in the Los Angeles area, we used a lapis-lazuli tile that was put through some stringent tests to be sure that it was feasible–it had to withstand several thousand degrees of heat. In my view, afflictions are also a kind of test. If we totally crumble in the face of afflictions, then that would indeed be pitiable because we will never know true peace of mind or gain a restful abode.

The *Commentary on the Abhidharma-kosha* says: "When the obstructions of *kleshas* are serious, further karmic obstructions may be generated; and these karmic obstructions may further generate more obstructions of different kinds-this process is based upon the first *klesha*, which is its root." When afflictions come, you must face them and dissolve them, for if you try to avoid them by hiding in your room, it will be of little avail. Afflictions are something that we cannot hide from; it is only by driving them out of our bodies and minds that we can claim victory over them.

Afflictions are a form of ignorance; they stem from not being able to reason correctly. When they come, it is as if a bad person had just arrived, for all of our good friends will quickly depart. Afflictions ruin our peace of mind, for they are like typhoons or cataclysms.

But where do they come from? Sometimes they arise from our external environment, like when one is unable to bear the words or actions of others; sometimes they arise internally, such as when suspicion, jealousy, or simple narrow-mindedness takes over. As the saying goes: "Fundamentally there are no problems in the world, for they all arise from our own worries." Most afflictions are thus of our own making.

Sometimes we speak without thinking and are criticized by others, and this of course is a source of affliction. Another kind of affliction arises when we are unhappy because others rebuke us for our own misdeeds. However, if we change our thinking and accept criticism as a lesson, then the comments of others will no longer become afflictions.

All too often we become troubled due to other people, events, or things someone says. But we must each have the strength to transform afflictions, to turn them into enlightenment. For the most part, human afflictions are the product of ignorance and lack of understanding. When afflictions come, we must rely on ourselves to dissolve them, because the advice and counsel of others is only momentary. Unless we can eradicate the roots of our afflictions, there will not be any good outcomes.

How then are we to overcome afflictions? Here are a few ideas:

1) When with others, do not compare yourself to them or be petty. Most afflictions stem from pettiness or unfavorable comparisons. If we do not compare or judge, then we will have fewer afflictions.

2) When an affliction arises because we feel someone is doing better than us, just wish them well. If someone you know buys a large building but you do not have enough money to buy your own home, so what? You can keep out of the rain by standing under the eaves of that person's building, so his or her good fortune may also do you some good. If you buy a TV set but I cannot afford one, so what? While you sit in front of it to watch TV, I can stand behind and watch for a while, too. If you build a large temple and I have only a small temple, so what? When I visit and stay at your temple, I will be able to enjoy a meal there. For the many things we may encounter in this world, as long as you can keep an open mind and accept them as they are without grudge or envy, then you will be free of afflictions.

3) It is best not to cling to things or insist that they turn out a certain way. Do not expect others to do things as we wish. People all have their own personalities and freedom, so if we get upset because others do not comply with our wishes, then afflictions will enter, just when our mental state is most vulnerable, obscured, and ignorant.

4) It is best to spend our time engaged in wholesome interests, work, and habits, because they can fend off innumerable onslaughts from the demons of our own intemperate behavior. The most important thing is to work hard at your job, for if you are busy you simply will not have the time to cause yourself so many problems. It is also important to spend time with wise and good friends and to avoid people who cause problems, for if we try to drown our troubles in drink while in the company of unsavory people, we will only make matters worse.

5) We must constantly self-reflect and be willing to tell ourselves: "I am not doing enough, I am not good enough." The Way to Buddhahood says: "Be ashamed of what you do not know and of what you are not able to do. Be ashamed of your defilements and enter upon the Mahayana path." If we only think about how good we are and are forever willing to forgive ourselves, we are likely to say: "That's just how I see things. It's the way I am!" This sort of thinking keeps us from improving and ridding ourselves of afflictions.

6) Be attentive to others, do good things, and say kind words. If we can keep these three wholesome practices in mind, we will have far fewer afflictions. The reason is that when you perform good deeds, say kind words, and maintain a wholesome mind, other people will praise and respect you. Of course, you will be free from afflictions.

Beyond these points, having afflictions is inevitably due to our own mistakes, so we must face them with courage and be willing to admit fault and make amends. A person with an illness must first admit that he or she is sick. How can you treat someone who refuses to admit this?

The most useful thing about religions is they help us to overcome ignorance and reduce afflictions. The Buddhist tradition is replete with a vast range of teachings. But no matter how numerous or how effective they are, if we fail to learn and apply them, it would be just like fighters who refuse to train. Though they may be equipped with the best knives, spears, swords, and halberds, if they do not learn to use them, not only will they fail to defeat the enemy, they will be subdued. For these reasons, we must use the tools of right mindfulness and right thought to conduct ourselves and deal with issues that arise. With right mindfulness, we can overcome the sources of delusion that produce afflictions. As the saying goes, "The Dharma can be understood in infinite ways, but foremost is purity as the foundation." If we understand how to purify our minds, afflictions will have nowhere from which to rise.

Finding Liberation from Fear

All people–men, women, young and old–have fears. For example, some fear death, some the dark, some ghosts, some other people, some strange things, some pain, some disease, old age, etc. What can be done to help overcome these sorts of fears?

People are mostly afraid of what they do not know. For example, we fear the dark because we cannot see what is there. If we understood everything, we would fear nothing. Most of us become afraid when we enter an unfamiliar environment. If we so much as see a blade of grass move in the wind, we fear that ghosts are wandering about.

When I was a young boy, I always felt that a ghost was following me when I went out walking alone. To overcome my fears, I would walk faster, but as soon as I sped up I felt that the ghost behind me was speeding up, too! If I was far from home, the ghost would follow me for quite some time, so I had to think of something to do. At that time I was quite small and had not yet become a monk. One day, I decided to stop and turn around. And when I did I saw that, of course, there were no ghosts behind me anywhere. So even then I learned how to discipline myself, for if there were no ghosts behind me, there was no reason for me to be afraid!

I think that the main reason people become afraid is they do not see the reality of the situation at hand. It is like the saying: "If we are bitten by a snake just once, we will fear rope for ten years." If a snake bites us one time, the mere shadow of a rope will cause us to overreact.

Some people are timid and lack courage; if you ask them to go on stage and give a talk, they say "I dare not!" If you ask them to greet guests, they say "I dare not!" Indeed, no matter what you ask them to do, they reply "I dare not!" Why do they not dare do anything? It is simply because they are timid. This is a character flaw, for we must have the courage to face anything that confronts us; because if we want to succeed, we must first work hard.

In Taiwan there is now a kind of training course called "losing-face training." No matter how unattractive a new daughter-in-law might feel she will still have to meet her in-laws. People must be able to withstand being embarrassed in front of others in order to become strong. If we buy an electrical appliance, it has to withstand our handling and tests before we know how durable it is.

Why do people become afraid? They fear losing love, money, power, social position, and honor. We fear losing that which we already have. Some people fear things like mice, even though it is really the mouse that should be afraid of us. How can anyone be afraid of a mouse? That is really getting things backwards! Then there are those who fear cockroaches, but cockroaches run and hide the moment they see a person coming. Why be afraid of them? It is strange that anyone should have such fear!

People also fear disasters, typhoons, earthquakes, and mudslides. Some fear being robbed, bad people, bandits, and so forth, but fearing these things does no good whatsoever! Trying to hide from them does no good either. If we know that a typhoon is coming, we need to reinforce our doors and windows. If there is a mudslide, we need to go to a safe place and wait it out. As for earthquakes, you need to understand what to do if one strikes.

For the most part, wooden buildings are very unlikely to collapse in an earthquake; instead, they simply sway back and forth because they are pliable. If you live in a tall building, the taller it is, the more it will shake. Even if you want to escape, there is not enough time. So there no need to panic. Instead you need to know what to do in such a situation. You might crawl under a table or stand near a supporting beam, or look for an open space where you can find safety. People who panic when a crisis comes in fact have a tougher time escaping it.

The truth is that no matter how serious a catastrophe may be, there is always something that can be done about it. What is more frightening is superstition, for superstitions cause people far more consternation. Some time ago there was a movie star named Lin Yan. She bought a house in the U.S., and though she had taken refuge in Buddhism, she was still very superstitious about feng shui. Accordingly, she asked a feng shui expert to come to her new home and look it over. The expert told her that three ghosts were living in the house. Since she was a single woman, she was fearful of spending her evenings alone with the ghosts, so she sold the house.

After she purchased another home, she asked the feng shui expert to come have a look at it as well. Although she expected that her new place would be trouble-free, the geomancer told her that the yin elements in her new home were very heavy! This made her even more fearful, and because she was unable to find peace of mind, she eventually used a gun to kill herself.

It is true that ghosts have places where they roam, so I am not saying that there is no such thing as feng shui, for as the saying goes: "Humans have human principles; the heavens have heavenly principles; emotions have emotional principles; the way has its principles; and the land has its principles." Nonetheless, you cannot tell if a property is good or bad simply by gauging the direction it faces. For example, there may be a number of businesses on the same side of the street, all facing east. Some of them may make money and others may not; do you think that their success or failure has anything to do with the direction they face? The success of a business is based on the product they sell, how the business is managed, and how well the owners have researched the marketplace. None of this has anything to do with feng shui, for all things are subject to the Law of Cause and Effect.

Superstitions can indeed be quite scary. When we must deal with fear, we should instead use wisdom and common sense.

If we understand typhoons, we will not be frightened by them. If we understand earthquakes, we will not be frightened by them either. We must recognize that ghosts have their world and animals have theirs. The situation is similar to that at Fo Guang Shan, where men have their own area and women have theirs. Each of us has our own world and because of this we do not obstruct each other.

Actually, ghosts will not bother someone without reason, and human beings should have no reason to go looking for trouble from them. Do not let yourself become obsessed with ghosts, and do not do anything to invite them into your home! People may have no problems at all, but due to superstitious beliefs, they might do things that actually attract ghosts to them! We have this situation in Taiwan among people who raise "pet ghosts," which in the end always create all kinds of problems. Thus, it is better to be wise than to be superstitious.

Once there was a bhiksuni who was bitten by a poisonous snake, and though she had a severe reaction to the poison and appeared as if she was going to die, she was not frightened. She said, "I am someone who contemplates emptiness. A poisonous snake can bite my body, but can it bite emptiness?" If we can identify with emptiness, we will have no fear. Once we are without fear, we are in fact more likely to avoid many kinds of calamities.

A person with compassion has no enemies and is welcome wherever he or she goes. If we have wisdom and can understand many things, then we will have no fears. If we have courage, belief in ourselves, right thoughts, and the ability to turn our attention where we want it to be, there will be no fear in our lives. When we have to walk along a road at night, we must depend on a light. If a person lacks courage, he can get other people to walk with him. It is fairly easy to deal with objective fears that come from the outside, but it is also important to realize that all fear arises from the timidity and ignorance of the mind. This is why we must train ourselves.

From a very young age, I trained myself to be courageous.

During the war of resistance against Japan, I slept among a pile of corpses. I also experienced the hail of bullets on a battlefield. When I first came to Taiwan in 1951, I needed a place to sleep at Shandao Temple in Taipei, so I made a space on the lowest rack in the room where human ashes are stored. At the time, there were no ashes being stored on that rack, so I was able to sleep there. That night, there was a huge earthquake in Hualien, and the shaking caused many of the urns above me to lean to the side. I said to the ashes: "You all, please don't fall down and hit me!" During that tremor, I did not worry about anything else and did not feel afraid in the least; the reason I remained calm is that I had only one thing on my mind—making sure the urns would not fall on me.

In the past, I read many stories about fox-fairies and learned that they are really very good beings and quick to repay a favor. If you are good to them, they will repay you many times over. Sometimes I used to think that it would be great to have a ghost for a friend. Naturally, I would rather have a Buddha or bod-hisattva appear to me, but if a ghost appeared, I did not feel that that would have been a bad thing. Since I was mentally prepared for such an occurrence, even if a ghost showed up, I don't think I would have been afraid.

I do not feel that ghosts are frightening. In fact, I feel that human beings are much more frightening than ghosts. In the section on the *Jin Dynasty* in the *Twenty-five Histories*, there is a story about a man named Song Dingbo from Nanyang who was hurrying along a road one night. In a very remote area, he unexpectedly came across a ghost. Striking a courageous pose he asked:
"Who are you? And why do you hop up and down when you walk?

"I am a ghost! Hey, and who are you?"

When he heard that, Song Dingbo thought to himself: "Oh no! How did I manage to run into a ghost today!" If he openly told the ghost that he was a human being, he thought he might have a big problem on his hands. So he lied: "I too am a ghost!"

"Oh, so you are a ghost, too! Where are you going?"

"I am going to the capital."

When the ghost heard that, he appeared quite pleased and said: "Great! I am going to the capital, too. Why don't we walk together?"

Song Dingbo had no choice but to agree to walk along with the ghost. After a while, they both became tired and the ghost said: "There is still a long way to go, and if we continue in this way it will be pretty tough. Why don't we take turns carrying each other; that way we can hurry along and one of us can rest as we go."

"O.K."

"Let me carry you first." As soon as the ghost stopped speaking, he hoisted Song Dingbo onto his back. "Oh, wow! How can you be so heavy?" he asked.

Song Dingbo quickly made up a lie to answer the ghost. He said: "Since I died only very recently, I am still quite heavy."

The ghost believed his story and continued carrying him along the road until they came to the bank of a river full of rough water. The ghost pointed to the river and said: "We had best swim across this."

And with a slight grunt, the ghost dove into the water and swam as lithely as a cloud to the other side, where he turned to watch Song Dingbo slowly struggling to cross the river with great effort and much splashing and sputtering. The ghost ran to the bank and in a disdainful voice asked: "Whoa! Why do you make so much noise when you're swimming? If any humans hear you, they will be really frightened. Why do you make so much noise?"

Song Dingbo realized that the ghost was getting suspicious and so again he quickly relied on human trickery to come up with a story. He said: "Since I just died, I am not that good at swimming yet."

After Song Dingbo climbed out of the water, the two continued on their way, but Song thought to himself: "I am really unlucky today for meeting a ghost. I better think of some way to get away from him." So Song put on a humble and deferential face and asked the ghost: "Say, older brother, since I have not been dead very long, I am not all that clear about the world of ghosts. For starters, can you tell me what it is that we ghosts fear more than anything else?"

"We ghosts are most afraid of human spit. If someone spits on us, we will be totally helpless," the ghost answered in a very sincere manner.

By this time dawn was breaking and the sky took on the paleness of a fish's belly. After a night of traveling, the two could see that they were almost to the capital. Taking advantage of a moment when the ghost was not paying attention, Song Dingbo let loose a thick gob of spittle on his body. Immediately the ghost began twisting and writhing in pain, and then just as quickly he turned into a small mountain goat. Song subsequently led the small goat to the capital and sold it for one thousand copper coins.

The truth is that ghosts are not terribly frightening; and surely they are not as frightening as some people. But there are still many timid people who fear ghosts. For someone who truly fears ghosts, developing a mind of wisdom will naturally allow one to overcome such fear. Otherwise, he or she will have to rely on outside help. Ultimately, though, we all must still rely on ourselves by making good connections with others often. With wholesome causes and conditions on hand, even if we end up running into a ghost in the middle of the night, some good person will surely come to our aid.

Eradicating Bad Habits

Most people have a fair number of bad habits, such as drinking, gambling, loving money, lust, the use of foul language, being argumentative, or gossiping about others. What is the best way to eradicate bad habits?

We often say: "Afflictions are easily overcome, but bad habits are hard to change." Some people say: "It is easier to change the rivers and mountains than it is to change a person's basic nature." Both of these sayings indicate how difficult it can be to change our habits.

In the Buddhist tradition, serious mental defilements are called afflictions, while less serious ones are called bad habits. Truthfully, it is hard for people to avoid having some sort of affliction or bad habit. In the *Explication of the Mahaparinirvana Sutra*, it is said even "an arhat may end all kleshas within the three realms of desire, form, and formlessness, but still have not rid himself of persistent traits." This means that even a great arhat who is enlightened may still like to look at himself in the mirror. The reason he retained that persistent trait is that he was a woman in hundreds of former lives and during that time developed the habit of looking in the mirror. One may become a monastic but still retain vain habits. All these are examples of the persistence of our habits!

Among the Buddha's ten greatest disciples, the ascetic Mahakasyapa still "got up to dance whenever he heard music," because it was a persistent trait. Gavampati had the habit of making a lot of noise when he ate; he sounded like a cow when he chewed food because in a former life he had been a cow and had had to masticate his food like other cows. This way of chewing became a persistent trait that reappeared life after life.

Some people lower their heads and do not look at others when they talk–this is a persistent trait. Other people frequently glare at others with a hostile look in their eyes. Still others love to eat certain kinds of foods or buy certain kinds of things–these are all persistent traits.

In the Chan tradition, it is considered best for people to possess as few things as possible, and thus we have the saying: "With clothing weighing only two-and-one-half catties and no more than the eighteen things a monk may possess." When people have fewer possessions, their desires will also be fewer, for the more we own, the more we are bound by things and the more afflictions they will engender.

People today have too many things, and they tend to become possessive and develop many greedy habits. This is not surprising, since as we sometimes say: "Not committing great transgressions, we cannot end our minor faults." In this case, the so-called "minor faults" are what I am referring to as persistent traits. Even great bodhisattvas who are but one step away from being completely enlightened often still do not become Buddhas. Now, why is this? It is because delusion remains to nourish life; they deliberately hang on to a bit of ignorance and a trace of their persistent traits so that sentient beings will be able to relate to them and draw near. To help liberate other sentient beings, the great bodhisattvas are willing to forfeit their own ambition of becoming Buddhas. So from this we can see that to become a Buddha, one must eradicate all afflictions and persistent traits.

Then how are we to deal with persistent traits? First, we must use introspection, or contemplation, to look into our own minds and see our faults. Most people put their critical focus on others, pointing out their mistakes and faults. According to the *Important Points of the Mahayana*, however, "habits are part of the mind." And thus, we should spend most of our time examining our own minds and our own faults!

Naturally, some people—such as alcoholics or drug abusers—require professional medical care, but even still, at some level they must decide to cut the addiction. People such as gamblers or those who frequently say mean things must also rely on their own minds to eliminate their habits. There is a saying describing good friends as being "straight-forward, forgiving, and knowledgeable," so some people assume they can always find a good friend to monitor or restrain them. It should be recognized, though, that if we rely on others to manage and counsel us, it is only useful to a limit. Self-restraint and self-awareness are the most important methods for curbing unwholesome habits.

Once there was a general manager who had a tendency to yell at others. Needless to say, the workers under his supervision were not happy. Even though he realized that his fits of anger only distracted his workers and dampened their morale and sincerely wanted to change his behavior, he just could not. At last he made a sign that said: "refrain from anger." He would use this motto to remind himself not to lose his temper. He was full of determination to change, but one day he overheard one of his co-workers say, "Our general manager has a terrible temper!" As soon as he heard those words, the manager became furious and immediately grabbed his sign and threw it at the person who had said that about him. As he did so he said, "I changed long time ago! How dare you say I still have a bad temper?"

The worst habit of all is not being able to see yourself. People often want others to be perfect while expecting little or nothing of themselves. Everyone is "strict with others, but lax with themselves." As time goes on, these sorts of limiting habits become persistent traits.

Then how do we change persistent habits? In my view, besides simply being courageous in admitting our faults and being determined to improve, we must also use wisdom and patience. There are three basic kinds of patience–patience of life, patience of dharma, and patience of non-arising dharmas. *Humble Table, Wise Fare* states: "If we eliminate one part of a persistent trait, we will attain one part of understanding. If we eradicate a great deal of klesha, we will attain a small part of the bodhi mind." When we have attained patience of non-arising dharmas, we naturally can overcome karmic obstructions and unwholesome habits. Our minds are like the surface of a mirror that must be kept clean, or like copper or bronze that must be wiped with oil from time to time. The mind must be washed like dirty clothes, or vacuumed like a dirty carpet.

If we only rely on others to remove our bad habits, we will never succeed. We must rely on our own resolve, willpower, and self-discipline. As the saying goes: "True gold must be smelted and white jade must be carved by a skilled hand." If we resolve to change and work hard at it, in time all of our bad habits will disappear.

Coping with disability

How should families cope with problems that arise when one of their members is developmentally disabled?

Though modern science is highly developed, human suffering has hardly been alleviated at all. Indeed, it often seems that the more societies progress, the more problems people have. For example, many people have mental impairments, physical handicaps, mental illnesses, amnesia, and so on. If a family member has some sort of difficulty like this, it can be a real burden and inconvenience to the rest of the family.

Then again, for many things in this world we can never be sure whether something is a blessing or a curse. There is a saying based on an old Chinese story: "Master Sai lost his horse, but who knows if it was a blessing or a curse?" For some families the presence of a disabled member may be a very good thing. For example, the President of the Chinese Association of Switzerland, Ho Cheng-wei, told me his entire family was able to emigrate to Switzerland from Vietnam, because the family had one member who was developmentally disabled. For this reason, they were given disability preference for immigration.

In Switzerland, welfare for disabled people is very good; the government gives about $3,000 per month to each disabled person, and this sum was enough to support that large family of ten. When I was in Switzerland, Ho Cheng-wei told me that their disabled child was a gift and savior to the whole family as the government stipend had saved them from poverty. There are many stories like this one.

There are parents who raise healthy children and after expending great effort, manage to get them admitted to good schools abroad. The children go overseas to study and after receiving their master's or doctoral degrees decide not to return home. Their parents end up with no one to care for them when they are old. Fortunately, in some of these cases, if there is also a disabled child in the family, the money provided by the government for this child may help support the parents. Parents in these situations often say: "Having a disabled child is our blessing."

Thus, we cannot say definitely whether it is a good or bad thing to have a disabled child. This is especially true in cases where families are inspired to practice the compassion of a bodhisattva due to having a disabled person under their care. Mrs. Yang from Hong Kong is a person of this type for her disabled child allowed her to fully see the suffering inherent in human life. This understanding inspired her to enter the bodhisattva path and make a vow of charity to benefit all sentient beings.

In this world, we can never say for sure whether something is good or bad, fortunate or unfortunate. As the Sadapaributha Bodhisattva said in the *Lotus Sutra*: "I dare not look down on you for one day all of you will be Buddhas." In the *Maha-samnipata Sutra*, it is said that even a bodhisattva must suffer from 108 kinds of discomfort. If a family has a disabled member, the most important thing is for the other members of the family to love the disabled person and not to avoid or abandon him or her. All things arise due to causes and conditions; if we use Buddhism to understand this kind of situation, we will come to realize that all events in this world are opportunities for us to develop compassion, for tests like these teach us to accept our conditions and face them with courage, love, and firm resolve.

Once when I was in the Fo Guang Art Museum in Taipei, I met two artists who had no arms. The artists—Yang Cheng-hua and Yang Cheng-lung—were brothers, and they asked to have their pictures taken with me. This type of person—one who is disabled but not wasted—is quite common. Their lives depend very much on how their families have treated them; if they have grown up in a loving home, they are often capable of doing wonderful things.

When I presided over the graduation ceremony at Nanhua University, there was a student, Lee Chi-chiang, who was born without hands, and yet he studied along with all of the other students. He now has a master's degree and is an expert software developer. He uses his feet to wash his clothes and eats without any help from others. He can even thread a needle by himself and types on a computer keyboard just as quickly as the next person.

I have seen disabled people in Mainland China who were very active; indeed, their disabilities seem to have made them even stronger and more determined. In Taiwan, there are many disabled people expressing themselves in the media, who have been highly respected and successful. Whatever heaven has granted us must be of use. With a good education and a caring upbringing, disabled people are capable of doing a great deal, so as long as they try their best.

"Just as the moon does not have to be full, a disability can also be beautiful. There is no need to possess a thing, for simply appreciating it is a kind of good fortune. A disabled life may also be brought to color as a beautiful verse." We should all sing the virtues of disabled lives and affirm their accomplishments. Gain and loss within this world can never be absolutely defined; though a blind person may not be able to see, he may compensate by having acute hearing. Similarly, a mute person may have a very clear mind.

Though human potential is normally expressed through the five senses and the four limbs, a disabled person can still do much. They can be disabled in body but not in mind, for as long as there is strength within the mind, people can do many wonderful things.

Preventing the spread of infectious diseases

If we become sick with a contagious disease–such as AIDS, hepatitis, skin diseases, or even a cold–how should we care for ourselves to avoid giving our illness to others?

If we are unlucky enough to contract a contagious disease, the important thing is to be mindful of others and follow the rules that keep us from spreading disease. During the outbreak of SARS in Taiwan, the biggest problem was simply that too many people failed to follow the rules that were designed to prevent transmission. For example, people who had contracted SARS were supposed to quarantine themselves, but some refused to do that. They went around passing on the disease to others, and all we can say now is that it was a real failure for Taiwan.

When people refuse to follow the rules and are unwilling

to be quarantined if they become ill, little good can come of it, for the self or others. If we promote the idea of following the rules, we will also be promoting the notion of respecting others while caring for the self. For example, when people wear gauze masks when they are ill, they are not only protecting themselves from pathogens, but they are also being courteous and taking others into consideration. If we have a contagious infection, we should not use things that are shared by the general public. Following these simple rules constitutes a sense of public morality and civic responsibility by which everyone should abide.

Of the contagious diseases prevalent today, AIDS is surely the one that frightens people the most. According to statistics, over 2,000 people died in Taiwan last year due to AIDS. The recent SARS outbreak caused some eighty deaths. Some contagious diseases are transmitted by physical contact, some through the air, some through blood transfusions, and some through saliva. Yet the SARS outbreak in Taiwan also brought some positive benefits in terms of public awareness of how to deal with contagions. People are better about washing their hands frequently, keeping their homes and environment clean, and generally respecting the needs of self and others.

During the period of time when Taiwan was trying to prevent SARS from becoming an epidemic, many people stayed at home and read instead. Actually, this motivated more people to develop a love for reading. During that time, many Humanistic Buddhism reading groups sprang up, providing more people with an opportunity to read and enhance their wisdom and knowledge.

When you think about it, where and when has there ever been a place that was not subject to some sort of contagious epidemic? Historically, the declines of both the Greek and Roman worlds were in some ways tied to epidemics. The demise of the Ming Dynasty in China was not due to the weakness of their army. Although some attribute their decline to the same problems that toppled other dynasties, it is not enough just to explain it in terms of corruption in the court or the manipulation of traitors. More importantly, the outbreak of an epidemic seriously affected social demographics and compromised the recruiting efforts of the Ming, which in turn caused it to fall. Thus, we can see the frightening repercussions that epidemics can have.

The truth is, there are worse things than the transmission of contagious diseases. The spread of distorted thinking, false information, and rumors can be even more frightening. If a person contracts a contagious disease, he or she should abide by public morality and follow basic social rules in order not to harm others. But today, we see a strange phenomenon in society. Quite a few people with serious transmissible diseases do not accept their fate graciously, and instead go out of their way to intentionally infect others. They think that it is too lonely to die alone, so they try to take as many other people as they can. This kind of deviant mindset shows a true lack of moral sensibility.

According to the *Sutra on the Collection of One Hundred Conditions*, the Buddha, during former lives "practiced compassion, made medicinal infusions, and gave them to all others. For these reasons, he received the reward of not becoming ill himself." Thus, if we wish for society to be strong and healthy and to be free from illness ourselves, we must be especially vigilant about advocating public morality in addition to following social rules and basic public manners. Nurturing a sense of lawfulness, restraint and morality, while demonstrating a mind of compassion and loving-kindness toward others, are lessons we cannot easily overlook.

Eradicating Karmic Obstructions

The Buddhist tradition often speaks of "diseases arising from karmic obstructions." When we become ill due to karmic obstructions, how do we eradicate these sorts of obstructions and heal ourselves?

The sutras state: "If we did not have heavy karma, we would not have been born in this saha world." Except for bodhisattvas who return to this world to fulfill their vows, almost all other people are here due to their karma. If it were not for heavy karma, they would never have been born in this world in the first place!

For each one of us, life is inextricably bound with our karma, for it is only due to karma that we remain trapped within the cycle of birth and death. Thus, it is only natural that the diseases we contract in this realm are also due to karmic obstructions.

What Buddhism calls "diseases based on karmic obstructions" are essentially ones we cannot name. In this same vein, those who suffer from afflictions caused by their own ignorance are simply "people of karmic obstructions." Things that should not have happened but occur anyway are called "matters of karmic obstruction." For example, it may seem that a person should not die, but nevertheless he or she dies for no apparent reason. This is an example of a karmic obstruction.

Some people become ill and nothing seems to cure them. Why? It is due to karmic obstructions. Two people live together, but one of them is always healthy while the other is often sick. Why? The difference is due to karmic obstructions! Not long ago someone jumped from a tall building and landed on someone who was walking below; the person who jumped did not die, but the person he landed on did. This is simply due to their karma!

There are also many examples of people–due to traffic or a last-minute invitation–who missed a plane that later crashed; or of people getting on an earlier flight than they had planned and dying when that flight crashed. These sorts of things are all due to the karma of the people involved–one person is saved, while another goes to die in his place; it is all simply karma. There are even cases of people sitting quietly at home only to be killed by a large truck that careened out of control and smashed into their house. All of these are due to karma.

There are two basic types of karma–collective karma and individual karma. Collective karma also has two subsets: shared collective karma and non-shared collective karma. Some people contract an incurable illness, but recover completely. Other people come down with a slight cold and die from it due to improper treatment. What Buddhist sutras call "an untoward death" is also based on karma.

The truth is that karmic obstructions produce much more than just physical illnesses. For example, poverty is a kind of karmic obstruction, as is having poor relations with other people. Feeling no joy in life or having no one to help us are also karmic obstructions. Some people have brilliant careers, but then one day their karmic obstructions manifest themselves and everything becomes as fleeting as a blooming flower.

Karma is produced by behavior. The *Maharatnakuta* says: "Even after one hundred thousand kalpas, karma is never forgotten. When conditions are right, we will receive our karmic due." Though the kinds of lives we have now are related to causes and conditions generated in former lives, we can still do much to eradicate bad karma by being repentant, doing good deeds, and cultivating beneficial practices. There is a story in Buddhist sutras about a novice monk who saved the lives of some ants. Though his karma was such that he was going to die very soon, due to saving the lives of those ants, everything changed. The merit of protecting life saved him from dying at a young age and rewarded him with longevity. Stories like these can be found in many Buddhist sutras, and they can also be found in the world today.

The *Commentary on the Awakening of Faith in the Mahayana* states: "Repentance can eradicate karmic obstructions; wholesome exhortations can eradicate demonic obstructions; sympathetic joy can eradicate the obstruction of envy; sharing and renunciation can eradicate clinging to extremes; and making vows can eradicate backsliding and forgetfulness." Thus, karmic obstructions can be eradicated by acts of repentance.

Eradicating karma can be compared to washing clothes with detergent when they are dirty, or cleansing our bodies with soap when we are dirty. It is like our need to brush our teeth and rinse our mouths everyday.

If you want to overcome karma, you must have a weapon or a tool to do it! We use tools such as making vows, doing good, storing up virtues, making connections, and doing things that lead to good fortune. These practices are a must when it comes to dealing with karma! If we do not repent and do good, but only implore the Buddha to remove our karma, we will be in a situation like the one mentioned in the *Agamas*: we will be like someone who throws a stone in a pond and then implores the gods to make it float! Or like a person who throws oil in a pond and implores the gods to make it sink! No matter how much you implore the gods, those things simply will not happen. These are natural outcomes consistent with the Law of Cause and Effect.

There is a saying: "If there is light, darkness will be removed. If there is the Buddhadharma, we will find peace of mind." During the outbreak of SARS in Taiwan, Fo Guang Shan monastery was closed for one month; during that time, we not only prayed for an end to the scourge, but also vowed to repent for all sentient beings and prayed on their behalf. This was akin to pulling up weeds with one hand while casting seeds with the other. By doing positive and wholesome practices like these, we began a process of generating good karma that, following its maturation, culminated in the eradication of karmic obstacles and an increase in wisdom and good fortune.

Developing a positive self-image

Some people think they are born with deficiencies. They might see themselves as too short, too fat, or unattractive; in other respects, they may feel less intelligent, less educated, and less privileged than others. People like that may feel inferior in many other ways. How can they form a positive self-image that will increase their mental strength?

No one is perfect, and yet many young people have low self-esteem simply because they feel they are too short or too fat. But being short or fat is not a bad thing; in fact, if the sky falls, it will be the tall people who have to hold it up. Short people's clothes require less material and being unattractive is really not a problem—monastics who are unattractive often achieve the most beautiful practice. Beauty is not necessarily a good thing, because beautiful people also suffer. "From ancient times, the lives of many women were cut short because of their beauty." Sometimes, merely because a person is beautiful, someone may throw acid in her face, or she may be raped or killed. Thus, it can be good to be a bit short, fat, or ugly. Indeed, life is often safer for these types of people!

Not being as educated as someone else is not a bad thing either. I often feel that people who strive to attain advanced degrees hurt themselves in the end, because "since it is always lonely at the top," by the time they finish their studies, they may have lost most of their friends and exhausted their future prospects.

There was a period in Taiwan when people who were looking for jobs did not present prospective employers with their college degrees, but used their high school records instead since it was much easier for them to find work if their education level was lower. The reason for this is that people who have higher degrees all want office jobs with high salaries, but how many jobs of this type are there waiting for you? The point then is to start with an entry-level job and not to ask for too much from your employer. This will in fact enhance your appeal.

Some people may feel they are deficient in some areas and not as well-qualified as others. But if they can accept reality, look inward, and develop their hidden talents, they can turn the situation around and create new opportunities. For example, although I may not be as smart as you, I may be more compassionate, determined, kind, and blessed with better friends. Similarly, if I am so ugly that no one will talk to me, it is not really such a bad thing, because I will have more time to read and improve my inner life.

Deficiency is also beautiful! For the column *Between Ignorance and Enlightenment* published in the *Merit Times*, I wrote a piece called "*Deficiency Is Beautiful*," in which I mentioned that though Thomas Edison was deaf, he still invented the light bulb and provided the human race with illumination. And although Helen Keller was severely disabled, likewise, she was capable of becoming a truly great human being.

In Hualien, Taiwan, there is an indigenous man named Tsai Yao-shing, who, though both of his arms are disabled, has managed to win three swimming championships; his feats are so amazing that people sometimes call him the "frog king without arms." And there is the author Liu Xia, who, though she suffers from severe arthritis, continues to produce first-rate work.

There is a saying: "Comparing people only makes them angry!" I believe that, though people with disabilities may be handicapped in some areas, if they are healthy psychologically, they are essentially no different from others in terms of their wisdom. It is similar to making vows. Since all of us who make vows are equal in this regard, all of us are equal on the path of spiritual cultivation. There are many distinctions that can be made in today's world, but if we can all continue to strive with a mind of equanimity, win others over with wisdom, and affirm ourselves with confidence, we will always be able to live with a sense of dignity, hope, and purpose.

Lighting the Lamp of the Mind

Some people have narrow and dark minds. They simply cannot see anything better or more beautiful. They do not see either color or light, or joy in anything. How is one to light the lamp of the mind in such people?

Every year the BLIA holds a Dharma function called "Chan, Pure Land, and Tantric Lamp Lighting Ceremony." However, the lamps lit during the function are lamps with shape and form; the most important lamp to light is, of course, the lamp within the mind. There are many things that can light up the mind, including books, other people, schools, and temples.

Contemplating the Mind says: "The lamp is used as a metaphor for awakening to the true mind and becoming enlightened by its wisdom. Thus, all who seek liberation should think of their bodies as the base of the lamp, their minds as the jar that holds lamp oil, their faith as the wick, and the increase in their capacity to live according to the precepts as the addition of new oil."

If a person can light the lamp of his mind, not only will he be able to clearly see the myriad phenomena of this world, but he will also be able to interact in a wholesome way with those phenomena. When the lamp of the mind has been lighted, people are able to clearly understand their relations with others and to improve them as needed.

And what precisely are the lamps of the mind? They include the lamps of wisdom, compassion, goodness and beauty, virtue, and repentance. Now, which ones do you want to light?

A person with learning is like a bright lamp that attracts many students. A person with virtue is like a lamp of virtue attracting all those who seek the way. A person with the ability and willingness to help others is like a bright lamp that in time will bring many good things to people near and far. A person with compassion is like a lamp drawing many people to him or her for support, without reservation.

Since anyone can be like a lamp to others, we should ask ourselves: Can I be a lamp to my family? Can I be a lamp to my community? Can I be a lamp that brings light to all of society? Can I be a lamp that shines upon all of humanity?

A lamp symbolizes light, and it gives people a sense of security. It is a bright star in the midst of darkness. In fact, the darker a place is, the more it needs a lamp. Sailors depend on lighthouses to find their way. Airplanes depend on lights to guide them to safe landings at night. The brilliant lamp before the image of the Buddha has given strength and purpose to all deluded sentient beings.

Why are forests high in the mountains a refuge for wild animals? Because those places are like lamps upon which the animals can rely. Fishes in rivers and oceans all seek unpolluted waters where they will be safer; they are like lamps around which they can gather.

Do not wait for others to light the lamp of your mind, for this is something that you must do on your own! Your spirit is like a flashlight that can be used at any time as a guide to greater understanding.

Contemplating the Mind states: "Brilliant wisdom is like an eternal torch, like a bright lamp of right awakening to the truth, and it can destroy the darkness of all doubt. With this one lamp, one can become enlightened and further light one hundred thousand other lamps."

Lamps give us light, and the value of light is that it helps us see where we are going. But, since so many people lack light in their minds, they suffer from the afflictions of ignorance. In turn, because of these afflictions, they obscure the light of wisdom, and thus feel there is no hope, future, joy, or excitement in life. These become both physical and mental maladies.

To cure mental and physical illnesses, we can count on the help of others for about ten to twenty percent of the problems, but for the other seventy to eighty percent we must rely on our own strength. The *Ksitigarbha Sutra* says that when we chant sutras for those who have died, the deceased receives about one-seventh of the merit, while the one who does the chanting receives about six-sevenths. It should be clear, then, that what is most important is to rely on our own efforts, for if we expect others to do everything for us, we put ourselves in a lower position than nearly everyone else. Thus, we must all learn to light the lamps within our own minds if we want to feel hopeful and look forward to the future.

Building Harmonious Relations

Selfishness and clinging are negative aspects of human nature. Some people are so self-centered, no matter what the situation, they only think of themselves. Some are so extreme in this respect that they stubbornly cling to their own beliefs, their greed, ignorance, jealousy, pride, and lack of repentance or remorse. People like this are always spoiling their relations with others; what can we do to help them improve?

Human life contains millions of afflictions, or *kleshas*. Our bodies must endure the afflictions related to old age, sickness, and death, while our minds must suffer from the tendency to be greedy, angry, and ignorant. Of all the human problems, the central one is the fundamental affliction of "clinging to the self." Clinging to the self is the commander of all of the other 84,000 afflictions that plague human life. Because people cling to the self, they also cling to doubt, jealousy, and their own views of the world-indeed, there is almost no end to the afflictions caused by clinging to the self.

The *Supreme Sutra on the Three Precepts* states: "Due to clinging, we are harmed by our intentions. Some concern things we like, some things we despise. When they harm us, it is because we are being deluded. Whether someone is harmed in the hell realm, the ghostly realm, the animal realm, or even the human or heavenly realms, it is always due to some sort of clinging."

When some people fall into water, they only want to live; then, the moment they reach land, they only want money. This shows that at times they cling to life even more than money. There are others who abandon kindness and decency to gain wealth and fame. This is because they have the twisted view that wealth and fame are more valuable than kindness and decency.

Bad habits are hard to change due to our tendency to cling to them. The habit of speaking and acting inappropriately is also difficult to correct due to clinging. In some cases stubborn clinging to thoughts or beliefs can be fairly harmless, if the beliefs are based on reason. But all too often, people cling to their beliefs even though they are based on irrational assumptions, twisted views, or other values that contradict the Dharma-and these sorts of people are quite difficult to deal with.

Most people expect others to behave like bodhisattvas, to be compassionate, and to treat others with tolerance. At the same time, they ask very little of themselves; indeed, they often allow themselves to be selfish, clinging, ignorant, and deficient in many other respects.

The truth is that everything in this world is mutual-how much you reap depends on how much effort you put in. Even if you were Sakyamuni Buddha, you would still have to undergo six years of austere religious practice before becoming enlightened under the bodhi tree. If you were Jesus, you would still have to suffer being nailed to the cross for the sins of other sentient beings before others would respect you. If you want to be a bodhisattva like Avalokitesvera, you will have to "save those who are suffering or in the midst of hardship," instead of waiting for others to save you! If you want to be Ksitigarbha bodhisattva, you will have to make a vow to stay in the hell realm until all sentient beings have been released from it. If we want to reap a good harvest, we must sow the proper seeds.

Many young people today are quite vigorous, but they cling to a strong sense of self, and are selfish and self-serving. They do not understand how to treat other people properly, and wherever they go, they cause disharmony. They often do not willingly accept the leadership of their supervisors and frequently have conflicts with their colleagues.

How are we to achieve harmonious relationships with others? I am now close to eighty years old and have only recently come to appreciate the full meaning of the phrase "treat others well." I was at Motosu Temple in Japan when a devotee asked me how best to interact with others and how to establish oneself in this world. My answer was simply treat them well. If you treat others well, they will be kind to you in return. This is an immutable truth. If you want others to treat you in a certain way, you must first be that way yourself. The biggest problem with people today is that they always want others to treat them well, but see no reason why they should do the same in return. This shows that they have a poor understanding of the Law of Cause and Effect.

When we treat others well, we treat ourselves well, too. Indeed, it is more important to be kind to others than to ourselves. Treating others well should not be done superficially, nor should it be done only on the spur of the moment; the attitude of treating others well is something that we need to cultivate on a regular basis.

There is a saying: "Those who respect others will always be respected in return." Do you want others to treat you well? Then you should take this desire and turn it into one that inspires you. Once you do this, you will naturally be able to benefit wherever you go.

Suicide

The most precious things in this world is life, and the cruelest act is to kill living things. In order to maintain life, people come up with all kinds of methods to preserve their health and nurture their lives. For example, for the sake of health, people not only ensure that they eat three well-balanced and nutritious meals a day, but also augment these meals with vitamin supplements and engage in various forms of regular exercise. In order to live carefree and comfortable lives, people apply various approaches to cultivating the body and mind. On the other hand, there are quite a few people who want to end their lives through suicide, something that is truly unfathomable.

Some suicides occur because of failed romance, financial difficulties, or long-term debilitating disease; others occur due to ill-fated love or jealousy, where one murders the other party and then commits suicide. Committing suicide is the greatest harm one can inflict upon one's own life, and at the same time, it creates an inestimable loss for one's family and society. Today, all advanced countries are treating suicide prevention as a serious matter. For example, in 1982, the World Health Organization of the United Nations, set the reduction in suicide rates as one of its policy goals, and in 1996, it reiterated the importance of preventing suicide. In 1992, Great Britain set out a goal to lower its suicide rate to 15% by the year 2000. In 1991, the U.S. began marking the annual National Depression Screening Day, and in 1999, it made the reduction of suicide rates an important national goal. From very early on, Finland, Sweden, Denmark, Norway, Belgium, and Australia made the reduction of suicide rates a national policy.

The problem of suicide has apparently become an underlying concern shared throughout the entire world. And, now, even animals have demonstrated suicidal tendencies. According to a report from the Australian Associated Press, there was a kangaroo in Australia that attempted to commit suicide by jumping into the sea. It was only after four lifeguards exerted considerable effort to coax the animal back to shore that they were able to save its life. The report jokingly pointed out that probably no one will ever know the reason why the kangaroo wanted to jump into the sea.

Countries around the world have committed social experts working to come up with solutions for stopping or even slowing the spread of suicidal trends. Regrettably, it is clear that the number of suicide cases continues to rise day by day despite these efforts.

Why do people commit suicide? What is the mental state of someone who commits suicide? How can we prevent ourselves from fostering suicidal thoughts? And how can we help those with suicidal tendencies escape the shadow of suicide and renew their hope in life? On July 6, 2003, Venerable Master Hsing Yun conducted a Refuge Taking Ceremony in Australia, in which more than 1,000 Australians and Chinese participated. After the ceremony and at the request of the lay assembly, a group discussion was held to address the problem of suicide. What follows here is a record of the discussions from that day.

Suicide & Morality

According to statistics, there are currently quite a few countries that are deeply concerned about the rising number of suicides year after year. This is especially true for Taiwan where there has been an upswing in the number of cases in which parents force their children to commit suicide with them. What is the Buddhist perspective on suicidal behavior and the problem of morality?

The Chinese have a saying: "It's better to live badly than to die well." However, there are people who feel that they have nothing to live for, so they consider ending their own lives. They think that such action would not harm anyone else and has nothing to do with others. Where's the moral issue in that?

From the Buddhist perspective, suicide constitutes the taking of life and is considered an immoral act. The Buddhadharma does not sanction suicide. This is because an individual's life is not the sole possession of the individual. This body of flesh and blood was brought into being and raised by one's parents from the beginning, and then later received from society what it needed to grow healthy and mature. The culmination in life was accomplished by the aggregate of conditions stemming from society as a whole. Naturally, one should give back to society, so everyone is obligated to make their lives happy and meaningful; but they do not have the right to destroy any living thing.

The three greatest philosophers of ancient Greece, Socrates, Plato, and Aristotle, all rejected suicide. Socrates and Plato did so out of a sense of religious belief, for they felt that life belongs to the gods, and without the decree of the gods, no one was permitted to kill oneself. Aristotle opposed it for social and ethical reasons; from his perspective, suicide burdens society with an unjust act, and shows a lack of moral self-restraint.

St. Augustine, a religious thinker during the Middle Ages, felt that one only has the right to employ and manage one's own life, but does not have the right to control, in absolute terms, matters of life and death. Another religious thinker, St. Thomas Aquinas, felt that killing oneself constituted a form of self murder, something that is morally unacceptable.

Is suicide really incompatible with morality? Western countries of the 20th century, for the most part, consider both suicide and attempted suicide to be an intolerable form of immoral behavior. Thus, some countries even punish those who fail in their suicide attempt as criminals, as was the case in Great Britain until about 1961.

On the other hand, although suicide cannot be considered moral, we should not make sweeping generalizations either. For example, many great sages of the past died as martyrs for a noble cause, preferring death to dishonor, or sacrificed themselves in order to secure some benefit for the country or humanity as a whole. How can we not consider such acts to be of the greatest moral order? If killing another person is an immoral act, then are judges who condemn criminals to death really acting morally?

When judges confer the death sentence upon criminals, their aim is to uphold order, fairness, and justice within society. Are these actions immoral? And then we must consider the morality of war, for as soon as war breaks out between two countries, people are killed. Buddhism does not sanction the killing of living things, but if killing the enemy means breaking this precept, then is killing in times of war inconsistent with morality?

Of course, killing another person out of anger and hatred is immoral. But if one kills another person with a compassionate heart so as to save others, it becomes the morality of a Mahayana bodhisattva. This is like a doctor who dissects human bodies for medical experimentation, or sometimes must transplant the organs of one person into the body of another. Cases like these are actions intended to save the lives of others based upon compassion. Are these actions in keeping with morality?

The standard for what is or is not moral should be determined by one's intentions. Actions that are beneficial to people are moral, while behavior that is harmful and without benefit to others is immoral. That is to say, deeds performed out of a sense of compassion constitute the ultimate in morality; conversely, even good deeds that are done without a basis in compassion would not be considered moral. As the ethicist Bernard Haring said, if a spy ultimately has to end his life in order to protect important secrets, this would not be considered suicide, because the action does not come from selfish motivations, but rather was done for the sake of protecting national defense and keeping the country safe. Ending one's life for the sake of a higher ideal is not suicide, but is instead dedication through sacrifice.

According to Bernard Haring's standpoint, only killing oneself for selfish motivations or some immoral purpose can be called suicide. For example, some people commit suicide due to failed romance, a failed career, financial problems, incurable disease, or because one has suffered some serious blow in life. In so doing, they avoid responsibility, and leave the problems for the world and others to deal with. As such, it is an immoral act.

Even more worthy of rebuke are cases in which some people not only kill themselves, but they also take others with them in death. This includes parents who kill themselves along with their children as mentioned above. There are lovers who end their lives together as a sacrifice to their love, or cases of enmity that lead to the death of both the good and the bad. These cases exemplify the behavior of people who have lost their minds, for it hardly arouses sympathy.

Not long ago, there was a middle-aged couple in Changhwa, Taiwan, who encountered some financial difficulties and succumbed to a moment of despair. So the couple first took sleeping pills and then kept their child with them as they burned charcoal, so that they would all die together from carbon-monoxide poisoning. Fortunately, their child began to cry loudly, which alerted the neighbors, who were able to rescue them all from the brink of death.

Another case involved a divorced woman suffering from depression, who jumped from the third story of a building along with her child. The child died at the scene, but the woman did not and ended up with many serious complications. As a result, her body is completely paralyzed, dooming her future to a living hell.

Committing suicide, as well as forcing someone else die with you, are delusional, deviant, and immoral actions. People should not project their pain and suffering onto others, nor should they infect those around them with their pain and suffering. Throughout history, we have seen many gentlemen of virtue, who, even if their own hearts were filled with pain, always maintained a smile before others, for they wanted to bring happiness to others and not infect them with their pain and suffering. Thus, in today's society, we should strengthen life education, moral education, humanistic education, and religious education. And, in particular, there must be appropriate religious faith. When one's faith is inappropriate and one lacks correct knowledge and understanding, one is unable to comprehend clearly the true nature and reality of the world. This easily leads to the pursuit of foolish acts, like those of some parents, who mistakenly believe that by having their children die with them, they are somehow sparing them from having to live alone in this world. They think that they are acting out of love as a kind of release. In reality, such behavior is incompatible with morality and ethics, and is actually a kind of crime, a selfish act that cannot be tolerated.

Generally speaking, people who commit suicide are only thinking of themselves, for they put the entire focus of attention on themselves. What they think about is only their own pain, their own troubles, and their own release. But if they had love in their hearts, they would consider their children and parents, their relatives and friends, or perhaps even the continuation of their own lives, and then they would not see life as so hopeless.

In Japan there is a place called the Aokigahara Jukai Forest, where people often go to commit suicide. In the attempt to reduce the number of suicides there, the Fujiyoshida police station has installed as special sign at the entrance to the forest, urging those who are contemplating suicide to reconsider: "Our lives are something precious that came from our parents; please calm down and think once more about your parents, siblings, and children. Do not let yourself suffer alone; please let us help you think things over."

We were born into our lives naturally, and we should also die naturally. Forcing oneself to live a meaningless life and giving up on oneself through the loss of all self-respect, are both wrong. Therefore, before considering suicide, people should take time to reflect and think it over. Problems can only be solved by living. How can anything be solved by dying? As long as you are willing to try, there are no problems in this world that can't be solved. Why the need to commit suicide as an escape? Therefore, in order to eliminate suicide, we must increase our moral sense and courage, and consider things from the viewpoint of our shared, symbiotic relationship with the entire mass of humanity. We must remember that there are always first, second, and third options for solving problems. Why consider suicide as the one and only way?

In short, all the myriad things in this world, from the sentient to the non-sentient, have life and vitality, and we should protect and honor them all. Consider how even ants have an instinct for survival; how much more so should humanity? Therefore, bringing an end to our own precious lives, and in so doing perhaps even drawing in and harming the lives of others, all constitute immoral behavior, behavior that should be proscribed and defended against.

Restoring Hope

As mentioned above, many people commit suicide because they encounter difficulties, look upon their lives as a failure, or have a pessimistic and hopeless attitude toward life. They feel that life is meaningless, so they take the negative approach and seek death as a release. How can we help those with suicidal tendencies to restore their confidence and help them live with a renewed sense of hope?

As the saying goes, "As long as the green mountain remains, there'll be no lack of firewood." In fact, suicide cannot solve problems; it merely leaves, to no good effect, even more and greater problems and pain to the world and those who remain behind. Thus, the German philosopher Immanuel Kant felt that suicide should not be permitted under any circumstances, because living is a necessary obligation for being human.

However, there are many people in society today who want to commit suicide and bring an end to their own lives. Why? As indicated by research into the causes of suicide, with the exception of those with mental problems or personality disorders, the two primary reasons most people commit suicide are that they suffer personal setbacks in life or that they do not understand the meaning of life. Thus, in order to guard against suicide, it is most important that we are able to live with a sense of happiness and hope, and in particular, that we are mindful of the world, sentient beings, karma, and what is right.

Life does not belong to each individual; life is the shared

possession of all living things in the world. An individual only has the right to offer oneself to the people and to make life as meaningful and valuable as possible, to the best of his or her ability; one does not, however, have the freedom to wantonly destroy life.

The meaning of life is to be found in serving people and in helping others to accomplish something. One cannot conduct life by considering his or her own benefit alone. We must realize that the meaning of life is found in making a contribution to society, serving others, facing up to one's responsibilities, and bringing happiness to other people. An individual has a moral obligation toward oneself, one's family, one's relatives, and to those who have benefited him or her, such as one's parents and teachers. You have not repaid their kindness yet, so your obligations are unfinished. How can you just end it all by killing yourself?

I once met a young man who wanted to commit suicide because of a failed romance that left him with unbearable suffering. When I went to see him, I wanted him to calm down, so I recited to him a short poem published in the literary supplement of the *Central Daily:*

> *There are hundreds of millions of stars in the sky,*
> *And there are more people in the world than stars;*
> *Oh, foolish one!*
> *Why kill yourself just for her alone?*

There are so many people in this world. How can you say that they are all unworthy of your love? Why be so miserable and kill yourself for the love of one person? Is not the value you put on life too limited?

Therefore, although many things in life are a disappointment, for we cannot avoid shifts in fortune throughout life, nor the ups and downs in our emotional life, once we realize that our emotions have sunk to a low, we must know that it is time to talk with spiritual friends and trusted companions. We must read books or listen to lectures—whatever helps us to relieve the stress and alter our feelings.

In the past, I had a five-minute program each day on China Television called "*Hsing Yun's Dharma Sayings,*" which was warmly received at the time. Some people who had originally intended to commit suicide became inspired to move on with life after listening to the show. There was also an eighth-grade student living in Kaohsiung who once wrote me a letter saying that he had fallen in with a bad group of friends and had become influenced by them. Because of this, his good friends and classmates no longer paid any attention to him. Although he realized his error and wished to change, that group of bad friends would not leave him alone. It was at this time of loneliness and desperation that he thought of committing suicide, when by chance he happened to read my "*Hsing Yun's Dharma Sayings*" published in the monthly magazine *Awakening the World* gave him encouragement. He realized that he was still a young man, and that there were many things he had yet to accomplish, so he could not so rashly put an end to his life. He thus decided that he must work harder to have positive feelings about life and take steps toward making a fresh start.

There is another story about a young man, who lost his job and was pacing back and forth in front of the Taipei train station as he stared blankly into the busy intersection full of rushing cars. He was planning to kill himself by jumping front of a rich man's car, so that his destitute mother would be able to live on the money she would receive as compensation for his death. Just when it seemed that he had lost all hope, an elegant and beautiful young woman passed in front of him. She nodded her head toward him with a delicate smile. This pleased the young man so much that he forgot all about trying to end his life. The next day he unexpectedly found another job, and thought no more about dying!

A very moving incident once took place at Fo Guang Shan's Taipei Dharma Center. One Saturday night when the monastics were preparing to start their chanting service, they suddenly received an extremely urgent phone call. The voice on the line said, "I must speak with the abbess! I want to kill someone!"

As it turned out, the caller had been running a small business when not long ago, his wife's younger brother had lost all his money, resulting in a financial crisis. The end of the month was approaching and his ten employees would be waiting for their salaries. He was so angry and upset, all he could think about was killing his brother-in-law as a way of venting his anger.

The Abbess Tzu Jung told him: "If you kill him, you will go to jail, and that would still not solve the problem!"

"Then I'll just kill myself!"

"After you kill yourself, how will your family endure it? Do you really want them to be burdened with debt?"

"Then, what can I do? What's to be done?" The caller's voice was getting hoarse from crying.

Abbess Tzu Jung gave him the address of the Taipei Dharma Center and asked him to come by.

In less than thirty minutes, the man arrived at the Taipei Dharma Center as promised. Venerable Tzu Jung consoled him, "There's no avoiding the ups and downs in life; having fallen down, as long as you are willing to stand up again, there is hope. Besides, we do not live for ourselves alone, for we must think all the more about those who love and care for us. Killing oneself and others only serves to bring pain to our family and happiness to our foes."

Seeing that his emotions had gradually stabilized, the abbess looked at the clock on the wall and saw that it was already ten o'clock. "You should hurry home! It's so late. I am sure your wife is quite worried waiting for you!" she told him.

"Oh!" He said with a sigh, and then went on to say, "My wife is a good and capable woman, but seeing her when I get home will just get me thinking about her brother, and that would be even harder for me!"

Abbess Tzu Jung continued her patient attempts to persuade him. After their conversation, the man unexpectedly requested that the abbess accept him into the monastic order as a monk. She asked him to fill out a form, saying that joining the monastic order requires information about one's family background. The abbess then secretly phoned the man's wife, using information supplied on the form.

"Mrs. Wang, please sit down."

When the middle-aged man heard these words, he looked back in shock. There was his wife coming through the door accompanied by the monk in charge of reception, her face full of deep sadness. The man could not help getting up and going to her. He embraced his wife and burst into tears.

Three months later, Mr. and Mrs. Wang both came to the Taipei Dharma Center and paid their respects to Abbess Tzu Jung. Mr. Wang happily said, "Thank you for saving my life, and for saving my family as well."

How can one escape from the shadows of suicide? How can we live with hope for life? Actually, to rely solely upon external support is rather limited. Some people go so far as to turn over their future to the protection of gods and deities, but this is not enough. The most important thing is for people to rely upon themselves. Of course, when a country has a sound social welfare system in place, including a solid health care system, an advanced system of transportation, and satisfactory public facilities such as drinking water, street lamps, and so forth, this naturally reduces some of the inconveniences people experience in life. But even if friends, family, state, and society supply us with external support, we must also be able to accept the support. Sometimes those with good intentions try to help, but their help is not always well received. Not only do some people become suspicious, they may even look upon the good intentions of others as some form of malice. People like this always look for the bad in every situation, and so others cannot help them no matter how good their intentions may be.

There are some people who, upon hearing a single word they do not like, refuse to listen to what another person has to say, no matter how hard they use kind words to reason and explain. People who only hold onto one negative comment and discount a hundred kind words are really just making trouble for themselves. Therefore, if we want to stop this problem of suicide, we must rely upon our own wisdom and understanding. Think about it: why should we become trapped by a single word, deed, or look from another person, and thereby suffer miserably because of someone else?

As a general rule, I feel that people should pursue their interests, such as reading, writing, gardening, travel, or volunteer work. Participating in more activities opens one's mind and is helpful to the body and spirit. In this way, people feel less isolated. If people feel too isolated, they become more and more confused. Given that society today is so open and full of possibilities, everyone should step out more and join in with society, join in with one's circle of friends, the institutions of learning, the activities of social groups, and the ranks of volunteers. Of course, joining any one of various religious faiths is also a good idea. In short, you must have many avenues for balancing your life and relieving stress, and in particular, have some good and helpful friends with whom you maintain active and cordial relationships on a regular basis. Get together for tea and conversation, for sometimes a certain word or phrase from others will wake us from our trance and be of great benefit to us.

There has always been suffering in human life. This suffering is sometimes due to desiring something beyond reach, which naturally leads to more suffering when it cannot be obtained. At other times, it stems from overly intense feelings of love or hate, so that one often feels he or she cannot be with those we love, yet are always in the company of one's enemies. This too will naturally lead to suffering. There is even the suffering of physical decline in old age, the suffering of debilitating disease, and the pain of death; and sometimes when we witness others suffering, we suffer with them. There is the suffering engendered by the natural world and by society; and even suffering brought on by the economy, our families, or interpersonal relationships. All kinds of suffering come crowding toward us from all directions, so much that words cannot fully convey.

However, we can turn suffering into happiness, just like a house that is originally dark can be lit up. All we need to do is light a lamp, which can turn darkness into light. Understanding how to make this turn is very important in life, for bad can be turned into good and wrong into right. By understanding how to turn ourselves around, by stepping back and thinking about life, we can experience a wider and more expansive world; and by understanding how to turn ourselves around, we will discover that the world behind us is incomparably spacious.

Someone once asked me—given that Buddhists take up beads to recite Amitabha's name—what name does Avalokitesvara recite with his beads. "Avalokitesvara," I replied. And why would you recite your own name? Because relying on others is not as good as relying on oneself. For this reason, the Buddha speaks of taking refuge in oneself and in the Dharma, meaning that one takes refuge in oneself, one believes in oneself, and one affirms oneself. If each person in society could develop their own power, so that one was not only independent, but also able to help others, this then would be the only way for society to be good and strong. If on the other hand, each of us waited, hoping that the country would take care of us, that society would help us, that parents would raise us, that teachers would guide us, and that friends would support us, then what would be the point of our lives? Therefore, in order to survive in this world, we must rely upon our own power, so it is most important that we strengthen and develop ourselves. Instead of looking to others to save and help us, it is always better to rely upon ourselves.

Many years ago, the famous writer San Mao suddenly became tired of living and committed suicide, arousing concern among society over the problem of why famous people commit suicide. Such situations often occur to famous and successful people, for when faced with unbearable difficulties, they consider death an escape. Actually, the way to dispel this is nothing more than developing a focus on death, for with that, the situation would not be so bad. If one is not afraid of death, then what indeed is there to fear in this world? Instead of destroying one's life by dying, it would be better to apply oneself to more worthwhile causes. Therefore, we should counsel those with suicidal tendencies or who have attempted suicide in the same way one helps ex-convicts rehabilitate their lives. It requires the concern of all of society as a whole.

Suicide & One's Beliefs

Most people who contemplate suicide do so because they do not value their lives and feel that their lives are full of unhappiness. However, some feel that upon death, they will be reunited with loved ones, while others end their lives because of their beliefs. What is the Buddhist perspective on the psychology of suicide, and in particular on those who commit suicide due to their system of beliefs?

Suicide reflects ignorance with respect to the value of life. Some people believe that those who commit suicide are brave individuals who do not fear death. Actually, suffering has created such desperate circumstances for those people, that they have already transcended the fear of death. They feel that death will relieve them of life's sufferings, and so they decide to commit such a foolish act. Such people do not even have the courage to go on living, so how can one say that they are not afraid of death?

When it comes to life and death, most people feel it is better to suffer in the world than to be buried in the grave. However, there are many people who, because of too much pressure in life, work, their studies, or relationships, head down the road toward suicide. Some may even do so because of warped beliefs, or after a burst of anger or upon hearing a personal insult that they could not bear at the time. Regardless of what the specific reasons are, suicide can be encapsulated by the following: first, a failure to appreciate the value of life; second, a lack of courage to face one's problems; third, a failure to comprehend how one's life is related to others through causes and conditions; and fourth, not knowing that killing oneself and others constitutes the same kind of wrongdoing.

In a word, people who contemplate suicide are selfish, incapable, powerless, and ignorant. They do not understand how to create happiness, nor do they know how to build a shared, symbiotic relationship with others; and they lack a true understanding of life. The meaning of life is something inextinguishable; only this is truly what it means to live. Because they have not truly seen life, those that commit suicide only think of death. So while they are alive, their thoughts are purely selfish, gray, and dismal. They are unable to see light or beauty, and so the shadow of death envelops them, while the hand of death holds them tightly in its grasp. Thus, once they feel some mental confusion and a weakening of resolve, the bonds of death will bind and hold them fast.

The thought of suicide actually lingers in our subconscious from time to time, and when we are at the weakest moment in our lives, it can easily be transformed into action and become reality. For Kawabata Yasunari, the first Japanese writer to receive the Nobel Prize for literature, the deaths of his parents from illness when he was two and three respectively, the subsequent deaths of his grandmother and sister several years later, and the death of his grandfather after that were experiences that created a deep sense of fear and overshadowed his entire life. In the end, three years after being awarded the Nobel Prize, he committed suicide by turning on the gas in his apartment, realizing what he himself had said before: "A wordless death is a limitless life." The famous Japanese author, Akutagawa Ryunosuke, who at the age of thirty-five was at the height of vigor, was so struck by the feeling that life is more of a hell than hell itself that he committed suicide by taking sleeping pills. The famous Japanese painter, Koga Harue, felt that there is no higher art than death, and thus resolutely ended his life. Although their philosophies of death varied, they all chose to end their brilliant lives in suicide.

Committing suicide means that one harms oneself. Modern people have come up with an endless variety of ways to kill themselves, like taking poison, jumping off buildings, hanging, jumping into rivers, slitting their wrists, cutting their throats, poisoning themselves with carbon-monoxide, and so forth. There are even quite a few words and phrases used to describe suicide, such as ending one's life, self-murder, killing oneself, self-destruction, hanging oneself, cutting one's own throat, slashing one's own throat, putting an end to oneself, and so on. Even the psychologies and motivations for suicide are too numerous to enumerate. I remember reading a news item in the paper, in which a certain individual raised a dog and lived with the dog so long that he formed an emotional bond with him. Even old dogs must die one day, and after the dog's death, the owner suddenly felt that life was meaningless. A few days later, the owner committed suicide, and thus joined his old dog in the hereafter.

Hundreds of years ago, when Prince Dan of Yan and Tian Guang were planning to assassinate the Chinese king of Qin, Tian Guang recommended Jing Ke, and the prince said, "The fate of Yan hangs on this action; you must keep it a secret." Tian Guang said, "I will!" Immediately upon his return home, Tian Guang committed suicide, showing by this act that the secret would not be revealed.

During one of the anti-Buddhist persecutions of the "three emperors Wu and the emperor Zong," when Emperor Wu of the Zhou dynasty abolished Buddhism, nearly all the Buddhist scriptures and statues were destroyed. At the time, a certain Dharma Master Jing Ai vigorously admonished the emperor to avoid the karmic retribution of destroying Buddhism, but the emperor did not believe him. Later, Jing Ai fled to Mt. Zhongnan, and because he was ashamed that none of his efforts proved beneficial to the Buddhadharma, he sat cross-legged on a rock, cut his own flesh, and died.

Wen Tianxiang of the Song dynasty led his troops in battle against the Mongol Yuan dynasty, but was defeated and captured. The supreme commander of the Yuan army, Zhang Hongfan, and the general commander, Li Heng, treated Wen Tianxiang to fine wine everyday, trying in every way to get him to submit. But Wen Tianxiang felt while death was not that serious, the loss of one's honor was a real matter of concern. Thereupon, he composed his masterpiece, the poem "*Passing the Lonely Sea*," so greatly admired by later generations:

> *All the hardships and misfortunes began with civil service;*
> *Fighting losing battles has lasted four years.*
> *The country lies broken as winds scatter the willow catkins;*
> *My life consumed by turns of fortune as rain beats upon rootless duckweed.*
> *At Fearful Rapids I spoke of fear;*
> *By the Lonely Sea I now sigh in loneliness.*
> *Who in life has ever been free of death?*
> *So I commend my loyal heart to the pages of history.*

Afterwards, he calmly went to his death.

As the saying goes, "One's death could be of great importance or a matter of little consequence." For some people in this world, preserving one's honor is something more important than death, so they will sacrifice their lives in order to fulfill their oaths of loyalty. Therefore, dying for a noble cause or sacrificing oneself for honor can in no way be compared to the common act of suicide. There are even those who are martyrs to their faith and those who die for what they believe, for their faith or purpose in life transcends life itself.

During the Buddha's lifetime, there were those among his disciples who at one time or another wanted to kill themselves or planned to commit suicide. For example, there was the Bhiksuni Simha who had practiced for seven years but had yet to quell her desirous thoughts. Disgusted by her own weaknesses, she contemplated suicide, but just as she was about to hang herself in the forest, she suddenly became enlightened. The Bhiksu Sappadasa practiced for twenty-five years but had yet to experience peace, and so decided to commit suicide. But when he put the razor to his throat, he sudden became enlightened. The Bhiksu Bhagari decided to commit suicide for the same reason and wanted to jump off a cliff so as to end his life, but just as he was about to leap, he suddenly became enlightened.

Another case is recorded in the thirty-ninth chapter of the *Miscellaneous Discourses of the Buddha*, where the Bhiksu Godhika had achieved enlightenment six times, but had regressed afterwards each time. Upon his seventh realization, he was afraid he would regress yet a seventh time, and so he wished to enter final nirvana while in that state. But upon reaching the seventh realization, he had already transcended the state of samsara and there no longer remained any delusive thoughts in his mind. So the Buddha permitted Godhika to carry out his self-attained final nirvana. Even the Buddha himself, while practicing during one of his past lives, "sacrificed his body to feed a tiger," while Ananda at the age of 120 chose to enter final nirvana because he no longer wished to hear any more vile words or idle gossip. Some of Buddhism's realized eminent monks faced death in a free and extraordinary manner, for they knew in advance their time had come and, looking upon life and death as the same, they passed into final nirvana while sitting in meditation. Such actions are not average suicides, in which someone flees from responsibility; nor are they comparable to mass suicides that have resulted from mistaken beliefs.

In recent years, there have been reports from around the world of people whose faith in cults has resulted in forms of mental aberration culminating in mass suicide. For example, in 1978, Jim Jones, an American preacher suffering from paranoia, led 914 of his followers to commit mass suicide in Jonestown, Guyana, representing the largest case of mass suicide in history. In 1991, a Mexican government minister named Ramon Morales Almazan, deluded in his worship, led twenty-nine followers to commit mass self-immolation in a church. In 1994, 1995, and 1997, members of the Solar Temple were involved in three incidents of mass suicide in North America and Europe, which resulted in the tragic deaths of more than one hundred people. In 1993, fifty-three Vietnamese villagers were directed to kill themselves with crude weapons by a blind person who devoutly believed in some perverse cult. In 1997, thirty-nine members of the Heaven's Gate cult believed that UFOs would take them to heaven, and so they committed mass suicide by taking sleeping pills. These events represent evidence of the great harm done by some cults.

Buddhism distinguishes between three kinds of wrongdoing, as listed in the tenth chapter of the *Treatise on Establishing the Truth*: there is wrongdoing, serious wrongdoing, and wrongdoing within wrongdoing. Among these, to commit suicide or to lead others to commit murder constitutes serious wrongdoing. The *Sutra of the Brahma's Net* also states that all living beings are our mothers and fathers; therefore, to kill living things would be killing our mothers and our fathers, and in this vein, to kill oneself would be no different from killing one's father or mother. Another example can be found in the *Treatise on the Perfection of Great Wisdom*, which states that no matter how assiduously one accumulates merit, if one fails to keep the precept of not killing living things, then such efforts are meaningless.

Buddhism unequivocally values life, and therefore opposes any approach that does harm to life, promoting the idea instead that we should spread life's light and glory during the time we are alive. By committing ourselves and serving all sentient beings, we can expand the meaning and value of life, and extend the hope and future for life. This is the only proper way of faith, and it is the only correct attitude toward human life.

What does suicide accomplish?

People who are determined to commit suicide all share a common psychology, and that is to rid themselves of everything by dying. Does suicide really accomplish this goal?

The mistaken belief that death brings an end to everything is a widely held view. So it often happens that when someone is unable to deal with difficulties and frustrations, they take the negative approach and want to commit suicide, hoping to rid themselves of all their problems by dying.

Actually, when we are reborn as a human being, we bring into this world our past karma. The successes and failures we experience in this life all represent the fruition of karma generated in our past and present lifetimes. We should just cope with it, for only then can we eliminate our karma as conditions arise. If, on the other hand, we were to commit suicide in the attempt to escape the problems and adversity we encounter, not only would the karma not be eliminated, but we also would be creating even more bad karma. How could we possibly rid ourselves of such bad karma? How can death bring an end to everything?

Therefore, committing suicide does not solve any problems! Suicide only generates more problems and adds to our suffering. If for example, I were to kill myself, I would immediately bring incomparable suffering to my family, friends, relatives, classmates, and even acquaintances. Sometimes there are unfinished obligations put upon them, adding to their burden. Moreover, the nation has educated me and society has supported me. Just when I could be of service to society, I die from suicide. This is a waste of social capital. Therefore, the suicide of one individual not only creates a loss for society, but also involves many other people, for one has failed the many people who hold concern and love for that person. This is truly unbearable.

Suicide leaves behind many complications. For example, if a family's ancestor committed suicide, then no matter how many generations elapse, the younger generations still feel some sense of shame, for not only does an unconquerable shadow linger in their hearts, in some cases it might even lead to imitation. Therefore, I believe that even though murder exists in society, to be killed by someone else is something that cannot always be avoided; but to kill oneself is simply unforgivable. To die because one falls victim to some external force is one thing, for there is no way to resist it, but to kill oneself is irresponsible. This is foolishness, because it happens out of a momentary inability to think things through; and owing to one's own foolishness, one inflicts loss upon one's family and society. So basically, suicide is not worthy of our sympathy or regret.

In particular, the suicide victim's emotional state at the time of the act carries some sort of wound to the spirit, and so the person dies with feelings of pain, grief, helplessness, hopelessness, worry, or even anger, hatred, and regret. Such thoughts will certainly lead to rebirth as a hell-being, a hungry ghost, or an animal, which is what the *Abhidharma-kosa-sastra* calls the path of karma.

The path of karma refers to the three karmas of desire, anger, and ignorance, in which desire leads to anger, anger leads to ignorance, and ignorance leads back to desire. What precedes serves as the path for what follows; a karmic path is produced through a cycle of these interactions. And so the paths leading to the cycle of birth and death of the six realms of existence are formed. This means that when we create karma, a force is generated that leads to a result. Karma is like a path or road; good karma will lead to a good place, while bad karma will lead to a bad one. Therefore, if we do not foster suicidal thoughts, we can avoid suicidal behavior and its resulting outcome.

Over the course of a lifetime, it is impossible to avoid problems. Although problems give us the experience of life's suffering, from another perspective, we come to experience both mentally and emotionally the unending cycle of birth and death, within which we can slowly make progress. We must never let a momentary difficulty lead us to consider death as a way of ending it all. To think that death can solve all one's problems is a mistaken idea. As long as we have confidence, courage, compassion, and wisdom, there is nothing in this world that cannot be resolved. So I hope that there are some good Samaritans within the community who can sponsor various activities of fellowship and group discussion on a regular basis, in order to develop a spirit of neighborly aid and support that promotes mutual concern and encouragement. Only by instilling a positive and optimistic attitude toward life can we prevent the tragic act of suicide.

Is Suicide Painful?

When people commit suicide and even after they die from suicide, is there any pain involved?

When people encounter troubles and pain and think about suicide, they hope that in so doing, they can end everything. There are those who, when faced with difficulties and setbacks, feel that death is better than life. So they think about suicide as a way of ending their lives. They think that they can find release in death, but after committing suicide, they will actually come to realize that life is better than death.

The *Poetry Anthology for Spiritual Edification* records the following story:

A certain individual surnamed Jiang from Wujiang County lost a bitter quarrel and then committed suicide by taking poison. Later, he communicated with the human world through his wife and reported the following: "I died when I should not have, and so I was punished by being sent to City for the Unjust Dead, where the beds burn with fire and copper pillars glow hot, in an endless variety of miserable suffering. Only then did I realize that one day of life is far better than a thousand years of death. So I urge everyone, it's alright to get boiling mad, but don't commit suicide, for doing so will only lead to endless regret." With that, his cried bitterly and left.

Clearly, suicide can only offer a momentary escape, but in so doing, one accrues even more endless suffering.

Another work, *Clearly Recognize the True Nature of Suicide* states that the pain suffered by a victim of suicide is a hundred or a thousand times worse than the pain suffered in life, something that cannot be put into words. For example, when people die by drowning themselves in a river, the water quickly rushes into through their mouths while the lungs try desperately to breathe; as these inner and outer forces struggle together, the victim experiences unbearable suffering. When people die by hanging themselves, their windpipe is sealed shut and the blood flow is reversed; it feels like the body is being cut with knives, and then they become paralyzed and suffer all manner of pain. When people die by poisoning themselves with such things as insecticide or hydrochloric acid, their internal organs are destroyed and they suffer extreme and unbearable pain. When people die by taking sleeping pills, they feel dizzy, their breathing is labored, and their internal organs become agitated. Sometimes their breathing ceases and their heart stops beating, a state that resembles death. After a while, they may slowly wake up, but they have already been sealed in a coffin, and with no way to get out, they toss and turn inside, dying in terror and pain.

Another study reported on the examination of exhumed bodies of those who died from intentional opium overdoses. The majority of their bodies were found lying face down, while others were lying sideways; but it was rare to find bodies lying face up. This was because the bodies thrashed about inside the coffins after burial, once the effects of the opium had worn off.

As indicated by the accounts above, although there are numerous and varied ways to commit suicide, invariably from beginning to end, the suicide victim experiences a great deal of suffering and when the point of death draws near, their consciousness becomes quite lucid and all the images from their past and present are clearly reflected back to them. Thus, the suffering they experience becomes even more profound.

People who commit suicide will certainly suffer pain before their suicide, for without the experience of pain, there would be no thought of committing suicide. It is because they can no longer bear the pain that they consequently seek resolution by suicide. But it is just at the point between life and death during suicide that they will discover that suicide is full of unbearable suffering, regardless of the method employed, be it hanging, taking pills, using a knife or gun, jumping into a river, leaping from a building, or inhaling carbon-monoxide. If one hangs oneself, one doesn't die immediately; the moment before death, one's breathing is cut off. There may be times when the person regrets what he or she has done and would like to stop, but lacks the strength to do so or even to cry out. The entire process of hanging oneself is truly full of indescribable suffering.

Not only do suicide victims suffer infinite pain during the final stages of life, but the pain experienced after death is a million times more than the pain experienced near death. And being saved from death brings even more pain. More and more people these days are trying to commit suicide with carbon-monoxide, for they think that doing so would mean leaving this world in a calm sleep. However, as indicated by doctors from the Mackay Memorial Hospital and the Chang Gung Memorial Hospital in Kaohsiung, Taiwan, those who survive this type of suicide may develop delayed nervous and mental symptoms due to acute carbon-monoxide poisoning, conditions from which some never recover. There are victims who developed consciousness disturbances or auditory hallucinations a full month after being rescued, and even suffered such symptoms as washing one's face with a dishcloth, trying to use a telephone like a drinking fountain, incontinence, and an inability to maintain personal hygiene. Some individuals were left with lingering complications such as slow responsiveness and memory impairment.

Suicide is also a violation of the precept against killing living things. Even if one successfully commits suicide, the karmic consequences of killing a living being cannot be avoided after death. Killing living things is a crime that cannot be tolerated in this world, and even the Lord of Death will not look kindly upon such a person. How can someone who commits suicide dare face anyone? Therefore, suicide is not the solution to one's problems, nor is death the end of pain, for death cannot bring an end to everything. Life continues on and on, according to one's positive and negative karmic retribution. So in Buddhism, we speak of a natural death, for it is only with a good, natural death, that we can find a good rebirth, which is the only way to achieve true liberation.

Depression and Suicide

Some people say that depression is the chief killer among mental illnesses in the 21st century, and there are already a growing number of people who have committed suicide because of it. How can we prevent people who suffer from depression from contemplating suicide?

According to a study by the World Health Organization, depression has become a global illness. There are 450 million people around the world who are afflicted with mental illness, and on average, one out of every four people that reported health issues has a problem with mental illness. And among all sufferers of mental illness, those troubled with depression have the highest rates of suicide. Growing numbers of people take the path to suicide because of depression, and it has become the third largest cause of death for humanity in the 21st century.

Why do people become depressed? There is an article entitled "*Lay Down Your Worries*" that states: "Students worry about their exams; young people worry about the future; parents worry about their children; old people worry that their tomorrows are getting fewer; poor people worry that there's not enough money; rich people worry about holding on to their wealth; sick people worry about their illness; busy people worry about not finishing all their work; people with nothing to do worry about being bored; lonely people worry about being lonely; fun-lovers worry that the party won't last forever; the not-yet-famous worry about living in obscurity; the already-famous worry that their fame will never again be so impressive; and even some mothers just worry to the point of tears because their child has been away for a few hours. So I ask you all: Who is without worry?"

The author's final conclusion was: "'Even those without immediate concerns must have distant worries,' is a truism that has withstood the test of time." The author describes how "worry is our shadow that follows us wherever we go, for it does not disappear despite the changes to one's place and environment."

Truly, it seems as if all modern people are living a

depressed, unhappy life. There is a lack of mutual trust, support, respect, and forgiveness between people. Such a cold and uncaring attitude has created a sense of psychological alienation. Additionally, young people today commonly live a comfortable, well-fed life, and they lack the ability to withstand pressure and accept hardship, and so they easily fall victim to depression. In Taiwan alone, there are as many as a million people who suffer from depression, and cases of suicide due to depression are also growing daily. Although it is true that not every person who commits suicide suffers from mental illness, yet the incidence of mental illness among suicide victims is about twenty percent, more than two thousand times that of the general population.

In a study published in 1999 by psychiatrist Dr. Cheng Tai-an, after interviewing the families of 113 suicide victims from eastern Taiwan and studying the suicide victims' past history and mental state, the results revealed that more than ninety percent of the cases were marked with some form of mental illness. Among these, the largest group included major depression and dysthymia (about ninety percent); there was also alcoholism and drug addiction (more than forty percent); and personality disorder (representing sixty percent). Some studies conducted abroad have come to similar conclusions that between eight-three and one-hundred percent of the cases were suffering from some form of mental illness before their suicide.

Therefore, experts suggest that one possible approach for reducing the rate of suicide is to treat suicide as a kind of illness rather than considering it to be merely a sign of weak willpower or unwillingness to value life. In their view, to look upon those who suffer from suicidal thoughts as having a problem with willpower, attitude, or morality might possibly make these people feel even more guilty and become less willing to seek help from those around them.

In Taiwan, many sufferers of depression are unable to seek treatment in a timely fashion during the early stages of their illness, and in some cases fail to identify the right specialists, thus losing the opportunity to seek help from their friends and family or doctors. The suicidal thoughts continue to magnify, leading to ever-growing rates of death by suicide. If we are able to observe and analyze ourselves and seek proper treatment early enough when we have emotional difficulties, this could lower the incidence of suicide among many groups. Having drawn this conclusion, institutions like Hsin Ying Hospital in Taiwan have already instituted special outpatient care for depression, and have also made available a score chart for depression, allowing the public to test themselves and help reduce the occurrence of suicidal thoughts.

At present, the world focus on suicide prevention is directed toward treatment of mental illness, especially with drug therapy. This is because, as many studies have shown, more than fifty to sixty percent of those who committed suicide were seen by doctors from gynecology or pediatrics departments or family practice doctors within three months prior to their deaths. Thus, the island of Gotland implemented a plan in Sweden during the 1980s, instructing family practice doctors how to recognize and treat depression. This resulted in a reduction of suicide rates among its citizens, and may represent the approach with the highest degree of proven effectiveness at present.

Most people feel that the onset of depression results from disturbances in one's external living environment. For example, unstable governments, insecure societies, economic downturns, high unemployment rates, and a high degree of stress in life will make one feel that life is only about suffering and that it would be simpler to free oneself from it all with death. But according to some studies, this is not always true. There are people who are born into wealthy families and whose life is a success, people who did not have to struggle in life. One would expect that these people should be able to live peacefully. But actually, such is not always the case, for after entering middle age, some begin to feel that life is meaningless, and not knowing why they are alive, they end up depressed and commit suicide.

In the case of Australia, not only is there a beautiful living environment, but there are also ample social welfare benefits such as medical treatment, retirement pensions, free education, and unemployment insurance. But people cannot free themselves from their worries, and still go on to take drugs, to self-medicate, and even to throw their lives away, to the point that Australia now has one of the world's highest suicide rates.

In reality, there are many people in society today who take drugs and abuse alcohol, damaging their lives over a long period of time, which also constitutes a slow-acting form of suicide. Others risk their lives doing dangerous activities; for example, some acrobatic performers regularly risk their lives performing, some young people drag race, some drive while under the influence, and so forth, all of which are subtle ways of trying to kill oneself. There are others who live in a fantasy world of make-believe, who, for example, consider suicide for the sake of romantic love to be a sadly beautiful act. This is a kind of abnormal illusory mental state, where someone imagines what it would be like to die; but in the end, a false illusion becomes a real act. Even more commit suicide because of personal setbacks or depression.

People commit suicide due to depression or personal setbacks when they lack the strength to resist external pressures. To resist external pressure and personal setbacks, one must increase his or her inner power to resist. For example, one can use joy, reason, or the consideration of others as forms of resistance; that is, do not always think of yourself only. One must, on a regular basis, nurture many kinds of strength, develop one's own wisdom, read more books, meet more positive role models, and participate in more social organizations or various religious activities, thereby obtaining encouragement through religion.

One can even try modern psychological counseling and therapy, as well as travel, exercise, herbal therapies, music therapy, animal therapy, learning new skills, developing interpersonal relationships, pursuing one's hobbies, encouraging one's confidence, talking to friends, creating hopes, being with all beings, opening up one's heart, going out for a walk, making oneself busy, and so on.

If one was able to make ready all the various weapons of war before one commits suicide or when facing life's pressures, then "the generals are prepared for any battle, and the earthworks are ready for any flood." And we would no longer fear that the demons of pressure would attack us, because we would have methods for dealing with and dispelling them.

Therefore, from time to time each individual must accept the lessons that hardship brings and strengthen the power to resist. We must do so, because from the past to the present, what living thing in this world has not suffered hardships? Many successful heroes were only able to succeed because they were able to overcome adversity. And so from childhood to adulthood, as we mature and grow, each of us must have strength and not allow ourselves to become upset by some matter or be overthrown with a single word. Many times, when we hear unhappy words, the person who said them forgets them quickly, but we become so angry that we can neither sleep nor eat for days-a truly pointless waste of time. Or when some people encounter some dissatisfaction or are faced with financial collapse, they then contemplate suicide. But as a matter of fact, there is always some way these matters can be resolved. It is important not to give in to a momentary impulse for suicide; it really is irrational.

Besides learning how to face adversity and having the ability to withstand pressure, each of us must have goals in life. With a goal in view, one can go far, and so a way to prevent suicidal thoughts is to seek out the meaning and value of life and live a life that is dignified and joyous.

One's life can only be lived once, and each one of us is totally unique, for no one can take the place of another. Therefore, we must come to terms with life's "non-repeatability" and its "non-interchangeability," and bestow importance and dignity upon our lives. Once a person understands how to respect life and comes to know how precious and rare living existence is, he or she will then be able to cherish life and will not allow some hardship to make one give up hope in oneself or even to lose the will to live.

Although experts say that depression will create widespread problems in the 21st century, we must not remain mired in it, for we must find a way to transcend it. A deep appreciation of the truths of the Buddhadharma will enable us to understand the true nature of life, giving us the power to bear, accept, and dispel what befalls us. Therefore, I hope that those contemplating suicide will have the courage and aspiration to attain enlightenment, and can transform their lives into one of service to all sentient beings. And wouldn't that be much better than trying to end one's life!

Suicide Trends

According to expert research, whenever a country or society suffers a serious natural disaster, as in the aftermath of the Taiwan earthquake disaster of September 21, 1999, incidents of suicide appear to increase among the residents of the affected areas. Is it possible for suicide to become a trend?

In our chaotic modern society, problems as gambling, drug addiction, robbery, kidnapping, domestic violence, and sexual assault are becoming more prevalent. But the most serious growing social problem is suicide.

Suicide is one of the ten major causes of death worldwide, and in the case of Taiwan, according to the statistics from the Department of Health for the year 2003, a total of 3,053 people committed suicide that year, meaning on average someone was committing suicide every three hours. Among these, the number of male deaths from suicide was twice that for females. In terms of age, the suicide rate for people under the age of twenty-four has increased eighteen percent over the rate in 1990, and the rate for people between the ages of twenty-five and forty-four has increased seventeen percent. Suicide has already become the third major cause of death among younger people, falling closely behind accidental death and cancer.

In addition, one source of statistics indicate that the suicide rate for major urban areas is far higher than for those residing in rural areas, and members of the middle class who commit suicide exceed that of any other social class. In terms of age distribution, suicide rates for young people between the ages of fifteen and twenty-five as well as people over the age of seventy-five are growing higher. In particular, the rate of successful suicide among older people is very high, but in recent years, the suicide rate among primary school children has been gradually climbing upwards as well. In terms of gender, the rate of successful suicide among males is three times higher than that of females, and yet the rate of attempted suicide among females is higher than that of males.

From a cultural perspective, the suicide rate among the advanced countries of Western Europe is far higher than among Muslim and Buddhist areas, and India. Reasons for this possibly include such things as alienation within interpersonal relations, the diminished position of religion, and the inflated modern consciousness for control over one's own life. As for a comparison between capitalist countries and socialist ones, there is no commonly accepted view as opinions vary. However, there are scholars who believe that the acceleration of suicide rates among the former socialist countries of Eastern Europe was much faster than in the West. Hungary, for example, had a suicide rate of 41.1 per ten thousand people in 1978, making it the highest in the world. In short, the results of empirical statistics show that the distribution of suicide is seemingly related to factors such as age, gender, and occupation.

Beyond this, the faster the pace of development among countries and societies, the higher the rate of suicide among its citizens. A trend such as this can no longer be reversed. This is especially true when the economy becomes unstable or some drastic upheaval takes place, for on such occasions the suicide rate clearly goes up. As mentioned above, during the years after the earthquake that occurred on September 21, 1999, the suicide rate for Nantou County, the epicenter, was the highest in Taiwan.

Not only can attempting suicide become a habit, for

according to one source of research statistics in the U.S., on average, each successful suicide was preceded by sixteen attempted suicides; but suicide can also become a trend, because people tend to copy one another. As people interact, their feelings affect one another, just like an epidemic, and become contagious. Added to this mix are the media's greatly exaggerated reports on suicide, which not only give negative lessons to society at large, but also create a secondary wound for those involved. This is because suicide already delivers a wound to the mind and body, but the added sensationalism of such reports are tantamount to killing that person all over again, and for this reason the media must not aggravate the situation.

However, the reason the media tends to emphasize such negative reporting is because they are trying to cater to the tastes of their audience. So society cannot just simply blame the media, for the mentality of the audience requires self-reflection, as well as learning self-control.

Let me tell a story: One day, the Lord of Death was passing judgment upon some criminals. First he said to Big Zhao, "During your life you committed murder and arson, bribed officials, and corrupted the law for your purposes. I sentence you to suffer in Hell for fifty years, after which you will find rebirth in the human world."

He then said to Wang the Fifth: "You are a learned person and in life you composed writings and wrote books; but the books you wrote were all volumes of pornography. Not only have you caused trouble with your fabrications, but you have also perverted the hearts of men, contributing no benefit whatsoever to the morals of humanity. So I sentence you to suffer in hell for the rest of your life."

Wang the Fifth objected: "Lord of Death, this is unfair. During his life, Big Zhao committed murder, robbery, and adultery, but he was only sentenced to a mere fifty years in Hell. I only wrote some stories, so why have you judged my crime so seriously?"

The Lord of Death said: "Because the books that you wrote are still circulating in the human world, and the harm your words have done to the hearts of men is still continuing and growing. This means that not until the influence of your writings has completely disappeared from the human world will it be possible to nullify your negative karma, and only at that time will you be spared this suffering."

Wang the Fifth was shocked and dismayed by what he heard. He had no idea that the momentary foolishness on his part could generate such negative karma on such a limitless scale, for there was no knowing when it would all be expiated.

This story reminds me of something else: One time a conference on the philosophy of life was held at the Taipei World Trade Center under the auspices of the Ministry of the Interior, and I was asked to give a speech. In my speech, I said something to this effect: "In society today, if we are virtuous in our writings, then that would be enough to save Taiwan; and being virtuous in our speech would mean that we could save ourselves." Do not think that words spoken to suit our own fancy can be so casually uttered and then forgotten. It is true that sound is impermanent and that the sound of our voice ceases to be, but the influence of our words will always remain, for the karmic power of cause and effect never disappears. Therefore, as a rule, do not say whatever you like to show off your verbal wit and do not cook up stories just to show off your writing ability, thereby serving as a bad example to others. Instead, one should speak good words, do good deeds, keep good thoughts, write good articles, and report about good people and good works on a regular basis. This will certainly save oneself, and it will also save society and the country. Therefore, the moral quality of a society must be built up by all of its citizens working together.

When it comes to suicide, the reason most people contemplate suicide is because they feel that living is too painful. And why do they feel it is painful? The reasons are: too much selfishness, too much thinking of only oneself, and lack of ability to deal with external pressures. If an individual only thinks of "me" day after day, "my" wishes, "my" wants," and "my" loves, then one would feel that life is limited. A person should love nature. Such a beautiful land of mountains and rivers; why would you want to leave it? A person should love the country, society, and sentient beings. Such an accomplished society; why don't you love it instead of wanting to leave it? Think of your family and friends; haven't they loved and helped you? How can you bear leaving them all behind? Thus, if you live with a sense of responsibility and consideration for others, you would not want to commit suicide. Especially if you keep the Buddhadharma in your heart, you will have the wisdom of patience, and as you develop step by step the patience for sentient beings, the patience of the Dharma, all the way to the patience of the non-arising of phenomena, you will naturally be able to lay aside the fickleness of emotion and the vagaries of social status in this human world, and thereby diminish your attachment to the world outside the mind. The world inside your mind would then become expansive and open-ended, and you would be able to live a more solid and free life, one in which there would be no thought of suicide.

In short, learning how to live freely is the responsibility of educators as well as the media; it is also the family's responsibility, as well as society's. Once a country has suffered a major disaster or calamity, protecting disaster victims from suicide during the aftermath is a serious issue that requires the close attention of all citizens working together.

Is Suicide Criminal?

The constitution clearly stipulates that killing someone is a crime. So does taking the life of animals and other life forms or destroying plants constitute a crime? Are unsuccessful attempts to kill others or commit suicide crimes as well?

This modern era is one that values the right to life, for not only do laws clearly prohibit the abuse of animals, but in particular some protected rare animals cannot be hunted or even taken from the wild. It is also a time of growing environmental consciousness, for not only have citizens joined in protecting natural resources, but the indiscriminate clearing of hillsides and cutting of forests has also been prohibited.

One could say that this era has already expanded on human rights to include the right to life for all things, for it is not just human beings that have life, but the earth with all its sentient beings, animate and inanimate, has life, which should be respected and protected. So although Buddhism is a religion based upon human beings, sometimes we may mindlessly harm such things as ants, mosquitoes, and flies; and even though such acts are not punishable offenses according to the law, they do represent moral transgressions. We should do no harm, from the mountains and rivers of this earth to animals and plants, since all of these should be well protected. To willfully destroy and harm them is killing life in its broader sense.

Buddhism is a religion with a strict precept against killing living things, for Buddhists believe that all sentient beings have Buddha Nature, and in the future they can each attain Buddhahood. Therefore, we should treat life as if we were attending to our parents; how could we possibly kill them? If we kill them, we would then be killing a future Buddha. The precepts against killing, stealing, sexual misconduct, lying, and intoxicants can be transgressed by committing them yourself, inciting others to commit them, or taking pleasure in seeing others commit them. The monastic precept against killing is described as follows in the "Ten Serious Pratimoksa": "Disciples of the Buddha are prohibited from personally killing, inciting others to kill, killing by expedience, admiring killing, taking pleasure in killing, killing someone by means of a curse, creating the causes for killing, creating the conditions for killing, creating the methods for killing, or producing the effects of killing; for all that is possessed of life must not be killed."

Buddhism does not merely prohibit suicide and the killing of others. It even prohibits facilitating others to kill living things or expressing approval of such killing. One may ask, "If killing people is a crime, is it also a crime to kill insects and animals? For example, is it a serious moral transgression to spray insecticide or DDT to kill mosquitoes, flies, and ants?" Generally speaking, the killing of living things is a moral transgression with karmic effect. Upon hearing this some people might say: "I am a farmer or I sell insecticide. I don't want to believe in Buddhism anymore, because Buddhism prohibits the killing of living things; if I don't kill harmful insects, how will I make a living?" Actually, even if you do not believe in Buddhism, once you kill living things, it is still the same transgression. Since Buddhism is a religion centered on human beings, even though there is a prohibition against killing all living things, the crime of killing people is treated more seriously than the killing of animals. Even so, we cannot use this as an excuse for the indiscriminate killing of living things, for even if such killing cannot be avoided, we must still maintain our compassionate mind by blessing all living things. For example, when eating chicken or duck eggs, we should think silently: "I now send you to the Western Pure Land, so that you will be spared the knife in this human world." Of course, it would be best if we did not infringe upon the life of animals at all, and that includes killing ourselves.

Suicide is the action of the weak, who have convinced themselves that therein lies their escape. In reality, it is not true that suicide can resolve all pain. For example, the suicide of young people today is comparable to a flower withering away before it has a chance to bloom; how merciless is that. Or how about those in the prime of their lives, who are just at the point they can accomplish things, but owing to a failed romance or some financial shortfall, they choose suicide as a mode of escape. And what about older people; although their long-term illness has not gotten better, modern medical treatment is well-developed and there is a healthcare system, so there is always some therapy that can prolong life. Even if one accepts that there are no effective treatments, death is a very natural process, a natural phenomena, and there is no need force it to happen. Therefore, whether it be killing others or suicide, these are all behaviors of the same class of moral transgression. Even unsuccessful attempts at suicide are crimes as well, because one has a mind to kill or thoughts of killing. With thoughts of killing, one is accountable for his or her mental process, and although the act may have been unsuccessful, one has already crossed over into danger since one's thoughts are the source of one's actions.

In short, killing others is a crime, which must be judged according to the penal code. Now is killing oneself a crime? The law does not punish suicide, but Buddhism holds that suicide is not only an act of ignorance, but it is also wrongful conduct. This is because the life of an individual is the accumulation of all the conditions within society. An individual has no right to destroy it. To employ violence to end one's own life or that of others violates the Buddhist precept against killing living things, and one has to bear the painful retribution of such actions. Therefore, those who want to commit suicide should have a sense of responsibility and be courageous; they should face their problems and apply wisdom to solve them. Never use suicide as a means of escaping problems.

Child Suicide

Recently, the age for suicide has been steadily dropping every year in countries around the world, and there are more and more young children with suicidal tendencies. What is the Buddhist view on this matter?

In the minds of most people, childhood should be that time in life when one has the least worries and cares; it should be the happiest and most wonderful chapter of life. But in the wake of all the changes in social structure and lifestyle, and influences exerted by the larger environment as mediated through the multidimensional and complex nature of the media, children everywhere are reaching mental maturity earlier. They are maturing without appropriate guidance; so now one often hears stories about primary and secondary students committing suicide due to such factors as schoolwork pressures, difficulties with interpersonal relationships, or family misfortune. This has caused the average age for suicide victims to drop steadily every year.

In Taiwan for example, a work entitled "*A Study of Factors Related to the Suicidal Ideas of Public Primary School Students*," by Chiang Yi-chen of the Institute of Public Health and Welfare at Yang Ming University, points out that twenty-six percent of Taipei's fourth-graders have had suicidal thoughts. Most of these resulted from too much schoolwork, emotional problems, a low level of family support, or relationship problems with their peers, while their knowledge of suicide methods came mostly from media reports.

In addition, according to a report by Nelson (1994), 2,151 children and adolescents across the U.S. died from suicide in 1980; children from five to fourteen years old constituted twelve percent of the total. A report from the Japanese Ministry of Education, Science, Sports and Culture points out that there were 192 Japanese children between the ages of six and eighteen who committed suicide in 2001, representing a forty-four percent increase over the 133 such cases the year before. Of these, fourteen percent were related to family problems, and seven percent were related to problems encountered in school.

The Xinhua News Agency in Hong Kong has also reported that in the last three years Hong Kong has witnessed a sudden increase in students with suicidal tendencies or who have attempted suicide, reaching as high as 507 cases. The reasons for such a sharp rise in student suicide attempts within the short span of three years are related to extensive reporting on cases of teen suicide by the media, which has spawned a competition among young classmates to imitate such behavior.

Therefore, the Hong Kong authorities felt that the problem of teen suicide had become a multi-layered social problem, and that various parties such as school, families, the media, society, and government must unite in common cause to solve the problem. Besides calling for more self-restraint on the part of the media when reporting on cases of teen suicide, the government at the same time has looked to the Education Department to provide various services to teachers, students, parents, and schools. These include:

1) Sponsor short-term classes, discussion sessions, and workshops for in-service teachers, so as to heighten their awareness of the suicide problem among students, and strengthen their guidance and communicative skills. And at the same time, compile tutorial materials and set up a hotline assistance service, so that teachers will be more prepared.

2) Add a new course to the primary school curriculum called "General Knowledge Course," and invite the Psychology Department of Hong Kong University to implement a peer support plan that it designed for twenty test schools.

3) Take the lead in establishing parent centers on a trial basis, to provide extra support for parents and teachers, and to go a step further in strengthening parental education.

4) Provide schools with support services, help the schools adopt a campus-based approach to guidance, and establish a positive, caring, and attractive school environment, which will enable students who are being harassed to better seek help.

The Hong Kong approach presents many ideas worthy of study and consideration. Given that the suicide rate in Australia is one of the highest in the world, and in particular, the suicide problem for young people is becoming more and more serious, it is important to study other country's responses to these social problems. Brisbane's Griffith University has spearheaded Australia's first university course on suicide prevention as a means of combating the problem of the world's highest suicide rate. This course of study called "Suicide Prevention" is specifically designed for guidance counselors, police officers, and social workers who deal with troubled teenagers, and instructs them on how to prevent and cope with suicidal behavior.

The suicide of children and teenagers constitutes a loss for the country and society; this is especially true in the case of gifted students who commit suicide because of schoolwork pressures, or children who merely want to experience what suicide is like out of a sense of curiosity, without realizing what death is all about. Furthermore, some children commit suicide because of depression. These are all serious problems that are worthy of our deep concern.

Most people live with a sense of hope, and because they are hopeful about the future, they are able to put up with short-term frustrations. But for a child afflicted with depression, tomorrow appears even darker than today and the future bleaker than the present. Since they have no hope for the future, they are more easily sucked into the deep abyss of depression and end up wallowing in thoughts of death. Factors such as setbacks, humiliation, or the death of a relative tend to aggravate the situation, pushing the child over the edge toward suicide.

Actually, the reason most children commit suicide is because they lack confidence and a sense of security. They feel isolated inside and earnestly hope that they can receive warmth from their families and the love of their parents. Therefore, the example set by the parents from day to day is very important. Parents should create more joy and harmony within the family, so that the children will come to honor life and appreciate life's preciousness.

This reminds me of a story: Once there was a child who always had to pass a temple on his way to school. One day, the child entered the Buddha Hall of the temple, and handed the monk in charge of the incense and lamps ten dollars for some incense and lamp oil. The monk asked him, "Where did this money come from?"

The child answered, "I found it."

"That's good," said the monk. "You have put the money you found to good use, which shows that you are not only mature, but also obedient." So the monk spoke many words in praise of the child.

The next day, the child came again to see the monk, "Master, master, I found another ten dollars today."

The monk said, "You are lucky indeed for finding money

on the street; and you are honest and courteous as well. You are really a good boy."

On the third day, the child came again, "Master, I found another ten dollars."

The monk wondered how the boy could be so lucky to find ten dollars lying around every day. So he asked, "Tell the truth, where did you get this money?"

The boy pulled a roll of bills from his pocket and said to the monk, "You see, my family has a lot of money. It's just that I'm not happy, because my mom and dad are always arguing, and when they fight, they yell at me in such an unpleasant way. Living with my family makes me so unhappy; so it's better to give you ten dollars everyday so that I can listen to your good words."

Therefore, parents should be careful not harm children when they speak; they should take their dignity into account. Although parents experience all kinds of suffering in order to live, exert all kinds of effort in order to make money and support a family, and deal with heavy pressures in order to struggle for their future, life is about being responsible and having strength and patience; otherwise it is hard to get by. For students of Buddhism, the most essential thing is to build the strength to be accountable and patient. There is a specific practice in Buddhism called "*ksanti-paramita*" or the "perfection of patience." Patience within the Buddhadharma is wisdom, and once the patience for sentient beings, the patience of the Dharma, and the patience of the non-arising of phenomena are complete, one will then have a clear understanding of the world and will naturally be able to detach from the fickleness of emotion, the judgments of good or bad, and the vagaries of social status in this human world. By attaining the meritorious power of patience, one will be able to generate tremendous energy and will thus know how to apply wisdom to resolve problems one encounters, rather than trying to escape through suicide.

Suicide is an act of weakness; it is the manifestation of ignorance regarding the meaning of life. The loss of every child's life is a loss for society, and for this reason, I hope families and society will strengthen the education of children and teenagers by not giving them too much pressure, and instead provide them with more space and understand how they think and act. All this will help children find a way out of their difficulties, and will let them know that life is not one's own possession, for each and every life is part of the shared relationships that exist with others. For example, each human life has a relationship with its parents, a relationship with its family members, and a relationship with its schoolteachers, as well as all the positive role models who have helped it grow and develop. Finally, each human life has a relationship with the country and society. So life is not one's own to do with as you please. Each person must feel concern for their parents, family members, and friends, for if one lives in this world without feeling concern for any other person, then he or she is living a life without value.

Therefore, parents, schools, and society should do more to strengthen the work of educating and guiding our youth, enabling them to develop an optimistic attitude, an outgoing character, and an outlook on life that strives forward in a positive way. In my view, this is the only way we can help children and teenagers find their place in society.

Strengthening the Mind

As mentioned above, the reason people commit suicide is mainly because they are psychologically weak and lack the power to withstand pressure. How, then, should we take care of our minds from day to day? And how can we strengthen the power within our minds?

According to Buddhism, "The Buddha teaches all Dharmas in order to quell what afflicts all minds; without all minds, of what use would be all Dharmas?" The mind is one's master; and if one thinks of good things, then one will naturally do good deeds; but if one thinks of bad things, then one's behavior will naturally become warped. If a person's mind is self-seeking and egoistic, and one only thinks of oneself everyday, this will certainly diminish one's living space.

There is a story of a young woman, who was pacing back and forth along a riverbank with a downcast spirit. In an instant, she mustered the courage to jump into the river, and with a splash, the river cast up a wave of foam. An old monk happened to be walking by and hurriedly rescued the young woman. To his surprise, not only was the young woman ungrateful, she was also angry. She said to him: "Why didn't you let me die; I hate you!" The old monk asked, "Why did you want to commit suicide?"

She said, "I look so ugly; everyone mocks me and criticizes me; nobody likes me. I don't feel there is any point to living. I just want to die and be done with it."

The old monk patiently instructed her, "People have two lives: one is selfish, for it only thinks of itself, putting itself first in everything. But that selfish life of yours died just now. People have yet a second life, which thinks solely of others; and now I have rescued that life. From now on, you must change the way you think and act, and help others at any place and at any time; you must be of service to others."

Having listened to the monk's words, the ugly girl began to do good deeds, serving others everyday. As a result, her good reputation and good deeds became known throughout the village. And since everyone praised her, imperceptibly her heart became more and more outgoing and her appearance become fairer and fairer. In the end, she did indeed find the man of her dreams and got married.

As the story of the girl shows, the old monk's words about the death of her selfish life and rebirth of her beneficial life allowed her to create a second life for herself. Therefore, as human beings, we must not be too selfish, and we should not only think of ourselves; we must think about and show more consideration for others. As long as one is able to develop faith and commit oneself to serving others, one will find that when the warming brightness of one's life expands, it will shine upon others, and as it does so, the lamp of one's own mind will surely be kindled.

As we each go from childhood to adulthood, there are two forces that help us grow: one is a positive force, like the loving concern of our parents and family members and the opportunities we are offered to receive an education, as well as the supporting conditions of society and all its people. All of this enables us to have a good job and so forth. The other is a negative force that comes from those who despise us, put us down, hate us, and push us away. This force often enables us to strive upwards, for like a ball when pushed down softly, it will bounce low, but when pushed down hard, it will bounce high; and so adversity and setbacks can help us discover that we are stronger than we thought possible.

However, very few people are able to understand this kind of negative force. There is the saying "to enjoy success while young," but that may not actually be the best thing, for on the contrary, the earlier one encounters difficulties, the easier it is to become stronger and more mature. But we often fail to see this aspect, just like what happened after the Taiwan earthquake disaster of September 21, 1999. Many people for a time were unable to deal with this negative pressure and trouble, and so they chose to commit suicide. In reality, all one needs is an understanding of how to transform things, so that even adversity can help us to mature and refine our will, enabling us to become even stronger. Even the best of seeds cannot mature without fertilizer, while a lotus flower must have mud if it is to grow and thrive.

There is indeed much frustration and adversity in this world, but to a capable person, these are not obstacles by any means, but instead can actually serve as supporting conditions. It is like after a heavy rainstorm; those trees that have withstood the test will grow even greener. And so even after natural disasters like earthquakes and mudslides, we can go on to build better and more beautiful homes.

The world is impermanent. Earthquakes and typhoons can destroy houses and damage buildings, but as long as our faith has not broken and our minds have focus and strength, even greater disasters will fade away, and tomorrow will be a better day. Therefore, we all must develop our own wisdom and strength. With wisdom, we can perceive clearly the true nature of the world, and with strength we can strive harder and advance further.

Consider bees, ants, and small birds; if the nests they build are blown away, they rebuild them again, and if necessary, they do it over and over again. Even such small creatures have the perseverance to struggle onwards; so how can humanity, the most intelligent of all living things, not measure up to these creatures? Therefore, all we need is faith, for faith contains within it a limitless treasure that can generate strength, and this strength can be passed on to others, enabling them to find the strength to fulfill all tasks. Thus, if we have the courage to overcome our difficulties, we will naturally find the strength to do so.

Our Intentions and Actions

Buddhism is a religion that condemns the killing of living things, but even the thought to kill must not be present. What is the relative severity between killing living things and the thought to kill, and how are we to distinguish between them?

The results of our actions, as expressed by our body, speech, and thought, can be either good or bad. There is a "morally indeterminate quality," in which action is undertaken without a good or bad intention.

As a matter of fact, it is sometimes very difficult to decide and distinguish between good and bad. There are actions that appear quite brutal, but upon careful examination of the situation, turn out to be well-intended actions to save someone else; and there are those apparently good works to help others and benefit society that bring harm to others. For example, killing someone is fundamentally a crime, but when a wicked outlaw whose evil knows no bounds is punished according to the law, it is the executioner who carries out the legal sentence of death. Now is this action ultimately good or bad? At the time he executes the criminal, the executioner perhaps may feel uneasy: "Heaven has given its care to living things, but today I have killed another person." It is the act of killing a person; but the wicked outlaw's killing of others was committed under the influence of ruthless and violent anger, while the executioner who carries out the law holds no grudge against the person he puts to death, for the executioner is only doing his job on behalf of the state, weeding out the wicked and protecting the innocent. The intentions behind the actions of these two people are not the same, and the resulting effect is naturally quite different.

Buddhism places extraordinary emphasis upon the nature of one's intention behind each transgression. Each precept is characterized by differences in what is approved and disapproved, and how it can be upheld and transgressed. A transgression against the same precept will result in different degrees of culpability and forms of repentance, owing to differences in intent, method, and outcome. For example, for killing someone to become a transgression beyond repentance, it must fulfill the following five conditions: that the one killed is a human being, that the intention is to kill a human being, that the perpetrator intends to kill, that the perpetrator employs deadly force, and that the victim dies as a result. This is similar in principle to the penal code in terms of what constitutes a crime and how to deter lawbreaking by emphasizing criminal intent and the facts of the crime. But the positive significance of the Buddhist precepts regarding intention lies in the requirement that individuals observe on their own initiative the motivations and thoughts behind the actions of their body, speech, and mind, so as to guard against Buddhist impropriety at the time such thoughts arise. This is more thorough than secular law.

Once there was a young novice (*sramanera*) who was walking one night and accidentally stepped on a frog, killing it. When his teacher found out, he scolded the young novice, saying: "How could you so carelessly crush to death a living thing? The retribution for such wrongdoing is grave indeed! You should climb the mountain and throw yourself off the cliff, sacrificing yourself as an act of contrition."

The young novice was thunderstruck upon hearing this, for only then did he realize how much trouble he was in. All he could do was tearfully bid farewell to his teacher, and with extreme sadness head for the sharp precipice on the mountain. Looking down from the cliff into the dark depths, the young novice thought to himself, "If I jump off, my body and bones will be smashed to pieces, and I will surely die; but if I don't, I will suffer the three lower forms of existence for many lifetimes in samsara, for one cannot escape the retribution of karma. What am I to do?"

The young novice thought about his predicament this way and that, stuck as he was between a rock and a hard place; in the end he could bear it no longer and started to cry. Just when he was crying in great distress, a pig butcher came by and was astonished to find the young novice crying as he knelt beside the road. The butcher asked what had happened. The young novice told him the story from beginning to end, and upon hearing it, the butcher suddenly felt sad, and spoke with a deep sense of regret: "Young master, all you did was inadvertently crush a single frog to death, and yet the retribution for your wrongdoing is so serious that only by jumping off the cliff and killing yourself can it be expiated. I kill pigs every day, and as I butcher them, my hands are covered with blood and gore. My guilt is far greater and beyond all limits; there's no knowing just how serious it is. Alas, my young master! Don't jump off the cliff; let me do it! For the one who deserves to die as an act of contrition is me!"

With this thought of repentance, the butcher leapt from the edge of the cliff without the slightest hesitation. As he began to plummet downwards, facing imminent death at the bottom of the gorge, a mysterious cloud slowly formed and rose up from the deep gorge, miraculously taking hold of the butcher's body and saving his life.

The implication of this "laying down the butcher's knife and becoming a Buddha right there and then," illustrates the extraordinary power of practicing repentance. And if a single thought of repentance can have such merit, then correspondingly, a single bad thought can lead to death. Although sometimes no action is taken, a single thought, all by itself, is enough to constitute a transgression.

Therefore, we should regularly avoid any thought of killing, and prevent a destructive nature that slowly develops from repeatedly tossing down bowls and chopsticks, throwing chairs and tables about, slamming doors shut, or punching holes in walls, resulting in killing others or killing oneself. And no matter if one kills oneself, kills others, or is pleased at others killing and being killed, these all will lead to the formation of bad habits.

The Buddhist precept against killing living things, also called the precept against ending human life, makes clear that even those who incite or convince others to kill other people or themselves, are transgressing the *parajika*, a grave offense. The S*utra of the Brahma's Net* is particularly specific and strict when it comes our obligation to stop wrongdoing. In the case of not killing, not only does the *sutra* forbid the taking of human life, it also forbids suicide, for it considers the termination of one's life by one's own hand as also breaking this precept. Nor is it permissible to encourage or direct others to kill. If one neither kills nor directs others to do so, but approves of such acts committed by others, such thoughts within the mind are forbidden and culpable. That is to say, this precept not only demands that the actions of the body be pure, but also that the actions of one's speech and mind are pure as well; otherwise, one is breaking the precept.

Actually, everything in the universe has life: some have life in terms of a body, some have life in terms of thoughts, some have life in terms of a career, some have life in terms of morality, and some have life in terms of time. Though they all differ in value, they all should be cherished. For example, it is better to wear an item of clothing for three years than three months; flowers can bloom for a month, but will wither in a day if you pluck them; for in doing so, you are harming life. If you take care of them, tables, chairs, benches, and sofas will be serviceable for decades; and in the end you can even take them to a museum or antique store, where their life will continue uninterrupted.

Therefore, in a broader sense, the killing of living things is not limited to the harm done by knives and clubs. Even abusive words and harsh looks in daily life can do harm to others invisibly and bring upon oneself serious guilt. On the other hand, there may be times when living things are killed, but without murderous intent, in which case the negative karma would be comparatively light. For example, those who dwell in certain places must rely upon fishing in order to make a living because their living environment makes it so. Though fishing is their livelihood, there is no murderous intent. On the contrary, they can from time to time generate the compassionate mind, and so the karmic effect would differ from other cases.

There are other cases, for example, in which sellers of pesticides will say that they sell pesticides that eliminate pests like mosquitoes, ants, and cockroaches. Are they guilty? The farmer will point out that since they grow fruit, they need to spray pesticides to eliminate pests in order to have a good crop. Are they guilty? Of course, I cannot violate the Buddhadharma and mislead others by saying there is no wrongdoing involved. But according to the Buddhadharma, eliminating harmful pests is not the most serious of problems, because when the Buddhist teachings speak about not killing living things, the main object is human beings, for it is the killing of human beings that is most serious. This is what the Buddhadharma specifically prohibits. If the purpose is to get rid of pests, then prevention is surely a lot better than destroying them. From a perspective that is focused upon human beings, though, the application of pesticides for the sake of survival is not that terrible a crime. Even if bhiksus who have received the monastic precepts commit this kind of error, they have, according to the Buddhadharma, only committed misconduct and nothing more. Instances of misconduct can be wiped clean through the power of repentance, something that is quite different from the killing of a human being to which repentance does not apply.

As a matter of fact, even if we kill living things during the course of our daily lives through our conscious and unconscious actions, it is usually only a mild sort of wrongdoing. And there are some actions that entail no guilt whatsoever. What is most important is not to kill living things out of anger or malice, for if one intentionally kills living things out of anger, then one will certainly fall into Hell and suffer. This shows how seriously Buddhism considers one's motivations and intentions.

Euthanasia

All Buddhist sutras are records of symposia. The twelve kinds of Buddhist sutras held in the *Tripitaka* contain a type in which the Buddha "speaks of his own accord without having been asked," which means that these teachings occurred without anyone asking the Buddha a question first. If we peruse the *Tripitaka*, we will find that, except for the *Amitabha Sutra* in which the Buddha speaks of his own accord without having been asked, virtually every Buddhist sutra is a record of someone, who represents the audience, asking the Buddha a question to initiate discussion. For example, in the *Diamond Sutra*, Subhuti asks the Buddha: "What should good men and good women rely on to subdue their minds?" In the *Vimalakirti Sutra*, when Vimalakirti talks to Manjusri and the other bodhisattvas about non-duality, they too are engaged in a most fascinating symposium.

There is a saying: "Great doubts produce great enlightenment. Small doubts produce small enlightenment. And no doubt produces no enlightenment." When Master Hsing Yun is invited to give talks, he often encourages people to ask questions. Sometimes, he compares himself to a bell—if you strike it, it will ring; if you have a question, he will answer it for you. Master Hsing Yun is incisive, commanding, energetic, clear, easy to understand, and skillful in his use of metaphors and parables, and he is particularly well-versed in handling questions on sensitive issues, like the ones discussed in this chapter. For example, the Director of the Australian Immigration Department, Phillip Ruddock, once asked, "Of all of the religious leaders in the world, who is the best?"

Master Hsing Yun replied, "The one that you like the most is the best!"

During his lifetime, Master Hsing Yun has presided over many insightful symposia. Those in attendance are always deeply moved by the benefits they have received from hearing him speak.

In a talk given on April 25, 2001 at the National University of Singapore Medical School, Master Hsing Yun answered questions on a variety of contemporary and often controversial issues, including euthanasia, abortion, and organ donation. He used the principles of both Buddhism and medical science in his answers and explanations. The talk was given to a large group of licensed physicians, medical school students, and students from other academic departments, as well as some participants from other institutions. Parts of this talk were first translated and published in short installments in the *Universal Gate Buddhist Journal*. However, the chapter below contains a complete record of the discussion that transpired that day.

Is Euthanasia Allowed?

What position does Buddhism take on euthanasia? Should euthanasia be practiced at all? This is a question of concern to people all over the world and one that has caused a great deal of contention. Some countries legally permit euthanasia, others flatly do not allow it, and still others continue to reserve judgment on the issue.

Chinese people have always thought that "heaven has the virtue of favoring life," so even if someone is ill and nearing death, they will do whatever they can to prolong his or her life. How could they be expected to help a person die sooner? Since most people think of living as wonderful and precious and dying as tragic and despicable, they tend to cherish life and fear death, which is normal. However, if we can look at life anew and come to understand its significance differently, we will be able to adjust our thinking concerning the process of life and death. We will come to understand that life is not necessarily so wonderful and death not necessarily so terrible. I believe that if we can achieve this, there will be fewer disputes about euthanasia.

Who actually has the power to decide whether euthanasia should be practiced or not? Who has the qualifications to determine if a person should be allowed to be euthanized? What legal repercussions accompany such a decision? These are complex questions that require study before they can be properly answered. For even if euthanasia is allowed by law, who gets to make the final decision about such a choice? Should it be the patient, a doctor, or the patient's family? I believe that those who love the person in question the most should have the right to decide. Yet, for all the matters in this world, while it is admirable to be motivated by a feeling of love for someone, how are we to determine if the person making the decision truly loves the patient in question? This is a problem that can have far-reaching consequences.

There was a wealthy woman in Taipei, who was physically healthy, but the people who claimed to love her most—her children—wanted her to die sooner rather than later, because they wanted to enjoy their inheritance as soon as possible. When we have children who should love their parents the most actually want their healthy parents dead, how then do we establish a standard for deciding who loves a patient the most? It seems as though those who are closest to the patient would have to form some kind of committee to elect one person, who loves the patient the most, to take responsibility for the final decision! The truth is, the person who requests to be euthanized must be in real pain, and that is why some look at death as a means to liberation.

Comforting the Patient

If a physician is called upon to administer an injection that will end someone's life, how should the physician attempt to comfort and respond to his patient?

If a general has received a debilitating wound on the battlefield and fears being captured and humiliated asks his subordinate to shoot him, he is doing so because he wants to preserve his dignity and self-respect. Similarly, a patient on the verge of dying who requests to be euthanized is similarly only trying to preserve his or her dignity and self-respect. When a person is healthy he feels like a hero, but when he is sick he feels like a puppy dog. Sometimes sick people feel that they look so bad, they do not want to be seen by anyone. So when people die, their families often cover their bodies because they do not want others to see how they look.

Some patients, upon discovering they have an incurable disease, do not wish to prolong their lives, but instead prefer to end their suffering by asking their doctor for an injection that will liberate them. However, this is not a decision the doctor is allowed to make on his own, even if he is a compassionate physician who loves and cares for his patients and is willing to end the suffering. Having such a perspective does not give the doctor the legal ground to take such an action. Thus, we have to rely on the patient's family or upon some future law to solve situations like this one.

Sometimes, a patient's condition may appear to be grave, and his doctor may have given him half a year, or only a month or even a week to live; yet, that sort of prognosis is never completely certain. Even people who have been sent to the morgue have been known to come back to life. This is something that I have observed with my own eyes quite a few times. If such a person had been given a lethal injection, he would not have had the opportunity to be revived. Thus, the issue of euthanasia involves many other complex considerations. The most important thing will always be to lessen the suffering of the person who is ill. For people who are approaching the moment of death, providing them with comfort, encouragement, and the willpower and strength to live so as to alleviate their mental anguish, is most crucial. As to whether they live or die, the result is up to nature.

Who makes the decision?

Above it states that the person who loves the patient the most should make the final decision about whether or not to euthanize. Why is this?

Buddhism unequivocally teaches non-killing, but this is not an absolute. Sometimes, it is an act of compassion and matter of principle to kill a vicious criminal who has killed many good people. After killing such a criminal, a person would have acquired merit as well as committed a transgression. Eventually, that person will have to face the unwholesome karma of killing, but the karma of killing in this instance is comparatively smaller than the positive merit acquired for having protected so many people.

In the sutras, there is a story about the Buddha, in one of his former lives, killing a murderer to save five hundred traders. This story illustrates that sometimes killing may be seen as a compassionate act. It is only within the Theravada tradition that we find Buddhists willing to sacrifice their own lives rather than to harm an insect. In contrast, within the Mahayana tradition, proper conduct is based on a judicious weighing of the pros and cons of each situation. For example, in a war between nations, a Mahayana practitioner would be willing to kill his enemies in order to save his own nation. Or, to save someone out of compassion, he would rather accept the karma for killing and sacrifice himself to save another. This is why we sometimes say: "When there is love, everything under heaven is at peace; where there is no love, not even the home is harmonious." Hence, love and compassion help us to decide what to do in many situations, which is in accord with an exhortation in the Mahayana tradition: "Bring benefit to all sentient beings." The person who loves the patient the most is best suited to make such a critical decision and is willing to accept the karmic result of his or her action as well.

How is death defined?

According to medical science, a person is defined as being dead when the heart stops beating or when brain function has permanently stopped. How does this definition compare with the Buddhist point of view?

What precisely is the moment of death for a human being? If brain function has permanently ceased but the heart is still beating, the person is not considered dead. If the heart has stopped beating but the body is still warm, the person is also not considered dead. If we cut an earthworm in half and both halves are moving even though there is only one life, which of those two halves is the real living worm?

In the Buddhist tradition, movement is merely a sign of life, while life itself is more complete. If life is a single entity, then which half of the earthworm is alive? This is a distinction we really do not need to make. Of course, science will have a much more detailed analysis of this question, and scientific conclusions may not always agree with Buddhist beliefs and tradition.

One morning, there was a group of people waiting to take a boat across a river on business. As the boatman pushed his boat off the sandy beach into the water, many small fish and shrimp underneath were crushed to death. When the boat left for the other bank, a group of passengers remained waiting for the next boat to arrive. Among them was a scholar who inquired of a monk, "Master, when the boat was pushed into the water, it killed quite a few fish and shrimp. Since the killing of these sea creatures must have incurred some unwholesome karma, I was curious who would receive that karma—the boatman or his passengers?"
The monk said to the scholar, "The unwholesome karma is yours."

"Why is it my unwholesome karma?"

"Because you are too meddlesome."

Buddhism is a religion that centers on humanity. Besides, "karma is fundamentally empty and is produced by the mind." Since karma is produced by the mind, there are many situations wherein unconscious behavior does not generate negative karma. At the same time, a person whose mind tends to generate distinctions or produces corrupt notions of differentiation will incur unwholesome karma. This difference is also recognized by the laws of most countries; if one person kills another unintentionally, his legal culpability is less than if the act were premeditated.

When people die, sometimes their hearts have not stopped and there are still signs of life in the brain and nervous system, but their ability to make conscious distinctions is gone. In these cases, the person can be considered dead.

The Buddhist tradition holds that when the consciousness and the spirit have entirely left the body, then one is truly dead. However, it is not that important for us to determine the exact time of death. I believe that it is far more important to help the dying person find peace and feel as little pain as possible than it is to know exactly when he or she has passed away.

Most people are familiar with MRI (Magnetic Resonance Imaging) technology, used for diagnosing medical problems. When they use this instrument, they place you inside a small chamber, which some people find quite frightening. I have had this procedure performed on me several times, and on a few occasions, because the results of the first test were not sufficiently clear, the whole procedure had to be repeated. That never bothered me at all. In fact, I felt so comfortable during the test that I even fell asleep. So, in this sense, how long it takes us to die is not necessarily that important. As long as we can feel comfortable at the time of death, I believe even the experience of dying can be beautiful.

Coping With Illness

Some people with mental disorders seek out psychics or fortunetellers when they become ill rather than visit a psychiatrist, which perhaps shortens their lives. What is the Buddhist perspective on this?

A person with a mental illness often suffers either from psychological confusion or profound delusions. In the Buddhist tradition, it is generally regarded as best to avoid people who are experiencing these problems. Buddhism teaches us to use the wisdom of the Dharma to help others, but it is also recognized that even if you are very wise, it is unlikely that you will be able to assist people with severe problems. Sometimes, I think that today's doctors are really admirable because they have tried to come up with so many methods to help cure mental illness.

Why didn't the Buddha devote more time to people who were mentally ill? Can it be that modern psychologists are more skilled than the Buddha in this matter? Of course, the Buddha was not a specialist of this kind, which is one reason. But the real question still remains–why do mentally ill people sometimes seek out superstitious or paranormal cures for their problems. Based on my understanding, seeking such cures is useless. It is merely a way to console oneself.

Many medical cures depend on the right treatment as well as the faith patients have in themselves. Indeed, it is really not a matter of entreating the Buddha or folk gods to cure them, but rather having patients cure themselves by strengthening their ability to have faith in oneself. Since supernatural or spiritual cures cannot be guaranteed to be effective and since they are based on the will of the patient, who must also bear responsibility for his or her own actions, seeking supernatural cures instead of medical treatment is wrong.

When a person becomes ill, what method should we use to cure him or her? Religion? Physical therapy? Medication? I believe counseling is very important. If a psychologist can offer a patient consolation and encouragement, the psychologist will be of great help to the patient. Psychological counseling can often be just as effective as treatment with medication! Buddhism is a religion that focuses on the mind. We have the saying: "All the Dharma taught by the Buddha is for the sake of curing the mind. If there were no mind, why would there be any need for the Dharma?" So when we speak of Buddhist cultivation, it means disciplining and enhancing the resilience of our minds. Once the mind is strong, then the medicine we take will be more effective, and even the water we drink will take on a more effective function. The strength of the mind can determine all things.

Once there was a doctor who wanted to understand just how powerful the mind can be, so he devised an experiment. He went to a prison and found a person who had been sentenced to die. The doctor said to him, "You've been sentenced to death and no matter how they kill you–whether they behead you or shoot you–your death will be quite painful. Now, if I use a needle to slowly draw out your blood so that you pass away peacefully, would you be willing to try that?"

Upon hearing this, the condemned prisoner immediately lay down on his bed to prepare himself to follow the doctor's plan. After his eyes were covered and he received an injection, the man began to hear the sound of blood dripping into a bucket. The doctor drew close to his ear and informed him, "You have already lost one-fifth of your blood and your face is becoming pale." Then after a while he said, "You have now lost four-fifths of your blood and your face is as white as a sheet. You are about to die!"

The prisoner closed his eyes tightly and as he listened to the doctor's description of his condition, he thought to himself, "My blood is draining from my body. I'm about to die." Then he began to feel very dizzy, his eyes blurred, and his whole body felt limp. As he imagined his own blood draining and his life slowly withering away, he passed away just like that.

The truth is that the doctor had not drawn any blood from the prisoner's body, but had merely allowed water from a faucet to drip into a container near his ear, simulating the sound of dripping blood. As he listened to the sounds of the water dripping and the doctor repeatedly saying that he was dying, the man was convinced that he was dying. His death was brought about entirely by his own mindset.

Therefore, we should not belittle the power of the mind, for the mind can rise to the heavens and achieve Buddhahood, or it may take us in its descent into one of the three lower realms. The mind is a limitless treasure trove capable of manifesting all kinds of things. The myriad phenomena throughout the universe have their fundamental unchanging suchness, but the moment the conscious mind begins to make distinctions among things, the vast landscape of rivers, mountains, and plains stored within it changes. This is the reason why most Buddhist practice is directed at cultivating the mind, because the power of the mind is truly incomparable.

How can we heal our minds? This is the most important question humanity faces in the 21st century.

Euthanasia and Abortion

Some women carrying fetuses with birth defects or pregnant due to rape are unwilling to give birth to such an undesirable seed. If you prevent them from having an abortion, then they would have to raise a child with birth defects for several decades, or they would have to live with a child they did not want to have while feeling they have let their husbands down. What can they do?

Actually, euthanasia and abortion are not problems that can be resolved by religion, morality, or the law. Only the people involved have a right to decide; they can make their own decisions and take responsibility with a clear understanding of the principles of karmic retribution through cause and effect, and willingly choose to face the consequences afterwards. One may even ask: Can euthanasia be considered suicide at all? Does abortion really constitute a crime for killing living things? There are no easy answers. When a person would be better off dying than living, it is tantamount to saying that their conditions on this earth are over, so there is actually no need for such heroic measures to continue life like inserting tubes or using oxygen; one should let life's passing take its natural course.

However, sometimes it is difficult to say whether person can recover or not as they hover between life and death. For example, in Taipei there is a lay Buddhist named Zhao, who is a very enthusiastic Buddhist teacher on television as well as a frequent visitor to prisons, where he teaches the Dharma to criminals incarcerated there. Many years ago, he accidentally slipped and fell, ending up with a brain concussion. He was taken to the Tri-Service General Hospital, where the doctors marked his chart in red, declaring that there was nothing they could do. They even had him sent to the mortuary, for they felt he was not long for this world. Yet today, Zhao is a vigorous and healthy man, still active among the various Dharma centers in Taipei.

Everyone listening to this example would surely think that Buddhism is opposed to euthanasia! But actually this is not completely true. Buddhism understands that, although heaven cares for every living thing and we must not terminate life that is able to be sustained, euthanasia applies to life that has reached a stage where there is no longer any meaning and where a feeble existence can only be prolonged for a certain period of time; and yet all the while, one's mind and spirit are suffering unbearable torment, where one can neither truly live or die. Such torment is more serious than death itself; so even the patient may wish to die sooner so as to be spared this pain and find release. Such a situation is different from suicide, for suicide is escaping responsibility and an unwillingness to face problems and resolve them, and so death becomes a means of escape. Euthanasia occurs when there is no other choice, when one can no longer make his or her own decisions; so loving friends and family must make a decision out of love and determine whether euthanasia is warranted or not.

Can euthanasia become law? Should abortion be legalized? Actually, there is no absolute yea or nay, good or bad, right or wrong, correct or incorrect for many worldly matters; and there are many questions in the world that cannot be totally resolved by the law, morality, or pubic opinion either. Therefore, the life and death question of euthanasia is one that those who most love the individual should decide with compassion. Because once a person becomes a human vegetable that cannot truly live or die, this is something unbearably painful! It is impossible for the law to resolve such questions, because it involves the right to life. Nor can doctors bring about a person's death, because that would be against the law. As a matter of fact, there are many sick people who are living in pain, and their care is a heavy burden for family members. Whether or not euthanasia should be carried out is something only those who most love that individual can decide, with love and compassion. Only in this way can such a difficult problem be resolved.

A similar consideration applies to the abortion question. Catholicism holds that abortion cannot be performed under any circumstances. Buddhism considers abortion to violate the precept against killing, in which there are inescapable karmic consequences, but if one already knows that the fetus has birth defects or is a pregnancy resulting from rape, then to unwillingly bring this child into the world would represent a heavy burden for society. And the mother would be trapped in a life of suffering as well. Thus, if the mother is willing to shoulder the karma of killing a living thing, then the right to decide should rest with the mother, and no one else has the right to interfere.

There are many teachings and expedient practices in Buddhism, but if all of these teachings and practices cannot be aligned with the compassionate mind, then they are nothing but a perversion. The Buddhadharma is based upon compassion; it neither absolutely denies euthanasia and abortion, nor does it resolutely affirm them either. We should make decisions regarding each and every life with a loving and compassionate heart, so as to let all living things continue a healthy existence. If it should so happen that there is no other choice but to perform euthanasia or abortion, then as long as one is certain that such actions come from the compassionate mind, that takes into account the suffering of the sick and the family, then there is nothing wrong. The key factor is whether or not the compassionate mind is one's starting point.

Animal Testing

When medical research uses animals in its experiments, is this considered killing? What is the Buddhist view on this issue?

When medical science uses animals in experiments, the goal is to save the masses. There is a saying: "Death can be as significant as Mt. Tai as insignificant as a swan's feather." All deaths do not have the same significance. When scientists pursue medical research, they have far-reaching goals in mind, so we should not let ourselves get caught up in small details. Furthermore, as Buddhism is a religion that focuses primarily on the needs of humanity, there is no absolute answer regarding the issues that are associated with the act of killing, for we must weigh the strengths and weaknesses of each case. We know that in a former life, the

Buddha killed one person to save the lives of five hundred. This demonstrates that Buddhist precepts are not strictly about being kind and passive; they are also about actively saving people. This is especially clear when we make distinctions between "mundane Dharma" and "supramundane Dharma." Since there is mundane Dharma, we must not ignore the practical needs of people's lives in society. Otherwise, why would people need a Buddhism that has become severed from the realities of modern life?

For example, some ten thousand people live on the Minor Ryukyu Island off the coast of Taiwan. There is a subchapter of the BLIA on that island, and its president is a school principal. Once when I was there on a visit, the president said to me, "Most of the people on this island make their living in the fishing industry. This contradicts the "no killing" precept in Buddhism. But if we were to ask everyone to stop fishing, we would all go hungry, so it is difficult to propagate the Dharma here."

I replied, "Although the Dharma says that we should not kill, there are different degrees to this. The main distinction is between 'the act of killing' and 'the intent to kill.' You fish in order to survive, and not because you have the pure intention to kill. This can be compared to cremating a corpse, because not only do you end up killing all of the tiny living organisms in the corpse, but also in the wood used for the fire. When we do that, however, we do not have the intention of killing, which means we do not have a mind to kill. So even if there is some karma being generated, it is less serious. Furthermore, we can still help ourselves through repentance."

Similarly, when a doctor gives a shot to an ill person, the shot may kill many germs. However, since the motivation is not to kill but rather to save the patient's life, and since it is done out of great compassion, this action cannot be considered breaking the precept of no killing.

In Tainan, a city in southern Taiwan, there was a notorious criminal who killed seven people and was sentenced by the court to be executed by a firing squad. However, since Taiwan had not had any capital cases in quite some time, no one within the prison system was brave enough to carry out the sentence. Finally, four military police officers from the Ministry of Defense were asked to carry out the order. Did these four police officers generate bad karma by their actions? No, they did not, for they were enforcing the laws of the country, not killing. Being too attached to the idea of not killing can become a sort of attachment to the Dharma. Thus, in the context of medicine, the precepts of Buddhism must be considered from many different angles.

Organ Donation

Today, many people can choose whether or not their organs will be donated to others after they die. What is the Buddhist position on organ donation?

Organ donation is about reusing available resources to extend life, and that is a manifestation of the oneness and coexistence of all life. In the Buddhist tradition, the body is not considered something that belongs to the self, but rather it is something that results from the illusionary synthesis of the four elements. It is like a hotel room that we rent for a temporary stay.

There is a famous parable relevant to this topic: Once there was a traveler who, having not found lodging along the way, ended up having to stay at the very remote and rustic temple of some local deity. In the middle of the night, a small ghost carrying a dead body suddenly appeared. Frightened, the traveler exclaimed, "I have seen a ghost!"

In that same moment, a large ghost appeared and pointing at the small ghost, said, "Why are you carrying my corpse?"

The small ghost replied, "This is mine. How can you say that it's yours?"

The two quarreled for quite some time, while the traveler trembled with fear. Then, the small ghost saw the terrified traveler and said, "Hey, there's somebody in there hiding under the altar!" It called to him, "Come out, come out. Don't be afraid. Please help us decide who the corpse belongs to."

The traveler thought to himself, "It seems like there's no escape and no matter what I do, I'm going to die. I may as well tell the truth." With that, he said, "This corpse belongs to the little ghost."

As soon as the large ghost heard this, it became enraged. It rushed forward and tore off the traveler's left arm, and in two or three bites devoured it. When the small ghost saw this, it thought to itself, "the traveler was only trying to help me, so how can I just stand by and watch?" With that, it tore the left arm off the corpse and stuck it on the traveler's body. In response, the large ghost became further incensed and bit into the traveler's right arm, consuming the whole thing in just a few bites. The small ghost tore the right arm off the corpse and again attached it to the traveler's body. The two ghosts repeated the same acts with the traveler's legs. After playing out this outrageous scene, the two ghosts walked away whistling, leaving the bewildered traveler to ask himself, "Who am I?"

This parable is taken from a Buddhist sutra, and though it is meant to illustrate that "the four elements are essentially empty and the five aggregates are without self," doesn't it aptly reflect today's issue of organ transplantation?

There are four key ways in which organ donation is meaningful and useful for society:

1) It extends lifespans: Life never ends! Though bodies grow old and die, life is eternal and without end like flame passing from one torch to another. Life is bound together by the force of karma, and the force of karma is like the thread that holds together a string of prayer beads through all time and space. When someone donates an organ, he or she is giving someone else a chance to live, while simultaneously allowing his own life to continue.

2) It demonstrates inner generosity: There are three kinds of generosity in the Buddhist tradition—material generosity, Dharma generosity, and the generosity of fearlessness. Material generosity can be further divided into internal and external generosity. External generosity includes the giving of money, property, and other material things, while internal–or inner–generosity is the donation of organs and body parts. In former lives, the Buddha cut away some of his flesh to feed an eagle and sacrificed himself to feed a tiger. There is a Buddhist saying: "Do that which is difficult to do, and bear that which is difficult to bear." Over two thousand years ago, the Buddha provided us with the best example of this teaching. Following his example, the entire human race should be willing to open themselves by giving their organs freely in order to bestow compassion to humanity.

3) It promotes the renewal of resources: In Taiwan, an organ donor may need to sign a donor's card in order to donate one's organs legally upon death. However, from the Buddhist practitioner's perspective, if there is the intention to donate an organ, then it is enough just to have family members sign on behalf of the deceased. The donation of organs is a renewal of resources, for it enables us to recycle usable parts of the body that would have otherwise been discarded. When you donate the cornea of your eye, you are giving the gift of sight. When you donate your heart, you are giving the vitality of life. Similarly, when you donate bone marrow, you are passing on the current of life to another person.

4) It shows the oneness and coexistence of all life: All of the myriad dharmas in this world arise out of causes and conditions. Human relationships also depend on causes and conditions to exist. Each of us depends on farmers and professionals to supply us with the things that we need to survive. Because we rely on the conditions provided by others in order to live, we should also give others supportive causes and conditions. Donating organs is a good way to break down the distance between self and others, and eliminate the superstition that a corpse must remain intact for the afterlife. It shows us a way to put a heart of compassion into action and to experience the coexistence of all life. If we have the will, all of us can become organ donors. Organ transplants allow us to assure the endless continuity and legacy of compassion and loving-kindness throughout the world!

In the past, the Chinese believed in the age-old notion of preserving the wholeness of a corpse, and that it should not be moved for at least eight hours after death. However, beliefs such as these no longer fit in the modern world. We must learn to adjust our thinking to keep up with the times. To support the cause of organ donation, I myself signed an organ donor agreement over thirty years ago. I hope that all people will respond to this dignified and noble endeavor, that society will continue to progress, and that all of us will build a beautiful world founded on oneness and coexistence.

Embracing the benefits of organ donation

So how can we transcend the belief held by many that the corpse must remain intact such that everyone will value the sacredness of organ donation instead?

Organ transplantation is a great achievement of modern medical science and technology. It has enabled many dying people to continue with their lives, and it has also ensured that the legacy of the compassionate spirit of the organ donor is passed on. But there are many controversies sparked by organ transplants, which everyone in contemporary society is unanimously concerned about and trying to understand.

Regarding organ transplants in Taiwan, the "Regulations Concerning Human Organ Transplants" were promulgated and implemented by the government as early as June 19, 1987, and some of these regulations were later amended in 1993. Among these, the sixth regulation stipulates that in order for doctors to remove organs from the deceased, one of the following three conditions must be met:

1) Before death, the deceased must have given written consent or left a will consenting to the procedure.

2) The closest relative of the deceased must have given written consent.

3) Before death, the deceased expressed willingness to be an organ donor, as certified in writing by two or more medical doc-

tors.

When considering the issue of organ donation and transplantation, we need to realize that the body actually does not belong to the "self." The body is a temporary combination of the four elements, just as a hotel room is merely supplied for temporary residence. Therefore, when a person's life comes to an end, it is better to donate one's organs and enable the life of another to continue living rather than allowing them to simply rot and decay.

An article entitled "*If You Want to Remember Me*" said it best: "There will come a day, when I will lie in the hospital beneath that white sheet; and there will come a time, when the doctors determine that my brain function has ceased. This shows that my life has already ended. At such a time, under no circumstances should you say that I am lying on my deathbed; rather, please call it my life-bed. This is because I want to offer my body as a way of helping others, so as to extend and enable their lives to become even richer..."

Organ donation encompasses such ideas as the extension of life, donating one's internal wealth, the resource for supporting rebirth, and living together as one. Therefore, true life cannot die! Though the body has its time for old age, sickness, and decay, life is a burning fire that is passed from torch to torch, eternal and unlimited. Giving others a chance to live by donating our organs also means that our own life will continue.

To be sure, advances in modern medical science have enabled many people on the verge of death to have an organ transplant and go on living their lives. However, it is important to remember that organ removal must occur during that short period of time after the declaration of brain death, but before the organs die. Yet many Chinese people today still maintain the outmoded belief that the corpse must remain intact and cannot be disturbed for an eight-hour period after death. For this reason, the idea of organ donation has never been widely popular among the Chinese, ensuring that demand for organs always outstrips supply. There are many people in desperate need of heart, liver, and kidney transplants, for example, who wait in vain for a kind soul to make a donation. This leads to all sorts of regret.

People should consider the generous spirit of people in Catalonia, Spain, which has the highest rate for organ donation in the world. Their citizens feel that if one donates his or her organs to others today, perhaps tomorrow when a relative or friend needs an organ transplant, other people will be similarly willing to donate theirs. One could say that this attitude is truly in accord with the idea of "coexisting together as one," and is worthy of our emulation.

In order to establish a new outlook on organ donation, the "Chinese Center for Organ Donation" in Taiwan has established the "Center for Information and Education" to get the word out through public service advertisements, promotional materials, community publicity, public broadcasting, and postal mailings. They also sponsor activities such as "Organ Donation Week." These efforts are being carried out in the hope of instilling the concept of organ donation in the hearts of all people.

Actually, a person living in this world cannot avoid imperfection, so why must one demand that his or her corpse be kept intact after death? As long as one has the willingness and generosity to offer his or her own body for the benefit of others, there is no need to worry that one will not calmly be reborn in the Pure Land because one has caused pain and anger by having organs removed. Not disturbing the body for eight hours after death and not donating one's organs are ideas that are no longer in step with the times. Our thinking should advance with time, which includes having an accurate understanding of life and death.

How should we consider birth and death? The process of birth and death is a lot like the process of how plants flower and bear fruit. Seeds are planted in springtime and the harvest is gathered during the autumn; this is birth and death. Going out in the morning and returning home at night, and going to sleep at night and waking up in the morning; this is birth and death. Death does not come only after we die. Are there not still the "thousand births and ten thousand deaths" we experience, both spiritually and mentally, several hundred times a day? Our minds shift among the ten dharma realms countless times every day; isn't this birth and death? Even the cells of the body are completely renewed once every seven days; isn't this birth and death? People today can get new corneas if theirs become damaged; if their skin is damaged, they can receive skin grafts; and if their kidneys fail, they can get a new one. Thus, life and death is but a series of breakdowns and fix-ups, births and deaths.

Our lifetimes are merely separated by "the confusion of birth"; that is, we do not realize that we are taking on another body. This is similar to a soybean planted the spring to be harvested next fall, not knowing that it was the same soybean that was harvested the previous fall. From the past life to the present one, and from the present life to the next one, it is only the physical body that changes; for in reality, these lifetimes are not without some connection.

The Chan School teaches transcendence from birth and death, while Buddhism in general teaches liberation from birth and death. To understand the meaning of life and to free ourselves from the fear of death represents liberation from birth and death. Thus, when a person gets old and dies, the organs are no longer of any use to him or her, so being able to donate them to extend the life of another is a truly wonderful act. Why wouldn't you be happy to do so? As early as thirty years ago, I even signed an organ donation consent form. It is my hope that everyone will respond to this sacred and solemn gesture and that society will become more and more advanced, so that we all can take part in creating a wonderful world in which we can live together as one.

Hospice Care

Introduction

If there is life, there most certainly will be death. There is nothing more natural than life and death. Yet ordinary people all cherish life and hate death. The joy of a new life often makes us forget our grief over death, while coming face to face with death can plunge us into such sorrow that the care of the mental and physical well-being of the person dying is compromised. Therefore, it is an important lesson in "life education" for us to learn how to care for and pay attention to the minds and bodies of the sick and dying in order to treat death with the dignity it deserves.

According to Buddhist scriptures, one's dying moment has an impact upon whether or not one will find a good rebirth in the future, for it represents the critical time that determines a rebirth in a higher or lower realm. For this reason, it is an extremely important period of time in our lives. However, when most people try to cope with a family member who is dying, the whole family gets caught up in all the hustle and bustle. They become paralyzed with fear and have no idea what to do. The dying family member is even more frightened and terrified, so the question of hospice care is not properly addressed. When the illness takes a turn for the worse, then the most family members can do is buy whatever their loved one likes to eat or try to satisfy his or her worldly desires. However, by this time, the sick often no longer crave food or wish for material things.

In recent years, developments in medical science and humanistic ideas have meant that advanced medical treatments can now postpone many illnesses that were once considered terminal, greatly extending the human lifespan. Yet precisely because of this, more people today are facing an extended period of time encumbered by the pain of old age and sickness. And even if modern medical science makes more progress, it must still confront the ultimate limitation, for in the end there is no avoiding death. Consequently, people have finally realized that the care of life should cover birth to death, and include the physical as well as the spiritual well-being of individuals. This is why hospice wards have been founded and why hospice care has become a subject about life, something to be researched, discussed, and publicized.

In today's society, there are many hospitals that have instituted hospice wards, which provide terminal care for the dying. Actually, Buddhism had its own system of hospice care very early on, known as the "halls of impermanence" established at India's Jetavana Monastery. The goal was to enable those suffering from illness to seek rebirth in the Western Pure Land, as based upon the ideas derived from the Pure Land practice of Amitabha Buddha. Chinese Chan [Buddhist] temples also established "halls of peace and ease," "nirvana halls," "courtyards of joy and ease," and "hospice centers." Each of these places had a director who was responsible for looking after sick monastics. Modern Buddhist temples and monasteries have established monastic and lay hospices, which serve those with serious illnesses. Therefore, Buddhists were perhaps among the earliest in society to initiate hospice care.

From ancient times to the present, Buddhism has always offered religious guidance to people regarding human life and the stages of birth, old age, sickness, and death, so that people might better understand the nature, reality, meaning, and cycles of life. The hope in Buddhism is for people to advance from merely recognizing life and death, to facing life and death with calm and acceptance. In addition to the finely detailed Buddhist scriptures on medical science and a history of monks with profound attainments in medicine, Buddhist followers have also undertaken various forms of medical service as charitable work. They offer substantial help that meets the needs of real life, and have developed a complete and positive form of care that extends from birth to death, including both the mind and body. These activities provide useful examples for those who are involved in hospice care today.

So, what then are Buddhist insights and methods regarding

hospice care? On June 15, 2001, the Venerable Master Hsing Yun was invited to give a talk at the Chang Gung Medical College in Taiwan. The Venerable Master addressed the issue of hospice care during a group discussion, with over two hundred students and faculty in attendance. What follows here is a record of the discussions from that day, as recorded by his disciple, Venerable Man Yi.

What is hospice care?

The issues surrounding life and death have always been with us, so why has hospice care only now become a modern social concern? What does hospice care actually mean?

Hospice care is a relatively new field representing life-and-death studies that encompasses various fields such as medical science, religion, law, ethics, philosophy, and morality. Its main goal is to enable the dying to face the final stage of human life, during which time patients will be guided by the best medical care and the power of religious faith. In this way, the dying can reach an understanding and acceptance of death, so that they do not experience fear or pain, and come to look upon death with calmness. At the same time, hospice care also gives spiritual support and encouragement to family members, helping them to pass through this critical time when loved ones become separated by death.

Hospice care is also known as terminal care, end-of-life care, palliative care, and so forth. Those receiving this care are primarily made up of terminal patients suffering from such serious illnesses as cancer, whose cases doctors have determined cannot be cured by any further treatment to the point where death is imminent. Patients can enter a hospice ward in a hospital, or they can stay at home and receive home care from medical practitioners there. Regardless of whether patients receive home care or care in a hospice facility, hospice patients are not merely waiting for death, for these patients receive the same complete medical service as other patients. The difference is that the medical care hospice patients receive does not necessarily have the goal of prolonging life. Instead, hospice care emphasizes four aspects of care.

First, hospice care provides for the *whole person*, which means that the patient's physical and mental condition is regarded as a whole, and the patient is not just treated solely in terms of his or her symptoms or a particular organ. Second, hospice care is for the *whole family*. This means helping family members and friends learn the techniques of care-giving, as well as helping them face together the grief of losing a loved one. Even after the patient has passed on, the spiritual counseling of the family falls within the scope of hospice care. Third, hospice care assists with the *whole process* of dying. Besides attending to the patient's last moment of life, hospice staff counsel the family on how to endure the low period after a patient has passed on. Last, hospice care provides a *whole system of care*. It brings together doctors, nurses, pharmacologists, nutritionists, physical therapists, psychologists, Dharma teachers, pastors, priests, nuns, and volunteers to provide the most complete mental and physical care possible.

It is worth noting here that when people are dying, they are particularly concerned about where they will go after death. Thus, Buddhist doctrines such as Pure Land thought, the cycle of birth and death, the eternality of life, and karmic retribution through causes and conditions become the ideal spiritual relief for patients and their families during this time.

In the past, many people believed that the primary role of a physician was to prolong a patient's life to the extent possible. But actually, death is also a part of life, for no matter how advanced medical science becomes, people in the end cannot escape death. Therefore, the greatest goal for hospice care is to help patients who are suffering serious illnesses and facing imminent death find relief from their mental and physical pain by means of medical care and faith, so that they may be able to live a quality life during the final stage of life.

The advent of modern hospice care began when Great Britain's Dame Cicely Saunders founded St. Christopher's Hospice in London in 1967, the world's first special service program for patients in the final stage of cancer. Later, with the strong financial assistance of the British queen, the hospice became a model teaching center and went on to establish other centers across Great Britain. Eight years later, a group of personnel from St. Christopher's Hospice went to the U.S., where they helped establish the first medical care institution for hospice care in the U.S. In February of 1990, the Danshui branch of Taipei's Mackay Memorial Hospital established the first hospice ward in Taiwan. In December of that same year, the Hospice Foundation of Taiwan was founded, making Taiwan the eighteenth country in the world to have an organization for hospice care.

At present, the world's aging population, people's concerns about death with dignity, and the increasing costs for all the various organizations involved in terminal care have spurred the rapid development of hospice care. Looking specifically at the situation in Taiwan, it was not until recently that the rising numbers of people suffering from cancer, many of whom experience acute pain during the final stage of cancer, led to the need for hospice wards to offer palliative care. It was only then that hospice care came to be treated seriously by the general population.

The director of the Educational Training Center for Hospice and Palliative Care at Taipei's Mackay Memorial Hospital, Enoch Y. L. Lai, has offered some statistics: "Cancer became the leading cause of death in Taiwan as early as 1982, and from then on the number of cancer deaths has continued to rise every year. For example, there were 16,558 cancer deaths in 1986; 19,628 in 1991; 22,323 in 1993; in 1994, they went from 23,240 to 25,841 in 1995; and from 27,961 in 1996 to 29,011 in 1997. The great majority of these people should all have received hospice care."

According to Director Lai's statistics, if we accept that there will be between 100 and 180 cancer patients for every 100,000 people, then each year there will be at least 10,059 to 18,900 patients requiring hospice care. Dr. Cheng-Deng Kuo, director of the Respiratory Therapy Department of the Veterans General Hospital in Taipei, concurs that there are likely between 100 and 10,000 people who require terminal care every year in

Taiwan.

Another factor behind Taiwan's rising awareness regarding hospice care has to do with changes in social structure. Today's families have shifted away from the large families of the past, in which three or five generations lived together, toward smaller family units with fewer people. The home environment has also changed, shifting from living in spacious family compounds with three- or four-sided courtyards to living in apartment buildings with less space. Thus, given the cramped living space most families experience today, issues such as where to keep the coffin pending burial have become a serious problem. Now, not only is it difficult to die peacefully in one's home in these high-rise apartment buildings, one also cannot be content staying in the hospital, due to the high cost of hospital care. Even for the rich who can afford high hospital costs, most of them do not like the idea of dying lonely and helpless in an intensive care unit surrounded by machines and wires. Thus, hospice wards came into being to meet the demands of the times.

Furthermore, owing to the shift from large extended families to small nuclear ones, everyone now spends their days living separated from one another, so that family ties are becoming increasingly weakened. Therefore, when a parent is facing that critical time between life and death, the children should be encouraged to give care and attention to the elderly and dying. They should do as people did in the past by watching over the sick during the night and helping them to take their medicine, so as to fully honor the bond between parent and child. This is a positive tradition that should be promoted.

In short, hospice care is respect for life, the recognition of old ties, and an acknowledgment of gratitude. Although advances in medical science have helped to prolong human life, the entire world is feeling increasing pressure from issues related to the aging of society. This is why a profusion of new approaches to hospice care have appeared, as well as new ways of coping with aging and end-of-life issues, such as reserving a burial plot, pre-need funeral contracts, retirement savings, living wills, and so on, which have spawned whole new industries throughout society. Hospice care is just one of these.

Actually, life does not require care only at the time of death. Care must be given during life as well, and even hospice care itself does not simply entail the medical care performed on behalf of the dying patient, but rather includes a kind of broadly defined education concerning death to be promoted throughout society as a whole. Such an education enables one to face the questions of life and death directly, rather than avoid any discussion altogether. Because where there is life, there must be death. The final moment before death is something each one of us must face. Since sooner or later we will come to that terminal stage, in one form or another, we should prepare for it as early on as possible, in terms of both spiritual and physiological aspects.

Even though we say hospice care is the kind of care provided to patients who are dying, we should not think that such care ends after the remains have been buried and everything returns to normal life. Rather, we should continue to give appropriate support for their spiritual legacy and the generations of children and grandchildren, so that those who have passed on may rest in peace and die feeling content. Therefore, hospice care does not mean caring about a patient only during life, nor is it only caring about the circumstances at the time of death or the questions of burial. What should be of greater concern is where one goes upon death and that one can rest in peace. This represents the true meaning of hospice care.

Helping people age well

Care is not only required at the end of life but during life as well. With the advances modern society has achieved in the areas of medicine and treatment, the human lifespan has been extended. But a society of people enjoying greater longevity has brought with it new problems associated with aging, a common issue throughout the world. How then can we help the elderly enjoy the declining years of their lives in comfort?

When considering issues regarding care for the elderly, not only is our aging society an important issue in today's world, but also the issue of seniors living alone has become a social problem in urgent need of a solution. There are many elderly people who do not have anyone to care for them in their later years, and sometimes they lie dead for days before being discovered by their neighbors. This is truly a miserable and unbearable way to spend one's old age.

What the elderly fear most is being alone, because just like children who must not be left alone in the house, it is difficult for them to live on their own. Fortunately, society today not only has daycare centers for children, but also daycare centers for the elderly. In addition, many foreign workers, including maids from the Philippines, Vietnam, and India, have contributed to the home setting of Chinese families, many serving as attendants to older people.

However, even if older folks are being cared for by foreign maids hired by their children, they are still very lonely in spirit. They have nothing upon which to rely and lack a sense of security. Thus, what older folks need first and foremost is spiritual consolation and living care, followed by economic support. In the past, Chinese society stressed the customary morning and evening greetings paid to one's parents and doing whatever it takes to please them. It is still considered very important to ask older folks how they are doing and to express your concern for them whenever possible.

China has always considered itself a land of propriety and righteousness, and the Chinese are a people who place extraordinary importance upon ethics and filial virtue. But now the concept of filial virtue is far less important than before. That is why people lament the passing of the old days and complain that their grown children do not behave as those in the past and that there are no filial sons at the bedsides of long sick parents. Many years ago, I stayed at the Taipei Veterans General Hospital to have surgery.

During that short stay of a few days, I saw everything that goes on in hospital wards, which left me with much to think about.

For example, parents were there giving care everyday in the children's ward, but throughout the geriatric ward sons and daughters hardly ever appeared. When some sons and daughters did make that rare visit to their parents, they came with tape recorder in hand. Rather than inquire about the sick person's health, they only asked: "How much inheritance will be left? Who gets the house? How is the estate to be divided?" After recording their answers, they just turned around and left. When some patients first entered the hospital, their children and in-laws may have accompanied them, but when they passed away, not a single one appeared. Indeed, "there are only compassionate mothers and fathers, but no compassionate sons or daughters."

Therefore, exactly how are older people to enjoy old age in comfort? You must make your own preparations. Everything should be taken care of sooner, while you still have time, especially when it comes to dealing with your estate. The best thing is to prepare a living will, which sets out what will be donated to the state and society, what will be donated to organizations that work for the public good, and what is to be divided among the children. This should only be done at your own free will. The sooner it is done, the better, thus helping to avoid any falling out among the children that might occur if they fought over the estate. This kind of fighting and bickering can lead to a situation in which the deceased cannot rest in peace.

Old age is a natural phenomenon within the cycle of life. As recorded in the Buddhist scriptures, when people age, they suffer distress and torment from the decline in such capabilities as vitality, strength, sense faculties, and lifespan. But there is also the expression, "for a family to have an elderly member is like having a precious jewel," for the experience and wisdom of the elderly is a priceless treasure, something which should be passed on to succeeding generations. Therefore, society should value the wisdom and experience of older people.

In Buddhist scriptures, there is a story about a country that once abandoned its elderly. In this country, there was an absurd law that stipulated that all elderly people must be driven from the country and abandoned in a distant land, for they could not be cared for at home. This was done because the king felt that elderly people were redundant, for they could not work and were a waste of grain. Therefore in this country, one only saw vigorous and healthy young people without a single old person in sight.

But there was a great minister who was a devoted son. As he watched his father grow old, he knew that according to the law of the land, he would have to drive his father out of the country, but he could not bear to exile his father to the forest. So he deceived his family and neighbors by secretly digging an underground cellar where he hid his father and took care of him.

Later, the behavior of this country angered one of the heavenly gods who wanted to exact punishment upon it, so he posed four questions to confound the king. As it turned out, no one throughout the entire country knew how to answer these questions, and just when it seemed that the country faced imminent disaster at the hands of the gods, it was saved by the wisdom of that old man hidden in the cellar. The king thereupon issued an order, commanding that old people were not to be abandoned, but that everyone must honor, obey, and care for the elderly; and if anyone disobeyed their parents or disrespected their teachers or elders, they would be condemned for having committed a serious offense. From then on, owing to the legacy of wisdom passed down from its elderly, the country that once abandoned its elderly was transformed into a prosperous, powerful, and peaceful kingdom.

The greatest and most precious asset that older people can offer is their rich experience of life. Such experience is the wisdom of how to deal with the world. This wisdom is also the most valuable treasure of the nation and society! Therefore, older people should offer their wisdom of life, and they themselves must understand how to enjoy their declining years. This is most important.

How can the elderly age without fear? I offer ten methods for growing old to consider.

1) Practice ten recitations when rising in the morning: When you get up in the morning, mentally recite the sacred names of the Buddhas and bodhisattvas, thus allowing your faith to become the support and hope of your mind.

2) Burn a stick of incense before bed at night: Before going to sleep at night, meditate for ten or twenty minutes, allowing the mind to become tranquil.

3) Consider the five contemplations before meals: When you take your meals, keep a mind of gratitude and maintain pleasant and happy feelings. Eat lighter foods so as not to overly burden one's digestion.

4) Learn to let go in life: Realize how all your honors, emotions, successes, and failures are as insubstantial as the wisps of clouds that pass before your eyes, and so slowly let go of all clinging.

5) Learn that old age and death are nothing to be feared: Dying is like changing one's clothes, moving to another house, or going to sleep. Though the physical body is extinguished, the true mind of Buddha Nature is not diminished. All you need do is positively foster merits and extend one's life of wisdom, and there will certainly be a bright future.

6) Maintain a repentant heart: People are not saints, and so who is without faults? When people reach old age, they will, to a greater or lesser degree, look back upon all the mistakes of their life and feel deep regret and remorse. If one can truly repent in one's heart, then it would be like being washed clean by clear water; one's character will be elevated to a higher level and one's heart will also be calm and relaxed.

7) Give with joy through one's generosity: When people get old, they always feel that they cannot be secure without money in hand, or they may have set aside property to give to their children and grandchildren. Actually, you cannot take anything with you except your karma, and if you have unkind children and grandchildren fighting over the property, you will find it even harder to bear. Why not offer your material wealth generously in all ten directions. By richly planting one's merits, one will attain a better life in rebirth, and it will also be a force for good in the lives of your children and grandchildren.

8) Make a vow of willingness to serve: After one retires, there is so much free time available. You can commit yourself to joining the ranks of volunteers and be of service to others, thereby expanding the scope of your life and creating broad connections with others.

9) Enjoy humor and laugh heartily often: It is said that a smile can dispel a thousand woes, so constantly be open-minded and joyous. In doing so, one not only fosters harmony and balance in one's mind and body, but can also increase the amount of joy in this world.

10) Exercise to maintain good heath: It is said that by walking a thousand steps after eating, one can live to ninety-nine. Exercise can allow for greater flexibility of the muscles and bones, while bringing vitality to the mind and body.

For the elderly, what is most important is the ability to organize their lives. They can set aside time each day to recite the name of Amitabha Buddha or read books. Those in good heath can travel, and others can enjoy conversation with friends or tend to their gardens. It is important for people to develop many different interests, so that they will enjoy old age naturally.

In particular, older people must keep in good spirits and be full of hope regarding the future. If one recites the name of Amitabha Buddha in the mornings and evenings, one can achieve spiritual support through faith; then, when facing the moment of death, one's mind will be free of clinging, one's thoughts will not be confused, and one can be without concerns or fear. Being able to liberate oneself from the suffering of calamity by means of one's faith is the best way to live out old age

In addition to the ten methods for growing old mentioned above, I offer four precautions for old age:

1) Finances: Earn money and reduce expenses in as many areas as possible as you get older, so as to prepare a retirement fund for yourself.

2) Health: Exercise often, regulate your life with set times for work and rest, and pay attention to a nutritional diet.

3) Faith: Possessing a faith of correct understanding and right view will not only be a refuge for one's soul and a support for one's spirit, but at the same time, it can also create broad connections by making friends with many others on the spiritual path.

4) Free time: Make proper arrangements for rest and activity, as well as the cultivation of one's pastimes or hobbies, which opens up one's circle of life.

In addition, there are four levels of living in retirement to consider:

1) Level one: Live in retirement by developing good connections.

2) Level two: Live in retirement by relying upon one's wisdom.

3) Level three: Live in retirement by saving up money.

4) Level four: Live in retirement by depending upon one's children and grandchildren.

Of course, it's best if the elderly can live out their retirement by relying upon their wisdom and the good connections they have made in the past, but for children to care for their parents is also a naturally ordained obligation. However, as Master Lianchi Zhuhong points out in his *Record of Worthy Buddhist Monks*, there are three grades of filial conduct: caring for one's parents in life and burial in death is the lowest grade; bringing glory to one's parents and ancestors is the middle grade; and guiding one's parents to freedom from suffering constitutes the highest grade of filial conduct. The *Sutra on the Past Lives of the Buddha* and the *Sutra of the Filial Child* are unanimous in stating, "Only by bringing moral improvement to one's parents can one truly repay their kindness."

The Vinaya canon also states, "If one's parents are without faith, help them to awaken it; if they are without the precepts, help them to keep them; if they are by nature miserly, then help them to develop wisdom. If you, as their child, can do this, then you have indeed begun to repay them for their kindness." Therefore, in caring for our elders, filial conduct must entail the simultaneous application of these three points. Give them good food and serve them well; gladden their hearts; and give them faith in reciting Amitabha Buddha's name, enabling them to have hope for salvation in the future. Only then will one have fulfilled the true meaning of caring for the elderly.

Helping the sick find mental and physical peace

Our minds and bodies feel particularly vulnerable when sick, thus it is often easier to generate faith in religion during such times. So then how can we help the sick to find mental and physical peace through faith? And, how can our visitations with patients be more in accord with Buddhist teachings?

We need Buddhism whenever we are confronted with questions of life and death. This is particularly true for the sick, for it is easier for them to accept the faith. Many years ago, there was a famous collector of books and paintings in Hong Kong by the name of Ko Lingmui. At the advanced age of eight-one, Ko Lingmui was ill and staying in the hospital. During that time, he had a family member contact me, hoping that I would be able to come to Hong Kong and preside over the ceremony for taking refuge in the Triple Gem. However, at that time my travel schedule was already full, and I was unable to find any free time to make the trip. So, I adopted the most expedient measure available to me at the time and performed the ritual over the telephone for Mr. Ko as he lay on his sickbed.

Although Mr. Ko did not think of taking refuge in Buddhism until the very end of his life, which was somewhat belated, such action demonstrates that when nearing the end of life, most people want to have some idea where their future lies. Even the renowned Professor Fang Dongmei, a philosopher famous for his penetrating study of the Mahayana Buddhist teachings and many contributions to the study of Huayan School, only very late in life chose to take refuge in Buddhism with Master Kuang-chin of Chengtian Monastery. This goes to show that even those of high intellect will in the end need to find their faith in the Buddha Dharma. Faith is the search for the ultimate meaning of life, for without faith, there can be no refuge in life. After the Sino-Japanese War of 1894, the Japanese Foreign Minister Mutsu Munemitsu went to China as the representative of Japan to sign the Treaty of Shimonoseki. Unfortunately, his daughter was ill at the time of his departure, so he instructed his family to contact him if the situation became serious. Just as the negotiations over the treaty reached a critical stage, Mutsu received a letter from home, informing him that his daughter was gravely ill and was hoping to see her father one last time.

The Prime Minister Ito Hirobumi consoled him saying, "Just go home and don't worry. I will be responsible for handling everything here." Mutsu left that very night and rushed home. When his daughter, whose breathing was already labored, saw her father, she happily said, "Father, soon I will be leaving you forever; but there is a question that has always troubled my heart, so I have been waiting for you to return and resolve it for me."

"What question is that? Just ask me," he replied.

"I am dying now, so where will I go after I die?"

Despite all his learning, this statesman Mutsu Munemitsu had no idea how to answer the question posed by his daughter from her deathbed. But Mutsu was more astute than most people, and so consoled his daughter by saying, "I really don't know where you will go after you die; but I often see your mother reciting the name of Amitabha Buddha, and so I think the Buddha will surely take you to a wonderful place." Upon hearing these words, his daughter left this world with a calm smile upon her face. Since he was unable to truly resolve the doubts that had cast their shadow over his daughter's mind, Mutsu Munemitsu thereupon began studying Buddhism. In the end, he chose Buddhism as his religion and joined the monastic order as a monk.

This story teaches us that Mutsu Munemitsu's daughter understood that religion is life's refuge, for even in the face of death one can be calm and happy, without the slightest amount of fear. A person may go out and, when it gets dark, not know where to stay for the night. This homeless feeling, the pain of pacing back and forth at some intersection, is surely hard to bear. Religion is like our home, the home that provides us with something upon which we can rely.

So, how can our visitations with patients be more in accord with the Dharma? Buddhism holds that visiting the sick is the "first field of merit." It is important to note, though, that there is an etiquette that should be followed when visiting the sick. First, visitations must take place at the right time, for it cannot be too early or too late, and the duration of one's stay should not be too long either. The volume of one's voice when speaking with the sick must be just right, and the subject matter must be discreet and proper. For example, it is not appropriate to speak of any person, matter, or thing that would excite the sick person's state of mind. In order to avoid causing excessive emotional reactions, one must not dispute or argue with the sick. Nor should one reproach the sick, for one's speech should be full of hope so as to give encouragement to them. When the sick are restless and agitated, one can speak of the Dharma as circumstances allow, which will bring consolation to their souls. One should patiently listen to the sentiments of the sick, so that they may relieve the sadness and pain in their hearts. From time to time, one can read to them from newspapers, magazines, essays, or interesting anecdotes to dispel loneliness and help maintain good spirits.

In addition, upon entering a patient's room, one's expression should be natural and free from grieving and crying, so as to avoid influencing the feelings of the sick and their family. Most importantly, one must maintain a compassionate mind and sincerely express one's concern. One should help the sick awaken their faith in Buddhism, allowing them to appreciate that the end of this lifetime is not death, but another rebirth. Being able to offer the sick faith in rebirth will encourage them to have hope for the future and help them to understand that as their ties to the world come to an end, they must not cling to the past and become muddled in thought. By no means should the sick become captive of memories, recollections, obstacles, and attachments, for only by taking rebirth through the peace and calm of the recitation of the Buddha's name can one become liberated and free.

In short, when visiting the sick, be careful not to speak of anything terrible or negative in order to avoid adding to the disquiet of the patient.

Facing the end of life

Since birth, old age, sickness, and death constitute a process we all must undergo, how can we face the end of life with serenity? Especially when one's closest family members become terminally ill, how can we treat such a situation with utmost care?

The Chinese have a saying about the end of life: "restrain your grief and surrender to the change." But once a member of one's family passes on to another rebirth, the entire household becomes trapped in an atmosphere of grief and sorrow. In particular, the closer the relationship and the more well liked the person, the more deeply felt, upon his or her passing, is the suffering of being parted from loved ones.

The Buddhist scriptures contain a relevant anecdote. When King Prasenajit's grandmother passed away, in his extreme grief he asked the Buddha to teach the Dharma, and the Buddha told him that there are four things that are truly frightening:

1) The living will grow old.

2) The sick will wither in appearance.

3) The consciousness will leave the body upon death.

4) The dead are forever separated from their loved ones.

Everything in this world exists because of causes and conditions. When conditions come together, there is life. When conditions are extinguished, life disappears. Even people as close as fathers, sons, mothers, and daughters must depart this world in the end, once the conditions are exhausted. Therefore, people must avail themselves of conditions when they exist, and work and cooperate with these conditions as best as possible. Especially while one's parents are still present and healthy, one should treat them with the utmost filial respect. By no means should one wait until, "The trees wish for calm yet the winds continue; the son wants to offer care but the parent cannot wait," so that one ends up regretting in vain.

Death is something that causes us grief, but birth, old age, sickness, and death are part of a process we all must undergo in life. We can die after an illness, but death is not that terrible. On the contrary, the pain, confusion, and afflictions felt during an illness are often more terrible than the illness itself. Therefore, when a person becomes sick, medicine can reduce the pain of illness and reduce suffering, but if a parent's conditions on earth have come to an end, it is not really necessary for his or her children to use extreme measures to save life through medical treatment and equipment. Living in this world means that life will inevitably lead to death; thus, living and dying is a problem that none can avoid. The only practical approach is to ensure the mental and physical comfort of the sick, so that they may reach the end of their lives without suffering.

Therefore, once a patient is lingering on the verge of death, family members should be considerate and keep calm, facing the situation with determination and courage. It would be best to teach the Dharma at critical stages of illness. With this in mind, I have composed several prayers that may be helpful: "*A Prayer for the Elderly,*" "*A Prayer for the Terminally Ill,*" "*A Prayer for Visiting the Sick,*" and "*A Prayer Before Dying.*" If family members were to read these aloud on behalf of the sick, it would go a long way toward helping not only the patient but also family members face the situation at hand. Here is one of the prayers.

A Prayer Before Dying

Oh great, compassionate Buddha!
I am sick.
I have been hopelessly ill for a long time;
Oh Buddha, I have asked other people to pray to you
on my behalf:
In this final moment of my life,
I, myself, realize that all worldly relations will end;
I no longer worry about relatives and friends;
I no longer cling to mind and body;
I no longer regret the past;
I no longer have wild desire for the future.
When my breathing gradually slows down,
When my beating pulse slowly gets weaker,
When my eyes, ears, nose, and tongue stop functioning,
When the organs of my body no longer work,
I will be like a traveler returning from far away,
Riding the golden lotus flower
To return to the bright Pure Land of Ultimate Bliss.
Oh great, compassionate Buddha!
I would like to have all my flesh
Returned to heaven and given to the earth
So that it will be transformed
Into warm gentle breezes and nutrients,
Following the cycle of nature, and nurture all things,
Year after year, month after month;
I would like to have all my intentions,
Given to all beings, given to all people,
Contributed to the Buddha, the Dharma, and the Sangha,
Transformed into a petal of a fragrant flower,
And offered to all ten directions everywhere,
time after time.
May those who hated me gain my blessings;
May those who gave kindness to me share my serenity;

May those who appreciated me spread my good deeds;
May those who miss me continue my vow.
Oh great, compassionate Buddha!
I finally understand clearly
That life is like a resilient seed,
That flowers fade, then bear fruits;
That birth and death are endless;
Therefore, the sad tears of relatives and friends
Are no longer the ties and constraints of love.
Oh great, compassionate Buddha!
I finally realize:
That life is like a small stream of flowing water,
That the sound of the Dharma is like a clear stream
that continues unceasingly.
Thus, I view the prospects for the future as
no longer uncertain and empty.
I finally realize clearly that, at this very moment,
I only bid farewell temporarily.
With the guidance and reception of all the Buddhas,
bodhisattvas, and excellent beings,
May I have the opportunity and condition
To follow my vow to come back again in future lives.
Oh great, compassionate Buddha!
All my worldly affairs have ended,
All my secular ties and affairs have been completed.
In this last moment of my life,
I am as joyous as a wanderer returning home,
I am as free as a prisoner set free,
I am as natural as falling leaves returning to their roots,
I am as clear and pure as spacious mountains and
the full moon
Oh great, compassionate Buddha,
Please accept my sincerest prayer!
Oh great, compassionate Buddha,
Please accept my sincerest prayer!

The Buddhist teachings include three practices for facing death that are both reasonable and sensitive. These are given below:

1) When someone is seriously ill, go visit him or her. Discuss the Dharma with the patient and his or her family and help them to find physical and mental comfort. You can chant the scriptures as a blessing and do repentance to eliminate negative karma. If the patient recovers because of this, then go and offer congratulations. Use the teachings according to the characteristics of the listener, and use examples to illustrate your points.

2) When someone is in the terminal stage of an illness and about to pass into the next life, recite Amitabha Buddha's name on the patient's behalf, so as to enable him or her to depart peacefully.

3) Upon the passing of the patient, and during the ensuing mourning period of forty-nine days, including the funeral and burial, family members can recite Mahayana scriptures on behalf of the deceased, so as to increase the store of merit as a resource for his or her next rebirth.

In short, birth, old age, sickness, and death constitute a process we all must undergo in life, for in being born, we will die; having died, we will be reborn. Life and death is circular. Death is not annihilation, nor is it eternal sleep. It is certainly not dissolving into some unknown or unconscious oblivion. Rather, it is going out one door and entering another, exchanging one environment for another one. Through this avenue of death, people can rise to an even brighter spiritual world. Thus, the concept of death is expressed in the Buddhist scriptures through many positive analogies, including examples such as: death is like leaving prison, death is like being reborn, death is like graduating, death is like moving to another home, death is like changing one's clothes, and death is like a metamorphosis.

The Pure Land School calls death "seeking rebirth." Indeed, seeking rebirth is just like heading out on a journey or moving abroad. By thinking of death in these different ways, does it not in a sense seem more pleasant? Therefore, death is not something to fear; it is merely shifting to another stage, the beginning of one life being entrusted to another body.

The meaning of life is not found in the length of one's lifespan; though the physical body undergoes old age and death, the real life never dies, just like fire that is passed from torch to torch without end. Although all the myriad phenomena of this world are subject to the process of arising, abiding, change, and extinction, and although life is subject to the cycle of birth and death, whether in the heavenly or human realms, where things come and go without certainty, ultimately the Buddha Nature of our true mind never changes. Therefore, what is important in life is to cherish each stage of our lives and to leave behind a history and legacy of merit. And in their fond recollections of a loved one, family members should commit to carrying on that person's worthy character and good work, and bequeath his or her loving testament of compassion to the human world. This, then, is the true way to remember our loved ones.

Putting our affairs in order

Today it has become very popular to buy pre-need funeral contracts and to draw up living wills, in which one puts in order all matters pertaining to his or her funeral and medical care while still alive and mentally alert. Doing so makes it easier to seek rebirth without worries or cares when death comes. So, what is the Buddhist perspective on such matters?

There are many things that people cannot predict or control in this world, especially given that life and death are impermanent. However, even though it is impossible to control matters of life and death, people can still make preparations in advance for their funeral arrangements. The pre-need contract popular today represents a new business that has arisen because modern people wish to make their funeral arrangements in advance.

The pre-need contract involves signing an agreement, either on one's own or through a family member, with the funeral home while one is still living and paying for the funeral ceremony in advance. This is done in preparation for one's eventual death, that is, to buy life's final insurance policy for your own funeral.

Pre-need contracts have been offered around the world for many years now. However, in the past Chinese people have by and large considered death to be too taboo a subject for discussion, and so it has been only in recent years that the practice has become commonly accepted by people in Taiwan, for example. Since its introduction, market response has been very positive, creating many business opportunities. With the growing popularity of such services, one could say that it represents a great conceptual break-through for Chinese people today. It demonstrates that people no longer feel restrained about broaching the subject of death.

At present, market patterns for pre-need contracts in Taiwan can generally be divided into three forms:

1) Insurance companies have incorporated the unique aspects of pre-need contracts into their business to promote life insurance policies with the same characteristics as pre-need contracts. Or they enter into an agreement with the insured to hold part of the insurance money in a trust, which will be used to pay for funeral expenses. In this way, the insurance companies improve market competitiveness and generate added value for their insurance policies.

2) Insurance companies work in cooperation with pre-need contract companies, wherein the consumer's funeral needs are outsourced to a pre-need contract company.

3) Funeral homes in general have sales representatives who directly sell pre-need contracts through various market channels.

Pre-need contracts are actually an extension of life planning, for in the great matters of life and death, it is certainly important to live freely, fully, and meaningfully during one's life. Being able to leave this world with peace of mind, to let go and be unencumbered by worries and concerns at the time of death must be arranged and planned for in advance. Thus, pre-need contracts are like an insurance card that can put one's mind at rest. Surely, this is a good thing.

The problem is, as with any commercial enterprise in the world, conflicts of interest are impossible to avoid, which lead to confusing claims. Thus, the benefits of pre-need contracts have been marketed in various ways, for example:

1) With their low premiums, the economic burden of pre-need contracts is small.

2) As value-based contracts, usage can be transferred to others; and they can also be treated as negotiable securities that can be expected to appreciate in value.

3) One can stipulate in advance the kind of religious ceremony one wants, guaranteeing the dignity of one's life to the very end.

4) Professionals are ready to take charge with a simple phone call, sparing one's family and friends the embarrassment of not knowing what to do.

5) It spares the family from suffering secondary pain resulting from unplanned expenses after one's death.

Pre-need contracts touch upon a broad range of issues, and among these are legal issues. For example, how can equal consideration be given to the wishes of the deceased and the customs, beliefs, and traditional practices of the family, as well as the interest of the service provider? At the time these services are performed, whose opinions take precedence? Can such contracts be terminated for a refund after being signed? Questions such as these often lead to endless dispute. And there are even quite a few unscrupulous service providers who accept payments for these services only to later abscond with the funds. All of these issues have produced additional social problems. Therefore, although pre-need contracts reflect a certain timeliness and necessity, it is best that these be managed by religious workers and not be subject to standard commercial practices.

Furthermore, because one's children and grandchildren may have different religious beliefs or belong to different religious faiths, people draw up living wills in order to make arrangements for their funeral beforehand and include such things as the division of property and the burial format. This is done in order to avoid disputes among one's descendants later on, which is a good thing by virtue of its reasonableness, openness, liberal-mindedness, and farsightedness. However, regardless of whether one draws up a living will or makes a pre-need contract, there are still often many disputes of various kinds. Therefore, the existence of these documents does not guarantee that these matters will work out as desired.

For example, you draw up a living will, and perhaps because you have a significant amount of property, your children and grandchildren may still fight over it. You make a pre-need contract, but the service provider may be unreliable, or both sides understand the contents of the contract differently. The time between the signing of the contract and the provider's fulfillment of the contracted services could extend over several decades. Following the social changes that would have taken place during that time, it is inevitable that there might be many variables beyond anyone's control. Thus, there is really no single contract that can provide protection against all possibilities.

On the other hand, the ultimate meaning of life does not lie in one's funeral and a proper burial. Throughout our lives, we should make contributions to society, leaving behind a legacy for oneself and fond memories for one's family. Although everyone will experience birth, old age, sickness, and death, true life never dies. In the past, Chinese people believed that raising children would provide against old age. If people did not have their own children, they would find a way to take on a godson or adopt a surrogate daughter, so there would be someone to care for them in old age and see that they have a proper burial.

However, as the saying goes, "beside the bed of a long sick parent, there are no filial sons." There are bad children and grandchildren who fail to take care of their parents and lack a sense of gratitude. Some even go so far as to wish for their parent's early demise, so that they might get their share of the inheritance that much sooner. Therefore, older people should not be too rich. It is better to develop virtue, wisdom, and karmic connections. This is the best way to take care of yourself in old age, and the best guarantee for your arrangements to be carried out according to your wishes.

As people age over the years, they learn new things and gain in experience, something that young people cannot attain. If one is able to detach oneself from external concerns in old age, one could write books, passing on to the next generation one's life experiences, what one has learned and experienced, or even key aspects of some skill or technique. One could teach younger generations what it takes to be a good person or how to do the right thing, edifying the human heart with one's rich experiences on how a good person handles situations. Such communication would naturally win the affirmation of all. Would you then still worry that growing old means becoming a lonely old person?

Besides understanding how to grow old through wisdom, we must also understand how to make connections for a better future. Relationships between people are maintained on the basis of karmic connections, so interpersonal human relationships are subject to the principle of causes and conditions. There is a popular saying that goes, "when connections are present, you will meet though separated by a thousand miles; but without such connections, you won't recognize each other even when you are face to face." The most precious thing in the world is creating broad connections for a positive future. Understanding how to support Buddhist activities on a regular basis will mean that after you grow old or are reborn, the Buddhist temple will naturally reward you. Try to become a part of some charitable enterprise on a regular basis or become a volunteer. Take the initiative to express concern for the poor, weak, and lonely, and develop interpersonal relationships through your love and joy. Then, as you grow old, there will be no need to worry about being friendless, nor will you worry about being deserted and uncared for by society.

Therefore, an individual's best guarantee is to make connections for the future, so that you can let causes and conditions help you after death. Obtaining help from others from day to day is very difficult, but as long as we create connections for the future and build causes and conditions, then they will easily find us. By creating connections for the future during our lifetime, those who have a connection with us will naturally appear to realize those connections after our death. This is the best and most effective way to solve problems. By contrast, if one is unwilling to make connections for the future, then no matter how much property you leave to your descendents, it is still possible that no one will see to your burial or recite the Buddha's name for you in the end. Thus, creating broad connections for a positive future is the most wonderful thing in human life.

In short, in life we should live joyously, and in death we should die joyously. No matter what happens, we should always be full of joy. This represents what is most wonderful and satisfactory. Therefore, it is best for us to put our efforts into creating broad connections for a positive future, rather than relying on some pre-need contract to plan one's funeral.

Understanding death

According to Buddhist sutras, people experience different ways of dying, such as natural death, dying of old age, dying an unnatural death, and dying young, owing to differences in karmic power. Some Buddhist teachings say "death is like a tortoise being torn from its shell." Can death really be so terrible?

For generations, death was the most taboo of subjects, but over time life-and-death studies have become a hot topic of conversation and are now considered a required course in some schools and for human life. Nanhua University, founded in 1996 by Fo Guang Shan, was the first to promote this trend in Taiwan and led the country in establishing the Institute of Life-and-Death Studies. This initiated a spirited debate on the subject in Taiwan, and applications for admission to the institute soared. There has been whole-hearted and enthusiastic participation of professionals from many areas, including the fields of education and nursing, religious circles, and social work. The level of competition to enter the institute was on a par with the ever-popular departments of science and engineering.

One could say that the establishment of the Institute of Life-and-Death Studies at Nanhua University represented a watershed in Taiwan's history of education. The institute belongs to the School of Humanities, and the institute's director, Venerable Huei Kai, has personally taught such courses as "Religious Tradition and the Exploration of Life and Death," "Discussion on the Fundamental Issues for Life-and-Death Studies," "Readings in Famous English Language Works on Life-and-Death Studies," and "General Introduction to Life-and-Death Studies." With academic specialties and research topics that include "Philosophy of Religion" and "Religious Life-and-Death Studies," as well as topics from the latter two courses mentioned above, he has led the way in focusing the public's attention on life-and-death studies.

The *New York Times* reported on research into life-and-death studies as early as July 1974. At the time, there were already 165 universities across the U.S. offering general education courses on the topic of death and dying. With a history of offering these courses spanning over twenty years, some schools now even include such courses within their core curriculum.

Life and death have always represented the subject most intimately connected with human life. Of the greatest problems in this human world, one is the problem of life and the other is the problem of death. In life we must live somewhere, and in death we must go somewhere; some people work hard for their life, while others worry about death. The study of Buddhism is indeed life-and-death studies. For example, in "saving those suffering hardship and distress," the Avalokitesevera Bodhisattva is solving the problem of life; while in "receiving those who go to rebirth," Amitabha Buddha is solving the problem of death. Owing to the "confusion that arises when birth separates one lifetime from the next," we do not realize anything about earlier or later lifetimes once we have changed bodies. For this reason, until more recently we have understood little about life and death, which constitutes the most difficult problem to resolve in the world. The sutras divide death into four main categories: death by exhausting one's lifespan, death by exhausting one's good karma for human life, death by accident, and death by self-fulfillment. "Death by exhausting one's lifespan" means a natural death, when one's body fails. Kidney failure, heart failure, and so on are examples in which the organs of the body no longer function, and the body becomes like an old, worn-out cart that cannot move quickly, or like broken tables and chairs that cannot be used. This is when the oil burns down and the lamp goes out, and one dies peacefully at home.

"Death by accident" refers to death brought on by suffering some accident or calamity, and is generally referred to as an accidental death. The *Sutra of the Medicine Buddha of Pure Crystal Radiance* describes nine kinds of accidental death: (1) contracting an incurable disease, (2) execution according to law, (3) having one's vitality sucked away by supernatural creatures, (4) being burned in a fire, (5) drowning, (6) being eaten by wild beasts, (7) falling from heights, (8) being poisoned or cursed with spells, and (9) suffering from thirst and hunger.

"Accidental death" can mean falling to one's death, drowning, being eaten by wolves and tigers, or dying in an airplane crash. It appears unbearable, but once karmic retribution comes into play, life can end in an instant. Though life is not prolonged, it can still be considered a natural death. In contrast, there are those who linger in their sickbeds at the hospital, with tubes inserted to keep them alive. How can this be considered a good death? Therefore, the meaning of accidental death versus natural death should be considered from another perspective.

People all wish for a good life, and even more so for a good death. One of the Buddha's ten epithets is "well gone," which explains why a "good death" is also the most supreme blessing in human life. Actually, dying in an instant is not really so terrible; it is only terrible when one has the time to directly experience death or ends up dying of fright. Dying immediately without pain or suffering and without any fear or dread is a natural death.

Can one really say whether or not death is like a tortoise being torn from its shell? Perhaps it is like that when undergoing electro-shock emergency treatment. But it is not if you can pass away with a smile on your face. Basically, as people are born, they will surely die, and after death, they will be reborn. Just like the circular dial on a clock or a round plate, birth and death and death and rebirth have neither a beginning nor an end. Birth and death constitute nothing more than an endless cycle. You reap what you sow, but planting is not really the beginning, nor is harvesting the end, for there is an ending in the beginning and a beginning in the ending. Therefore, death is not really terrible.

Of course, in death we have the so-called "good death" or "bad death." For some people, death is like falling asleep, from which they never awake. Some Chan masters in the past died in the fields holding a hoe; some died while still receiving bows of farewell; some passed away as they played the flute while riding in a boat; while others bid farewell to their relative and friends before passing on. As the saying goes, "they came into this world for the sake of sentient beings, and went out from this world for the sake of sentient beings." All the comings and goings are nothing for us to worry about. It is just like exchanging a new set of clothes when the old ones are worn and threadbare; or substituting a new house for one that is worn and damaged. We even replace old cars with new ones. So why can't we, as our bodies become advanced in age, just exchange them for another?

Francois Rabelais, a representative figure of the French Renaissance, once said, "Let down the curtain: the farce is done!" He expressed a view of death that was unconventional and free-spirited, without any regrets over loss. The philosopher Jean-Jacques Rousseau consoled his wife as he lay dying: "Do not be sad. Look to the bright sky; that is where I am going!" He was the very model of a life unconstrained and at ease.

Many Americans enjoy an affluent material lifestyle, but they do not think death is so terrible. By contrast, the Chinese people have suffered endless adversities, along with political suppression and constant warfare, yet they fear death and hope that they can live forever and never grow old. This is a very interesting phenomenon.

Actually, it is best to follow the natural course in everything, and the same goes for death. Death is nothing to be afraid of; it is just that upon death, we become like immigrants. Will you have the capital to survive when you move on to that other country? As long as you possess the Dharma wealth of your merits, why should you be afraid after you have gone to some other land?

Arranging funerals in accord with the Dharma

The Chinese have many taboos and superstitions regarding burial practices. After a loved one passes on to another rebirth, how do we arrange his or her funeral in accord with the Dharma?

There are the so-called "great matters of life and death," and since ancient times the Chinese people have always considered life and death the two greatest matters of life. They have also emphasized "in life, treat others in accordance with the rites; in death, bury them in accordance with the rites." Serving one's parents is an expression of filial piety, but providing a proper burial constitutes an even greater filial act, and so death has always entailed an elaborate funeral. During the time of Confucius, there were more than fifty different ceremonies that had to be performed during the period from death to burial. Just as the German philosopher Ludwig Feuerbach (1804-1872) remarked, "The Chinese are a people who worry most about the dead." Thus, there are always many detailed forms and complicated rules for funerals, and there are many outmoded customs, superstitious elements, and taboos. For example, most people believe that the dead will most certainly become ghosts. In order to ensure their loved ones are not without travel money while on the way to the nether realm, it is customary to burn paper money for their loved one to use on the journey.

Westerners have the custom of placing flowers on the coffin of the dead as an expression of remembrance. As with this custom, there is nothing essentially wrong with the sentiment behind the Chinese people's burning of spirit money. However, now the custom has expanded from the burning of spirit money to include the burning of paper houses, automobiles, and home appliances. Even paper representations of servants are burned. Some of these practices are open to debate, because in burning paper representations of houses and villas for the dead, for example, if there is no land after death, then where are the dead expected to put these things? In burning representations of automobiles, if the deceased were killed in a car accident, then wouldn't you be setting up the deceased for yet another accident in his or her next life?

The Buddhist sutras state that people can be reborn in any of the six realms of existence. If they advance to the realm of the Buddhas and gods, a paradise of riches, what need would they have for paper representations of money? If they are reborn in the human realm, one cannot know the country of their rebirth, so should they receive Taiwan currency or U.S. dollars? If they are reborn as hell-beings or hungry ghosts, they will face such limitless suffering that paper money would be of no use to them. Therefore, it is better to print Buddhist sutras, perform acts of charity, and do good deeds on behalf of the dead. Only the dedication of merit to the deceased represents something of substantial benefit for them.

The Chinese people have also always stressed the ideal of dying peacefully at home. So they often believe that if a person dies in a car crash, his or her body cannot be brought back home, for doing so would be inauspicious. Actually, in the agrarian societies of the past, most people spent their entire lives at home, but in modern industrial society, many people go abroad to make a living. For this reason, greater numbers of people are dying in accidents away from home. Dying abroad is already something quite sad, so why not let them come home? If we changed our perspective, we might think in this way: "For someone to die away from home is quite sad, so if you can get that person back home as soon as possible, he would feel the family's love and be at peace." This way, there would no longer be anything unacceptable.

In accordance with another Chinese custom, when a family member passes away, the children must provide a proper burial by carrying the spirit tablet respectfully and holding an open umbrella. There is a story behind this custom: during the Qing Dynasty, a period when the Chinese were under Manchurian rule, there were some holdovers from the Ming court who were not happy about becoming subjects under the Manchurian regime. They swore that "my feet will not touch the ground of the Manchu Qing dynasty, nor will my head be covered by its sky." Thus after they died, their children covered their bodies with an umbrella so that they would not be covered by the Manchu sky. But haven't we reached the modern age? Do we still need this umbrella?

The Chinese people have traditionally stressed ethics, which has engendered quite a few customs. For example, after a person dies, over the course of many days his or her grieving family members cannot shave or change their clothes, their children must crawl in on their knees when they return home, and so on, as expressions of their grief. None of these practices are natural. Even people whose astrological chart conflicts with that of the deceased cannot participate in the burial; and when one's husband dies, a wife cannot participate in the graveside burial, for doing so would indicate her willingness to remarry, something which would be considered infidelity.

Another phenomenon that often appeared within traditional agrarian society of China is that whenever there was a death in a family, relatives, friends, and neighbors all came over in droves with their suggestions. Even gossipy matchmakers and fortunetellers got into the act. One would mention this custom, another would speak of that requirement, while the obedient sons and grandsons are left scratching their heads, not knowing what was the right thing to do.

My family lost contact with my father as he was returning home during the Japanese invasion of China. Later, we concluded that he had probably been killed. I do not know anything about his death. However, when my mother passed on at the age of ninety-five, I did not let anyone give me suggestions. Since it was my own mother who had passed on, there was no need for others to come up with all manner of confusing and conflicting ideas. Therefore, I believe that my mother surely passed on in peace.

There are many outmoded ideas and practices related to the traditional Chinese funerary ritual. Practices such as using feng shui to pick an auspicious burial day, leaving the corpse undisturbed for eight hours before being laid out in the coffin, and making lavish funeral arrangements that include recorded music, flower-adorned cars, a procession, graveside weeping, and so on should be refined and improved. Not only are such things a waste, but they also ruin the solemnity of the occasion.

Then, how should we handle today's funeral rituals in ways that are in keeping with the times? Funeral practices should be sensible, reasonable, and legal. Examples include following the methods for funerary ceremonials published by Taiwan's Ministry of the Interior, or following the practices of one's own faith, like what is advocated and practiced at the Buddhist monasteries with respect to funerary ritual.

What the Buddhist perspective on funerary ritual emphasizes first is to establish the correct understanding and right view. For example, birth, old age, sickness, and death constitute a process we all must undergo in life, but there are very few people who can face death serenely. This is because they often neglect the important moment we experience during the "dying stage." The dying stage is that critical juncture between "rising up" and "sinking down." It is that most precious and decisive moment which determines how one approaches rebirth. If family members are crying and wailing at this time, their actions will stir up sad feelings in the patient, which will drag the person down and make him or her lose the opportunity to seek rebirth in a positive realm. There is nothing helpful in this, only harm. Therefore, if someone passes away in your family, there should be no wailing or loud crying, no tugging at the dying patient, no placing money in the hands, and no bowing at the feet; and the killing of living things as offerings must be particularly avoided. As the *Ksitigarbha Bodhisattva Sutra* states, "On the day someone dies, be careful not to kill living things or to create negative connections for the future... Why is this? The living things you have killed and prepared as offerings are of no benefit whatsoever to the deceased, but only serve to create negative connections for the future, in turn making the unwholesome karma much worse." The *sutra* also states, "If after the body has died, one can widely perform many good deeds during realms and to take rebirth in heaven or human realms, where they will experience excellent and profound happiness. The benefits for the surviving family members are likewise immeasurable."

Thus, to do good deeds on behalf of the deceased over the course of forty-nine days of mourning creates the most meritorious benefit. This is particularly so when the sick person reaches the terminal stage of illness. The best thing we can do then is to invite monastics or fellow Buddhist practitioners to join the patient for chanting. Visiting family members should join in with the chanting, for this will help the dying person obtain rebirth in the Pure Land of Ultimate Bliss. One can also invite a virtuous elder who excels in teaching the key points of the Dharma, someone whom the sick person respects, to come and give consolation and Dharma explanations. Such a person can encourage the sick to recite the name of Amitabha Buddha and seek rebirth in the Pure Land.

There are a few other points regarding funeral ritual that should be especially observed, which I have listed below:

1) Don't put on an extravagant show: When people arrange funerals these days, they often attempt to outdo one another in vain ostentation. They want theirs to be better than anyone else's, and so many people become involved in competitive extravagance. Actually, what is most important is just to honor the wishes of the deceased.

2) Don't go overboard: Some people in Taiwan, for example, get caught up in details such as how many marching bands will perform or how many flower-adorned cars there will be in the funeral entourage. But there is no need for this. A funeral is the business of an individual family, so what is the point of mobilizing a crowd? Something solemn, mournful, and respectful is much better than jarring noise.

3) Don't be superstitious: Preparing a funeral is simply a matter of having the dead be at peace and the living fulfill their love and duty. Expressing one's grief and sadness is what it is all about. There is no need to make anything more out of it.

In short, life and death are the two greatest matters of human life, and from a Buddhist perspective, life is nothing to rejoice about, nor is death something to grieve over. All that is required is to apply your solemn feelings in helping the dead to smoothly find a positive rebirth, something that is more important than any magnificent ceremony.

Understanding the cycle of life and death

Buddhism speaks of death as "taking rebirth," and also speaks of life as the cycle of birth and death through the three periods of time. How can we be sure that there are previous and future lives?

All the myriad phenomena in the world must obey the principle of cyclic existence: the stars of the universe that circle about; the progression of the seasons through spring, summer, autumn, and winter; the passage of the hours through the day and night; cyclic existence through the six positive and negative realms of sentient existence; and the human body with its birth, old age, sickness, and death; as well as the transitions of the three times over the past, present and future. All of these are like the cyclic turning of a wheel, proving the principle of cyclic existence.

Since ancient times, society has recognized the existence of the cycle of birth and death. Ancient India's *Rig-Veda* within Brahmanistic culture suggested that the soul reincarnates after death. Later works such as the *Brahmana*, the *Upanisads*, and the *Bhagavad-gita*, all articulate a mature theory of reincarnation. In the West, ancient Greek and Roman philosophers carried out active research into the doctrine of the soul, and among these, Pythagoras and Plato proposed the idea that the soul after death reincarnates as a human being or some other thing, depending upon the good or bad committed during the previous life.

Even today, all religions accept the existence of rebirth in one form or another. Among these, Daoists advocate immortality, Protestants and Catholics believe that the goal of life is to enter heaven and be with God, where one attains eternal life, and in most folk beliefs there is a strong yearning for an immortal life. Buddhists believe that the ultimate goal of life is to realize the state of "no rebirth," nirvana. The state of no rebirth is one in which cyclic existence has been transcended and one no longer experiences the suffering of life and death. From the Buddhist perspective, a long life, an eternal life, or an immortal life, is still subject to the sufferings of cyclic existence. Only with the state of no rebirth can one be free from the torments and sufferings of life and realize the pure life of ultimate happiness.

There are many people today who believe in the existence of the cycle of birth and death and are studying its principles. There are some people who actively seek out their previous lives, as well as those who are unable to free themselves from the sufferings of cyclic existence as determined by the functioning of karmic power.

Buddhism presents a penetrating analysis of rebirth, revealing the mysteries of the cycle of birth and death, and explains the truth regarding the significance of human life as well as the path for avoiding suffering and obtaining happiness. After the Buddha attained enlightenment, he began his profound teaching career to bring salvation to all sentient beings. He presented many ideas concerning cyclic existence, such as the *Sutra on the Contemplation of the Mind* that states, "Beings transmigrate through the six realms of sentient beings like the wheel of a cart that has no beginning nor end." The *Treatise on the Perfection of Great Wisdom* states, "Beings are reborn due to the power of karma; they cycle through the sea of birth and death."

Buddhism considers the "alaya (storehouse) consciousness" to be the subjective component of cyclic existence, while what determines the inclinations of cyclic existence is "karmic power." The alaya consciousness is the root consciousness that takes rebirth in life. It is not a soul, nor is it a spiritual entity. Upon encountering external objectivities, a life produces various forms of positive and negative behaviors. The seeds resulting from the effects of these behaviors then exert their influence in the alaya consciousness, which is where these seeds are stored. When the physical body dies, the alaya consciousness is the last to depart. When life reincarnates in another rebirth, the alaya consciousness is the first to do so; for this reason, the alaya consciousness is the fundamental subjective component of cyclic existence. As sentient beings act through their body, speech, and mind, the resulting behavior produces positive or negative karma. These karmic causes and conditions form two kinds of force, which compete with each other in a kind of tug-of-war. If the power of the positive karma is greater, then that individual will take rebirth in the three positive realms of gods, human beings, and asuras; but if the power of the negative karma is greater, then that individual will suffer by being reborn in the lower, negative realms of the hell-beings, hungry ghosts, and animals. Therefore, karmic power is the determining factor for cyclic existence.

From ancient times to the present, both in China and abroad, examples of the cycle of birth and death through the six realms of existence abound. When the situation presented itself, the Buddha would often give accounts of his own practice over many kalpas; the *Sutra on the Collection of the Six Perfections*, the *Jataka Sutra*, the *Sutra on the Original Vows of Ksitigarbha*, and so on, all contain tales of the Buddha's life. In Great Britain, there was a man named Arthur Flowerdew, who from an early age could often recall things that had happened more than two thousand years earlier in the ancient city of Petra in Jordan; later, he assisted archeologists in locating relics and antiquities. In China, accounts relating to rebirth over the course of history are far too numerous to enumerate.

In Taiwan, there was the February 28th Incident that occurred in 1947 when native Taiwanese were massacred by Nationalist troops. Even today, there are people whose hearts are filled with hatred and still seek revenge over this incident. Couldn't these people be the victims of the February 28th Incident who have reincarnated in this present lifetime? The Buddhist Esoteric School also upholds the doctrine of reincarnating Buddhas. Though this doctrine has turned into a customary tradition, it is not without basis, for it presents many aspects that are believable to a certain degree. And there are modern psychologists in the West who have employed hypnosis to help patients recall memories of past lives. Such significant developments show that the cycle of birth and death can no longer be doubted.

Life is like a seed that cannot be removed and cannot die. Believing in the cycle of birth and death through the three periods of time enables us to realize that we cannot simply focus on this present life of ours, for we must pay attention to the future. We must create broad connections for a positive future and cultivate meritorious causes and conditions; only in this way will the future turn out to be wonderful.

Understanding heaven and hell

Buddhism talks about the ten dharma realms. Do heaven and hell really exist among these dharma realms? Where are heaven and hell located?

In this wide and vast universe, most people think about and are conscious of this present world upon which their existence depends, and after that, heaven and hell. This is because, in the view of most people, upon death one either ascends to heaven or falls into hell. Heaven and hell are situated above and below the human realm of existence, respectively; one represents the enjoyment of happiness and the other represents the experience of suffering. This constitutes what most people understand about heaven and hell.

Where are heaven and hell? During my years of preaching the Dharma, I have often been asked this question. My usual response is as follows: Where are heaven and hell? This can be addressed on three levels:

First, heaven is located in the place of heavens, while hell is located in the place of hells. Buddhism divides the universe into ten distinct dharma realms or dharmadhatus. These are the realms of the Buddhas, bodhisattvas, pratyekabuddhas, sravakas, gods, humans, asuras, animals, hungry ghosts, and hell-beings. Among these, the realm of the gods refers to heaven, which includes the Twenty-eight Heavens of the Three Realms; and hell is divided into the Eighteen Hells. Therefore, heaven is located in the place of heavens, and hell is located in the place of hells.

Second, heaven and hell exist right here in the human realm. In this world, some people live a life of luxury, dwelling in homes surrounded by gardens and riding in automobiles instead of walking. In this sense, they seem to be living in heaven. Others live in hardship, in cramped and crude hovels. The misery they experience from powerlessness and lack of money is like living in hell. Those who suffer from cold and hunger would seem to be living as hungry ghosts; while those who suffer from flaming volleys and burning infernos would appear to be living in something like the nether world of the ghosts.

Third, heaven and hell lie in a single thought. Actually, the real heaven and hell exist within our own minds. Many people habitually compare themselves to others, their hearts filled with doubt and bitterness as they spend their days consumed with greed, hatred, and delusion. They may be burdened with worry and grief, as if they were living in hell. However, if they could hold a pure heart, keep an open and generous mind, and be accepting of all and experience from time to time happiness, satisfaction, joy, and peace, then this would be like living in heaven. In the course of a day, each one of us will sometimes find ourselves in heaven and sometimes in hell, going back and forth who knows how many times. For this reason, I believe that heaven and hell lie within a single thought.

The various religions all believe in the existence of heaven and hell, and even Buddhism affirms the fact that heaven and hell exist. Even so, according to the Buddhist teachings, upon death a person will not necessarily ascend to heaven or fall into hell, for heaven and hell are but two realms among the ten dharma realms. In order to ascend to heaven, one must have the causal conditions for ascending to heaven; in order to fall into hell, one must have accumulated the karmic power for falling into hell. These two represent karmic retribution through the Law of Cause and Conditions and the Law of Cause and Effect that cannot be confused or overturned.

There are even people who say that the Christian Heaven is the same as the Buddhist Pure Land. Actually, these two are in no way similar. You can articulate their differences in at least four ways:

1) In the Pure Land, everyone is the same; there are no distinctions between rich and poor, high and low.

2) In the Pure Land, one must still practice and improve before the flower of one's mind opens to reveal its full Buddha Nature. Being reborn in the Pure Land does not mean you are done with your cultivation.

3) Being reborn in the Pure Land means ascending to the Buddha land. The Buddha land is not heaven, for if you exhaust the reward of being in heaven, you can still fall into the lower realms.

4) The Pure Land is a place of purity without desire, while heaven is still tinged with desire.

Where are heaven and hell? Right in this human world in

which we live. Everyday in this world we can see the horrors of hell. For example, just go and visit a market or a restaurant, and you will see chickens, ducks, pigs, and sheep strung upside down or hanging from hooks, having been skinned and cooked alive. Isn't this the Hell of Hanging Upside Down, the Hell of Sharp Knives, or the Hell of Roasting in Fire? Go to an operating room or a patient's ward, and everywhere you can hear the anguished cries, the very terrors of hell that are observable to all. In contrast, in today's society, most people also have enough to wear and eat, are elegantly dressed and richly fed; some people live in high-rise luxury apartments that not only have carpets on the floor but air conditioning as well. Going out the door, one can ride in an automobile instead of walking, fly in an airplane, or sail in a ship, covering a thousand miles in a single day; in the area of communication, one can instantly contact distant friends on the telephone. While enjoying a documentary on television, one can see what's going on beyond the myriad miles of ocean and mountains all in an instant; and the usage of computers and remote controls enable you to achieve what your heart desires in a free and easy manner. We enjoy so many meritorious causes and conditions, living a life of ultimate peace and prosperity. Is this not heaven? And so, even heaven can be realized in this world of ours.

Where are heaven and hell? They lie in our mind. Tiantai philosophers say that in our minds, "one thought contains three thousand dharmas;" the Mind-Only philosophers say that all the myriad phenomena "are transformed by mind-only." Our minds change in the blink of an eye, being so elusive and unpredictable; suddenly we have the mind of all the Buddhas and sages, then just as suddenly, we have the mind of beings from the three negative realms of existence. Through the course of a day, our minds bob and sink among the ten dharma realms, going back and forth between them countless times. Therefore, hoping for Buddhahood or becoming a sage depends upon one mind; falling into rebirth in samsara is also tied to a single thought.

The *Flower Adornment Sutra* states: "The mind is like a

skilled painter, who can depict various objects." Our minds are like a painter, who can portray beautiful things and can also depict ferocious beasts. According to the *Vimalakirti Sutra*: "The land is purified as the mind becomes purified." If we can hold a mind of purity from time to time in our dealings with everything in the world, then this world becomes heaven, a Pure Land. Therefore, heaven and hell are not in some faraway place; they are right here in this present thought.

"Heaven and hell are in a single thought." If we can understand the profound meaning in this, then we would then come to appreciate that, in life, we must not simply focus on how we live outside of our minds, for it is most important that we establish a heaven within our own minds. But if we have not established heaven within the mind, we will be letting the hell of worry, sadness, and misery remain there instead, which will bring a life of unspeakable suffering. Therefore, living in this human world we should see ourselves as dwelling in heaven, but if we cannot recognize its beauty, then heaven will become transformed into hell. If you apply the Dharma in dealing with adversity and transforming bad luck, then hell can also become heaven.

The Buddhist scriptures tell us: without good karmic retribution, one will experience the "five signs of decay" that precede death even in heaven; but with the aspiration for compassion, even hell can become heaven. Just like the Ksitigarbha Bodhisattva vowed: "I vow not to become a Buddha until hell is emptied out," and so over the kalpas he has been laboring hard in hell to liberate sentient beings. But I think of the Bodhisattva Ksitigarbha as always living in heaven, because the hell in his mind was emptied out long ago. Although the Buddha came into this corrupt world, we should not think that the Buddha lived in a degenerate age characterized by the five impurities, because the Buddha lives in the Pure Land realm with its Dharma nature. There is also the Avalokitesvera Bodhisattva who upholds compassion and brings salvation to those who call out to her, thereby transforming burning flames in fresh lotus blossoms. The Venerable Purna kept to his purpose with determination, bringing salvation to the uncouth peoples of the border regions, and so what others saw as a hell-like border land became in his eyes a heaven-like place of enlightenment with all its freedoms.

A popular saying goes, "the world is what our minds make of it." Everything is transformed by consciousness and appears to us as mind only. There is the "one mind and its two aspects" discussed in The *Awakening of Faith in the Mahayana*, in which the aspect of the mind in absolute terms is Buddha Nature and the aspect of the mind in phenomenal terms represents the state of the ordinary person. The difference between a Buddha and an ordinary person rests solely in the one mind, within which there can be the sages of heaven or the demons of hell. In conducting ourselves in the world, if we can treat others with a Buddha mind, then the world will follow us in transforming it into a Buddha realm; but if we deal with the world with a demonic mind, then the world will become a realm of demons. The difference between a Buddha and a demon lies in the one mind. Do you want to be a Buddha? Or would your rather be a demon? Be careful!

Meeting the demand for hospice care

In today's society, there are quite a few treatment centers and philanthropic groups that have instituted hospice wards to meet the demand for hospice care. What types of places are best suited to offer this service? And what sort of things require the nursing staff's attention?

Following the widespread recognition of hospice care, currently in Taiwan there are treatment centers that have established hospice care, including the Lotus Hospice Care Foundation and the Hospice Foundation of Taiwan. In addition, many hospitals have established hospice wards, such as National Taiwan University Hospital, Mackay Memorial Hospital, Cardinal Tien Hospital, Taipei Veterans General Hospital, Changhua Christian Hospital, and Buddhist Tzu Chi General Hospital. These organizations are huge, drawing their staff from doctors, nurses, nutritionists, pharmacologists, and physical therapists, who use various methods to reduce and mitigate the physical pain of the patients. These ranks are swelled by social workers and religious workers, who enable the sick to eliminate their fear of dying, and through their religious power, make sure the dying obtain comfort and guidance. The main goal of hospice care is to help the patient to complete life's final journey with dignity. Therefore, when performing nursing care, one should be mindful of the following:

I) Recognize the psychological changes of the dying patient. The emotional changes the dying undergo vary from person to person. Family members, volunteers, charity workers, and religious professionals should all understand this process, and provide the appropriate help. Examples include:

1) Fear: Develop methods for helping the dying to feel joyful, and to be without fear and confusion.

2) Anger: Comfort the dying and help them to calm down, so that they can let go of all their concerns and not become caught up in likes and dislikes.

3) Guilt: Enable the dying to be free of guilt; teach them that negative obstacles can be eliminated by reciting Amitabha Buddha's name.

4) Attachment: Urge them to refrain from greedily clinging to their family and worldly possessions.

5) Worry: Help the patient to gain peace of mind by assuring them that it is not necessary to worry about trivialities.

6) Helplessness: Help them to realize that there are many family members and friends to give them spiritual support.

7) Giving up on oneself: Encourage them to strengthen their faith; by reciting Amitabha Buddha's name, they will surely be reborn in his pure land.

8) Loneliness: Do not allow the patient to suffer from loneliness.

9) Despondency: When the patient is about to depart this

world, one should offer the appropriate comfort when dealing with despondency or frustration.

10) Ignorance: Tell them that they are going to a pure, peaceful, and wonderful place; help them understand that their future is full of boundless hope.

II) Correctly observe the needs of the dying patient. Serving as a hospice caregiver, one should either create a profile based on a frank conversation with each patient in order to understand his or her individual needs and wishes, or come to know what they want through observation. Understanding their needs might include:

1) Their wishes about knowing the nature of the illness.
2) Their wishes about obtaining the forgiveness of others.
3) Their understanding about forgiving others.
4) Their wishes about the care others give them.
5) Their wishes about visits with friends and family.
6) Their understanding of life.
7) Their pursuit of religious faith.
8) Their wishes regarding their funeral.

III) Provide assistance to the dying patient. Serving as a hospice caregiver, one should have a high degree of compassion and patience, possess all the necessary abilities and knowledge to assist patients in completing their life's journey without regrets, and design for them a beautiful ending. Examples of ways you might assist them include:

1) Listen to them whole-heartedly and with a caring attitude.

2) Allow their loved ones to give care at appropriate times and to keep company with the patient.

3) Respect the religious beliefs of the patient.

4) Tell stories about and explain the principles behind salvation through repentance.

5) Arrange to have a monastic or religious worker speak

with them, or explain the Dharma to them.

6) Satisfy their heart's wishes to the extent possible.

7) Discuss with them their hopes.

8) Inform the doctor when they are in pain, so that they remain conscious and lucid.

9) Help patients and families maintain their regular lifestyle, as well as prepare for the funeral.

10) Maintain the patient's peace of mind.

11) Join in with the recitation of Amitabha Buddha's name on their behalf, enabling them to engender the right thought, so they can pass away peacefully.

As soon as we are born we have two problems: one is life and the other is death. When we are born, our parents raise us and our teachers instruct us. We grow up, get married, have kids, enjoy a career, and perhaps become rich and famous. In old age we must be looked after, when sick we must be cared for, and when death comes, there's the funeral, the eulogy, the cremation, the interment, and so on. The children and grandchildren of the dead must see to many things before this last event in a person's life is completed.

In light of this and in order to bring a satisfactory resolution to the final problem of human life, Fo Guang Shan built the Longevity Memorial Park in 1983, which included the implementation of an overall plan in certain stages. The third to the sixth floors constitute the Wanshou Pagoda, where the bones of the deceased are interred and the spirit tablets are kept. The Gongde Hall on the first floor is reserved for funeral ceremonies. Altogether there are four memorial halls, both large and small, known as the Nine Grades Hall, the Lotus Flower Hall, the Completion Hall, and the Longevity Hall, which are where the remains are kept pending burial and where memorial services can be held. There are also two separate halls on either side that provide a place where followers can make inquiries and where the family of the deceased can rest.

The Wish Fulfilling Residence on the second floor is

where terminal patients and caregivers from the family are housed. Each unit is equipped with a kitchen, bathroom, and treatment room, and there are enough units to handle six patients at the same time, named Wish Fulfilling Residence, Virtue Residence, Bodhi Residence, Prajna Residence, Fortune & Wisdom Residence, and Harmony & Joy Residence, respectively. Family members of dying patients can keep company and live together with them, so that they can devote their full attention to caring for the dying. If their condition improves, they can return home; but once the patient passes on or at the final moments of life, there are monastics there who can join in with the recitation of Amitabha Buddha's name of their behalf. Arrangements for the ensuing funeral, from casket preparation, eulogy service, cremation to internment, are all provided as a service by Fo Guang Shan, so that the funeral is concluded satisfactorily.

In light of what happens during most funerals, over the course of illness and death to the burial itself, the family is exhausted from rushing around doing various tasks, and so Fo Guang Shan provides, from life to death, a whole series of services with respect to the completion of a life. In addition, besides the morning and evening chanting services that take place everyday, two Buddhist memorial services are held each year during the spring and autumn, which not only benefit the living and the dead, but also purify the popular trend towards extravagant funerals.

In regard to the completion of life, Fo Guang Shan follows the ideal of "benefiting society through charity." So it provides care for the old and young, the living and the dying, and the old and infirm by operating orphanages, Fo Guang viharas, Fo Guang clinics, memorial gardens, support services, and winter relief for the poor. In addition, by pursuing cultural, educational, social-educational, and event-oriented avenues at the same time, Fo Guang Shan hopes to make a contribution through the transformative teachings of the Dharma, thus helping to purify the human mind, improve social trends, elevate humanistic thinking, enrich spiritual life, and to develop wisdom and compassion.

However, there are some uninformed people in society who are unaware of the contributions Fo Guang Shan has made to the development of Buddhism and the moral transformation of society. They often criticize Fo Guang Shan for becoming too commercialized and point out that Fo Guang Shan has a lot of money. Actually, it is not that Fo Guang Shan has a lot of money; rather, it knows how to spend the money it has. This year's money has been spent; even next year's and the following year's money has been spent, too. Living a life in which "each day of challenging circumstances must be each day lived," we spend every penny of the charitable donations we receive on Buddhist work, such as training talent and preaching the Dharma for the benefit of sentient beings. Fo Guang Shan does not feign to look upon money as something sinful, nor do we waste or hoard money so that it becomes a source of negativity. It is our belief, that by employing the power of Buddhism, we can take this mundane world of suffering and build from it a prosperous and happy Pure Land on this Earth. This would allow the life of each and every individual to be completed within the Fo Guang Pure Land, rather than waiting until one dies before any thought is given to Buddhism and one's refuge for the future. It is our hope that everyone will be able to live a full and complete life within this Pure Land of Buddha's light.

Changing funeral traditions

Among the ancients there were those who suffered the pain and sadness of having to "sell themselves in order to bury their father," and although today's society is economically prosperous, there are still people who are destitute and "can't afford to die." For example, they can't afford to buy a burial plot or to pay funeral costs. Moreover, given that "the dead and the living are contending for land," one sometimes cannot find a plot of land even if one has the money. For these reasons, more and more people today are advocating cremation, water burial, burial by planting trees with the ashes, burial by spreading the ashes, and even sky burial by feeding the body to birds. What is the Buddhist perspective on these changes to funeral rituals?

When people die, their main wish is to be buried in the ground to rest in peace; this is a deeply entrenched idea for the Chinese people. Thus, when most people have to deal with a death in the family, every one of them hurriedly tries to find a gravesite. Some people have already made preparations while living, further reducing land availability. In particular, some wealthy individuals often build large mausoleum complexes, creating a situation in which the dead and the living are contending for land. Given the modern explosion in population and the housing crunch now felt in many cities around the world, the issue of the dead and living contending for land has become a problem worthy of serious attention.

The Chinese people like feng shui, so they will make sure the burial site is just right, in order that their decedents will be able to become rich and famous. In the past this has even included hopes of becoming a ruler, general, or prime minister. Hence, the disorderly layout of grave sites in Taiwan has created a uniquely Chinese landscape, for not only do these sites impair the scenic beauty, but they also create a situation in which hillside property cannot be utilized, constituting a serious environmental protection issue. In comparison to the park-like trend in public cemeteries throughout Europe and the U.S., there are surely lessons worthy of attention, highlighting even more the need for positive improvement of the Chinese-style funerary ritual.

Fortunately, with the rise in modern consciousness for environmental protection, Taiwan's government is actively promoting natural and environmentally friendly ideas for burial such as burial by planting trees with the ashes, burial by spreading the ashes, and burial at sea. The Taipei municipal government was the first in Taiwan to open up an area of 1,200 square feet in the Muzha Fude Public Cemetery as an experimental area for burials by planting trees with the ashes and by the spreading of ashes. Others include the Hsintien Public Cemetery in Taipei County and the Linbian Village Cemetery in Pingtung County, where areas designated for burials by planting trees with the ashes and by spreading of ashes will soon be open. At the same time, the government wishes to encourage "clean burials," by greatly expanding its subsidies for local government planning in this area. These are good trends well deserving of praise.

From its beginnings in India, Buddhism has advocated cremation; later, Tibetan Lamaism adopted sky burials. Cremation is better than sky burial, burial at sea, burial by planting trees with the ashes, or burial in the ground. At the time after his final nirvana, the Buddha himself was cremated by the true fires of samadhi. Now, most people accept the idea of cremation. In particular, followers of the Buddha will have their bones interred, after cremation, in columbarium mausoleums at Buddhist temples and monasteries, which is truly is the most perfect resting place from life.

The Buddhist columbarium mausoleums differ from the average secular ones, in that besides providing substantive solutions for practical problems, the Buddhist setting is instilled with the profound significance of faith. Therefore, besides operating orphanages, homes for the elderly, and mobile clinics, Fo Guang Shan's charitable work also includes setting up memorial halls where followers can inter their cremated remains. In this way, Fo Guang Shan provides comprehensive care that covers the birth, old age, sickness, and death of Buddhist followers, so that one's entire life can be spent in the complete care of the Buddhadharma.

Some people, however, make a career selling niches in columbarium mausoleums in open competition with religion. From time to time we even hear of cases in which funeral homes have snatched the bodies of the dead, representing a total breakdown in human decorum! Actually, columbariums were once solely a religious enterprise. We hope that in the future the government will pass new laws and regulations, giving the precious columbariums back to the purview of religious faith, and not allow them to degenerate into a commercial business.

Death constitutes a process we all must undergo in life. It is also a sorrowful and vexing matter. After a person becomes old and sick, medical care is applied first. When medicines are no longer effective, then preparations for the funeral must be made. There are many people today of whom it may be said, "they cannot afford to die." This is because most people live in apartment buildings with other families nearby. So, when there is a death, not only will all the wailing and crying impact the neighbors, it is not clear how one would perform traditional funeral rituals due to social pressure from neighbors and relatives. This is how all the modern funeral services, such as funeral parlors, burial providers, morgues, and columbarium mausoleums, came about as a response to the times. Moreover, according to statistics from Taiwan's Ministry of the Interior, the average cost for a funeral in Taiwan is somewhere between 300,000-400,000 Taiwan dollars. About forty percent of the families are unable to come up with such a sum of money right away.

It is not only that people can't afford to die, but also that some cannot afford to raise a family, pay for housing, obtain an education, get married, or go on vacation either. Actually, as long as we understand how to be frugal, we can afford to do anything, but if we are extravagant and wasteful, then you cannot afford anything. Therefore, Buddhism approves of cremation, because burials in the ground lead to disputes over land and also symbolize too much attachment. As for water burial, burial by planting tress with the ashes, burial at sea, or burial by spreading the ashes from the air, they all seem too heartless, always leaving one feeling uneasy. Therefore, cremation is the best, for not only is it clean and economical, since the wooden coffin for transporting the corpse does not require high quality materials nor take much to build. Cremation also saves time, for all one needs is a hearse from the funeral home to take the body to the crematorium; it is done in less than two hours; and the costs for cremation are low as well. Most poor families can even apply to the government for a reduction in costs. There are quite a few private charitable organizations whose good work entails providing coffins for free; they also volunteer to help the destitute take care of this important matter of death. For example, to enable those in hardship to rest in peace, Fo Guang Shan has set aside 2,000 niches at its Longevity Memorial Park so that the poor and indigent will have a place where their cremated remains can be interred.

Although there are many good points to cremation, there are still quite a few people who insist on burial in the ground. They cannot bear the thought of burning the body after death. But isn't it a hardhearted thing to bury the corpse in the ground instead of cremating it, where the body will decay and putrefy and be fed upon by insects? Burial in the ground requires retrieval of the bones according to Taiwanese custom, and even the most good-hearted filial descendents would find the bones so rotten that they would not dare to get close to them. There's nothing wrong, however, with placing the cremated remains at the head of your bed as you sleep. In this world, there is nothing so dirty that washing with water or burning into ash will not cleanse. There is no need to give offerings to the Buddha image at home or to recite Buddhist sutras; instead one can use cremation itself is an expression of respect. In the same way, after cremation, the rotting dead corpse becomes clean ash. Now isn't that better?

In truth, it is just as Zhuangzi said, for no matter what form of burial is employed–burial in the ground to be eaten by insects, being left in the open ground to be eaten by birds, or burial at sea to be eaten by fish–it all amounts to the same thing. Therefore, regardless of the form of burial, as long as it does not create trouble for others or waste money, then any way is the best way. Plain and frugal does not mean a lack of solemnity. Therefore, whether one employs cremation, burial by planting trees with the ashes, burial at sea, or burial by spreading the ashes from the air, any and all possibilities help us find a solution for this last great event of human life. If one can identify the most economical approach with the greatest practical benefits, then that would be the most important consideration in my view.

GLOSSARY

Amitahba Buddha: The Buddha of Infinite Light or Infinite Life. Amitahba is one of the most popular Buddhas in Mahayana Buddhism. He presides over the Western Pure Land.

Avalokitesvara: Literally, "He who hears the sounds of the world." In Mahayana Buddhism, Avalokitesvara is known as the Bodhisattva of Compassion. He can manifest himself in any form necessary in order to help any being. He is considered one of the great bodhisattvas in Mahayana Buddhism. In China, he is usually portrayed in female form and is known as "Guan Yin."

Bodhi: It means enlightenment. In the state of enlightenment, one is awakened to the true nature of self; one is enlightened to one's own Buddha nature. Such a person has already eliminated all afflictions and delusions, and achieved *prajna*-wisdom.

Bodhi mind: *Sanskrit, bodhicitta.* The mind that seeks enlightenment.

Bodhisattva: Refers to one who is seeking the attainment of Buddhahood or liberation, and one who practices all perfections. Bodhisattvas remain in the world to help others achieve enlightenment. The concept of the bodhisattva is the defining feature of Mahayana Buddhism.

Bodhisattva path: Indicates the cultivation of the bodhisattvas in Mahayana Buddhism. The main philosophy of the bodhisattva path is to attain Buddhahood and liberate all sentient beings through the practice of the four means of embracing and the six perfections.

Buddha: Literally, "enlightened one." When "the Buddha" is used, it usually refers to the historical Buddha, Sakyamuni Buddha.

Buddha nature: The inherent nature that exists in all beings. It is the capability to achieve Buddhahood.

Buddhahood: The attainment and expression that characterizes a Buddha. Buddhahood is the ultimate goal of all sentient beings.

Buddhism: Founded by Sakyamuni Buddha around 2,500 years ago. Its basic doctrines include the Three Dharma Seals, the Four Noble Truths, the Noble Eightfold Path, the Twelve Links of Dependent Origination, the six perfections, and the concepts of karma, impermanence, and emptiness. Its three main traditions are the Mahayana, Theravada, and Vajrayana. While Buddhism has been a popular religion in South, Central, and East Asia, it is currently gaining popularity in the West.

Cause and condition: Referring to the primary cause (causes) and the secondary causes (conditions). The seed out of which a plant or flower grows is a good illustration of a primary cause; the elements of soil, humidity, sunlight, and so forth, could be considered secondary causes.

Cause and effect: This is the most basic doctrine in Buddhism, which explains the formation of all relations and connections in the world. This law means that the arising of each and every phenomenon is due to its own causes and conditions, and the actual form, or appearance, of all phenomena is the effect.

Chan: The Chinese transliteration of the Sanskrit term, *dhyana*; it refers to meditative concentration.

Chan School: One school of Chinese Buddhism. It was founded by Bodhidharma, emphasizes the cultivation of intrinsic wisdom, and teaches that enlightenment is clarifying the mind and seeing one's own true nature. Another major tenet of the Chan School is that the Dharma is wordlessly transmitted from mind to mind.

Dependent Origination: The central principle that phenomena do not come into existence independently but only as a result of causes and conditions; therefore, no phenomena possesses an independent self-nature. This concept is also referred to as interdependence. The twelve factors of dependent origination are: ignorance, karma, formation of consciousness, mind and body, the six senses, contact, feeling, craving, grasping, becoming, birth, and aging and death.

Dharma: When capitalized, it means: 1) the ultimate truth and 2) the teachings of the Buddha. When the Dharma is applied or practiced in life it is referred to as: 3) righteousness or virtues. When it appears with a lowercase "d": 4) anything that can be thought of, experienced, or named; close in meaning to "phenomena."

Dharma-body: *Sanskrit, Dharmakaya*. Refers to the true nature of a Buddha, and also to the absolute Dharma that the Buddha attained. It is also one of three bodies possessed by a Buddha.

Dharma realm: *Sanskrit, dharma-dhatu*. It indicates the notion of true nature that encompasses all phenomena. As a space or realm of dharmas, it is the uncaused and immutable totality in which all phenomena arise, abide, and extinguish.

Emptiness: A basic concept in Buddhism. It means that everything existing in the world is due to dependent origination and has no permanent self or substance.

Five aggregates: Indicates form, feeling, perception, mental formation, and consciousness.

Five Precepts: The fundamental principles of conduct and discipline that were established by the Buddha for wholesome and harmonious living. They are: 1) do not kill; 2) do not steal; 3) do not lie; 4) do not engage in sexual misconduct; and 5) do not take intoxicants.

Four Noble Truths: A foundation and essential teaching of Buddhism that describes the presence of suffering, the cause of suffering, the path leading to the cessation of suffering, and the cessation of suffering.

Impermanence: One of the most basic truths taught by the Buddha. It is the concept that all conditioned dharmas, or phenomena, will arise, abide, change, and disappear due to causes and conditions.

Kalpa: The measuring unit of time in ancient India; a kalpa is an immense and inconceivable length of time. Buddhism adapts it to refer to the period of time between the creation and re-creation of the worlds.

Karma: This means "work, action, or deeds" and is related to the Law of Cause and Effect. All deeds, whether good or bad, produce effects. The effects may be experienced instantly, or they may not come into fruition for many years or even many lifetimes.

Mahayana: Mahayana, literally means "Great Vehicle." One of the two main traditions of Buddhism, Theravada being the other one. Mahayana Buddhism stresses that helping other sentient beings achieve enlightenment is as important as self-liberation.

Medicine Buddha: In Sanskrit, "Bhaisajyaguru." The Buddha of Healing. He presides over the Eastern Pure Land. In previous lives, when he practiced the Bodhisattva Path, he made twelve great vows to help sentient beings eliminate the suffering of physical and mental illness and to guide them towards liberation.

Noble Eightfold Path: Eight right ways leading to liberation. They are: 1) right view; 2) right thought; 3) right speech; 4) right action; 5) right livelihood; 6) right effort; 7) right mindfulness; and 8) right concentration.

Parinirvana: A synonym for *nirvana*. It is the state of having completed all merits and perfections and eliminated all unwholesomeness. Usually, it is used to refer to the time when the Buddha physically passed away.

Prajna-wisdom: *Prajna*-wisdom is the highest form of wisdom. It is the wisdom of insight into the true nature of all phenomena.

Pratyeka-buddha: Refers to those who awaken to the Truth through their own efforts when they live in a time without a Buddha's presence.

Pure Land: Another term for a Buddha realm, which is established by the vows and cultivation of one who has achieved enlightenment.

Saha world: Literally, *saha* means endurance. It indicates the present world where we reside, which is full of suffering to be endured. The beings in this world endure suffering and afflictions due to their greed, anger, hatred, and ignorance.

Sakyamuni Buddha: The historical founder of Buddhism. He was born the prince of Kapilavastu, son of King Suddhodana. At the age of twenty-nine, he left the royal palace and his family to search for the meaning of existence. At the age of thirty-five, he attained enlightenment under the bodhi tree. He then spent the next forty-five years expounding his teachings, which include the Four Noble Truths, the Noble Eightfold Path, the Law of Cause and

Effect, and dependent origination. At the age of eighty, he entered the state of *parinirvana*.

Samadhi: Literally, "establish" or "make firm." It means concentration; a state in which the mind is concentrated in a one-pointed focus and all mental activities are calm. In *samadhi*, one is free from all distractions, thereby entering a state of inner serenity.

Samsara: Also known as the cycle of birth and death or transmigration. When sentient beings die, they are reborn into one of the six realms of existence. The cycle is continuous and endless due to the karmic result of one's deeds.

Sangha: Indicating the Buddhist community; in a broad sense it includes both monastics and laypeople. Specifically, it refers to the monastics.

Sentient beings: *Sanskrit, sattvas*. All beings with consciousness, including celestial beings, asuras, humans, animals, hungry ghosts, and hell beings. From the Mahayana view, all sentient beings inherently have Buddha nature and therefore possess the capacity to attain enlightenment.

Six dusts: Indicating the six objects reflected by the six bases (sense-organs), which then produce the six consciousnesses.

Six perfections: Also known as the six *paramitas*. *Paramita* in Sanskrit means "having reached the other shore," "transcendent," "complete attainment," "perfection in," and "transcendental virtue." The six perfections are: 1) giving charity; 2) upholding precepts; 3) patience; 4) diligence; 5) meditation; and 6) *prajna*-wisdom.

Six organs: Refers to the eyes, ears, nose, tongue, body, and mind.

Six realms: Or the six realms of existence, indicating the realms of heaven, human, *asura*, animals, hungry ghost, and hell.

Tathagata: One of the ten epithets of Buddha, literally translated as "Thus-Come One," meaning the one who has attained full realization of suchness; i.e. the one with the absolute, so that he neither comes from anywhere nor goes anywhere.

Ten wholesome conducts: The ten wholesome actions are: no killing, no stealing, no sexual misconduct, no lying, no duplicity, no harsh words, no flattery, no greed, no anger, and no ignorance.

The Way: Refers to the path leading to liberation taught by the Buddha.

Three Dharma Seals: Also known as the Three Marks of Existence. They are as follows: 1) all phenomena are impermanent; 2) all phenomena do not have a substantial self; and 3) nirvana is perfect tranquility.

Three poisons: Greed, anger, and ignorance.

Three Realms: The realms where sentient beings reside and transmigrate: 1) the realm of sense-desires; 2) the realm of form; and 3) the realm of formlessness.

Three Studies: Includes precepts, concentration, and wisdom. Precepts can prevent one from the unwholesomeness of body, speech, and mind. Concentration can help one eliminate distracting thoughts with a singly focused mind, see the true nature, and attain the path. Wisdom can enable one to reveal the true nature, eliminate all afflictions, and see the Truth.

Tripitaka: The *Buddhist Canon* known as "Three Baskets." It is divided into three categories: the sutras (teachings of the Buddha), the *vinayas* (precepts and rules), and the *abhidharma* (commentaries on the Buddha's teachings).

Triple Gem: Indicating the Buddha, the Dharma, and the Sangha, and also called the Triple Jewel, or the Three Jewels. The Buddha is the fully awakened or enlightened one; the Dharma is the teachings imparted by the Buddha; and the Sangha indicates the community of monastic members.

World-Honored One: One of ten epithets of a Buddha. Traced back to the original Sanskrit term, *loka-natha* refers to the lord of the worlds, or *loka-jyestha* means the most venerable of the world. Today, it is usually translated as "the World-Honored One."